The Last Shot

Jacqueline Lonsdale Cuerton

The Last Shot

Acknowledgements

I would like to acknowledge all those, past and present, who travelled with me for short and long journeys. Thanks to those who helped me through the rapids, applied balm to the bruises; enjoyed my music and talked with me about the endless things that constitute a life. To those who cried with me, laughed with me.

I look forward to meeting those who might call by in whatever time I have remaining.

More prosaically, without Steve Wilson and his class of life-writers, my life story would not have been told. Thanks to all of you for your encouragement, suggestions, and sharing pieces of your stories which helped me over the hard parts of mine.

The Last Shot
ISBN 978 1 76041 598 3
Copyright © Jacqueline Lonsdale Cuerton 2018
Cover image © Vladimir Borozenets – Fotolia.com

First published 2018 by
GINNINDERRA PRESS
PO Box 3461 Port Adelaide 5015
www.ginninderrapress.com.au

Contents

13. 03. 1941	7
At the beginning	9
Looking back	19
Arrival – and after being nine	20
The house – and a farewell	34
Work	63
Return visit: south to north	106
Sun and snow	119
Mary	121
Student life	129
And yet again	130
The family	134
First marriage	165
My son's father	179
My story	182
A miscellany	188
Solomon moments	193
Ten days of normal	234

'If ever there is a tomorrow when we are not together…
There is something you must always remember.
You are braver than you believe,
Stronger than you seem,
And smarter than you think.
But the most important thing is,
Even if we're apart…
I'll always be with you.'
From *Winnie the Pooh*, A.A. Milne

for my three sons

13. 03. 1941

on the day I was born
there was a partial eclipse
of the moon;
Germans attacked the Brits
in North Africa,
the construction of Auschwitz camp
began;
236 Luftwaffe bombers
attacked Glasgow
and again against Liverpool –
major bombing wiped out the golf course in Hull;
Palestinian poet and writer
Mahmoud Darwish
was born:
but not much to celebrate
in England
that day

At the beginning

Some memories must be mine alone, as no one else could think them up and, even if they did, they wouldn't have passed them on to me. Such as when I was somewhere between three and five and had the strange experience of being enveloped by light and the realisation that I was more than physical flesh. I sensed another me, outside of my body, which was the creative intelligence of me. Of course I didn't think in those words then but I knew I had another, more important, self. Many today would say my 'higher' self. I did feel protected by this knowledge and, while my life has not been one of blissful happiness and ease, I have always felt safe. I was, at the time, in a space between the kitchen and scullery, a place I would not normally be; it had no direct light from outside.

The Second World War was not finished. My father, as yet unmet, was still overseas. We had been bombed out of the home we had in Scunthorpe, north-west Lincolnshire, where I was born, and had the next house damaged. My brother, almost five years my senior, had, at different times, spent time away with another family and my mother's lover had been killed in a direct hit on his place of work. His daughter, my half-sister, was born prematurely soon after, when I was two-and-a-half. Her birth certificate says we were living in Dean's Close, Grimsby.

We had our narrow escapes, as the time when an airman friend of my dad's was staying with us for a short leave. His wife had come across from Wales for the few days her husband, Owen, had before going overseas with the RAF. Dad's overseas service started exactly nine months before I was born and didn't end until well after the official end of the war. The air raid siren sounded but my mother kept on doing whatever she was doing, making no attempt to get my brother or me from our beds and go to the shelter. The Welsh wife became hysterical and her husband persuaded my mother we should go. It was the first and last time she made any attempt to do so. She suggested she would fetch my brother. Owen could collect and carry me down. Mother and brother were down first but didn't get any further than the cupboard under the stairs. Owen, carrying me, had just rounded the newel post when the heavy front door blew in and up the stairs, missing us by a breeze. Later, they inspected the house and found my cot broken and the sheets cut to shreds.

Another time when we were bricked in and a neighbour kept knocking on the broken wall shouting were we all right and my mother calling back that we were, but couldn't move. The neighbour saying help was on its way and in the meantime she'd bring us a cup of tea and then both women laughing at the ridiculousness of the offer. Tea and laughter, it was said, got the Brits through the war.

My father had joined the Royal Air Force rather than wait to be called up and be put into the army. He said he couldn't bear to see the person he was about to kill, so he would do it at a distance. My mother had wanted to join one of the women's services or at least become an ambulance driver but my grandparents refused to care for my brother. Had they, I might not have happened.

According to my mother, she and I had mild TB (tuberculosis), she, perhaps, worse than I. I would have been very young. My brother caught whooping cough, so I had that as well. My understanding is that she had no help from her mother or sister, so looking after my sister who was ill all the time and coping with other diseases must have been very hard for my mother.

I was away staying with friends when my father was finally demobbed and coming home. He came to fetch me. As I said, I'd never met him. I'd known my sister's father as my own until I was two-and-a-half but I saw my dad crossing the road when I was playing in a red pedal car and I knew who he was. I ran across the road and up into his arms. I was almost six and had never felt so comfortable.

My father accepted the extended family and life went on. He was a good man married to the wrong woman, just as my mother was married to the wrong man. Doctors had told my parents my sister would not live through another English winter and needed a warmer climate. Being born approximately twelve weeks too soon, her respiratory system was not fully developed; nor had her body completely unfolded. She had plastic surgery on her jaw and ear and grew into a slender, lovely-looking woman.

England's dampness meant severe asthma and bronchitis. In 1943, beds, space, energy were being used up by the war-injured; the medical staff could do nothing for my sister and she and my mother were sent home after the regulation ten days' confinement. My mother kept her alive by breathing into her, no one knew about CPR then, and putting the tiniest drop of brandy onto her tongue, causing my sister to gasp and thus take a breath for herself. The family doctor had offered medication that would comfortably bring my sister's life to an end, because no one thought she was going to survive anyway but also because of the social aspects of my sister not being my mother's husband's daughter in the remote event both should survive the war. My mother refused.

My parents decided to move to Australia. My grandfather suggested Brisbane as our destination rather than Tasmania, where Dad had been offered a job. My father never really wanted to leave his country but did, for his stepdaughter. That was the only reason ever expressed but I think there were deeper ones.

I would make no more snowmen near a window from which my sister could see it; no more bowls of snow brought in so she could feel it. No more toboggan rides down my grandmother's hill or, in the summer, sliding down on metal trays. No more snow being pushed down my back by rowdy boys as we all made our way home from school. No more school dinners, which were actually nice but of which I ate little, resulting in letters home worried that I wasn't eating enough. No more Guy Fawkes' nights with huge bonfires and spectacular fireworks on a cool November night. I still have the image of my teacher, last day, sitting on her desk in a pinky-grey plaid skirt, brown brogues, feet crossed at the ankles, addressing the class, farewelling me. And my friend Michael James, who was going to become a sheep farmer, travel to Australia and rescue me. He didn't and didn't.

There seemed to be no emotional connection within the family. In age I was closer to my younger sister, with almost two and a half years separating us; we should have been friends but she was always ill and our relationship consisted of my being her carer or teacher or, in my way, making some sort of social life for her. She was never well enough to go to school, nor did she ever have any long-term employment. She was never anything but our sister until our mother died in 1995, when she said she wanted no more to do with us.

A memory is more than a stored fact. It is coloured with feeling, emotion, and can change according to circumstance.

An alternative title for this missive was *Splendide Mendax*, which translates as Noble Untruth.

Earliest memories

The Second World War finished when I was going on five, so it is difficult to know what I remember of it and what has been told. I have an image of my brother, in his pyjamas and unclosed dressing gown flying out behind him as he ran back and forth across the garden 'shooting' at the planes flying overhead. It is a story told about my mother and her father standing in the same garden shaking their fists at the enemy aeroplanes. Both would have preferred more active roles. I do remember the giant 'crochet' that stretched across the kitchen in my grandparents' home. I suppose 'giant tatting' might be more correct and it was fishing nets, I think, that my grandfather wove, his contribution to the war effort.

Somewhere in my memory there is a large set of buildings. It could have been a school, as I remember the space around the buildings and the low stone wall. It was opposite a house I knew well but whether it was the house I lived in, my aunt's house or my grandparents', I really don't know. What I do remember are the uniformed men who occupied the buildings and how they would sit on the stone wall and talk to anyone prepared to give the time. They must have been Americans as they were the only military men who gave the children bars of chocolate and other sweets. My teeth suffered from the chocolates left on my pillow at bedtime.

It is a story of how I, in my pram, was wheeled by my mother down the back lane, to the shops. She tried to return by the same route but was turned away. An unexploded bomb had been found in the lane. My mother argued that she had gone past it on the way out, why shouldn't she walk past it to go back. She didn't win and had to retrace her steps. The piles of bricks and debris, the holes in the ground, the rubble that was once a house, were real enough. And noise. I do not enjoy fireworks displays and the attendant noise.

Everything was still rationed even when we left in 1950, but not as strictly as it was through the war, and we could get ice cream, which was now available once a fortnight. Walls ice cream slices, wrapped, came with wafers. It was probably more ice than cream but it was a treat for us children. My mother told us, when she knew war was inevitable, perhaps in 1937/8, she started collecting things, particularly food, tinned and packeted, that would not spoil for the keeping. My parents were not wealthy and whatever my mother was able to store wouldn't have amounted to a great deal and would soon have been depleted. We still went without many things, although I understand my maternal grandmother was not above buying a pig on the black market when she heard one was available.

I remember the long summer evenings and looking with envy from my bedroom window at the older children playing in their gardens below. I was reminded of those long evenings when I moved to Tasmania almost a lifetime later.

On Friday evenings in those post-war times, my brother and I, or just one of us, would go to the local fish and chip shop and get tea for the family. There was usually a queue trailing down the street so we'd go early. I remember the summer light, the stamping of cold feet in winter and looking forward to our feast when we took it home. Occasionally my dad and I would go together.

Walking home from school in the winter, I fancy I can still feel the icy coldness down my back when boys grabbed me and shoved snow down. I'd get to my warm house and the aroma of fresh-baked bread. There was always a warm roll for me, which I'd eat with butter and golden syrup. Years later, when I was pregnant with my second or third child, I craved hot rolls, butter and syrup. My husband warmed bought rolls and applied the toppings but they just didn't taste the same. In spring and summer, everywhere was green and I'd walk over the common enjoying life and chewing on a piece of liquorice stick. Not the sticky black stuff but the actual liquorice root. I would often spend my penny bus money on that in a Boot's chemist, and walk, chewing the flavour from the fibres until there was nothing left but dry threads. Autumn, of course, was full of the colours of the season and I loved the sound of crunching leaves.

I have photos of me in my primary school uniform, my stockings wrinkled, probably threatening to fall down, a dark blazer. I liked going to school but for some reason I would not eat the hot midday dinners provided and if I were to eat at all I would have to make the trek home and back again. We didn't take packed lunches to school then and I don't know if schoolchildren in England even today take them. I went back to see the school but I didn't remember the building at all.

It always seemed to be autumn when we picnicked in the woods. Perhaps it just felt like autumn in the reduced light of a wood. I do remember the leaves underfoot, the giant oaks, beeches, elms, sycamores and other trees, around which we would run and hide, the collections of leaves and making up stories about the ghosts and fairies who came out at night. Summer picnics seemed to have been on grassy meadows, with trees to climb and inquisitive cattle over a fence. These were always bigger affairs than the family in the woods, with aunts, uncles, friends. We'd play French cricket or rounders (I think Americans call it baseball). I was terrified of Aunt Alice, who seemed big and loud. Mother would have called her common. The daughters, although around the ages of my sister and me, were much bigger and heavier and, of course, our games were different. My sister and I were not into the rough and tumble boisterousness that they were. We considered them rough, they thought we were soft.

The house smelled of the roses that grew in the front garden while we ate the peas, beans, cabbages that grew at the back. Sometimes I would look out of my bedroom window late at night and see my mother working in the garden. (Neither of us were early sleepers.)

My maternal grandparents had a cottage garden, full of soft, colourful flowers in the front. My sister was the only one permitted to pick any, which usually meant pulling the heads off. My grandfather had apple trees in the back garden, the fruit stored in the attic, where I would go to read a book. I must have left scores of apple cores behind. Rhubarb grew over the air-raid shelter which I think wasn't used for anything else. Recently something came up about black and white Scottie dogs which reminded me of the bottles which held the whisky my grandmother drank. The labels featured two dogs of that breed, one black, one white. My grandfather did not drink alcohol at all.

We had rosewood furniture and I remember the reflection of bowls of fruit; not a lot of fruit and not a great variety and none of it for me. It was reserved for my sister. I didn't covet it, it was just a fact of life. I first saw a banana when I was six or seven and I remarked on its strangeness and asked if one ate the skin. The adults laughed. I think I was hurt by that; it was a legitimate question requiring a simple answer but their laughter intimated I was stupid for not knowing. Throughout my years of attending classes of one sort or another, I have made a point of asking the first question, when that embarrassed silence has gone for long enough. There's always something everybody thinks everybody else knows and so doesn't want to show ignorance by asking it. And of course, ask one question, the rest follow. When I had children no question went unanswered; we had a much-thumbed encyclopædia.

My mother had not been an approachable parent. It was a case of 'don't bother me'. There was one time we were walking somewhere, my sister in a pram, me walking by the side and chattering. It might have been inane, non-stop chatter but I just remember being told to 'please be quiet'. One event I would wish to forget but can't was towards the end of our life in England. I was playing with friends in our back garden. A toilet had been replaced and the broken one was put next to the back wall of the house waiting to be collected. Somehow one of the girls slipped and fell on it, slicing a large piece of flesh, a narrow ellipse, from her calf. My mother was the closest adult but I had been told not to disturb her; the other girl and I supported the injured girl on either side and took her to her home. I never saw either girl again and didn't ever learn of the outcome, medical, legal, or any social, psychological, aspects.

My grandson asked me, one day, what I had played with when I was little. I explained about the war and the scarcity of everything and forced my mind back to think what I did play with. Books I've mentioned but I remember the last Christmas we had in England. My sister and I might have had cloth or knitted woolly dolls but that year of 1949 we each received a proper doll that went to sleep and had arms and legs that moved. Our aunt had knitted beautiful outfits for them. I do think, though, I was a bit like my mother and I really didn't know what to do with a doll. That night they were put to bed and left near the fire. In the morning we came downstairs to find melted lumps.

I did make dolls' houses out of boxes and my sister had a big one, made for her by our grandfather, from matchboxes. Papered, they looked like bricks. The inside was covered with wallpaper and filled with hand-crafted furniture. I made dolls – not for the house, mine were not good enough, but families, soldiers, any kind of group, from dolly-pegs and scraps of fabric. We played cards and draughts, did jigsaws and read. We drew and I wrote stories for the people I made. I put together a little book for the enlightenment of my grandsons. I do not remember reading or having been read to, from the popular children's books – *Winnie the Pooh* comes to mind, as the A.A. Milne books were among the ones I bought for my children. I read *Anne of Green Gables* as an adult, although I did read Enid Blyton's books for older children as an older child and the Noddy and Big Ears ones to my children.

It must have been during the last summer we had in England when we all, as a family, went to a Scouts' picnic. My brother was a Scout and this day, it might have lasted longer than one day and my brother might have been away camping, but the rest of the family was there for that day, and all the children had taken part in races as well as joining other games like cricket, tennis. I think I'd been riding a bicycle and skidded on gravel, causing me to fall. My skin was broken the length of my thigh. I was taken to the first-aid shelter, where the doctor said he would have to clean my leg and get all the bits of gravel out of the cuts. He told me not to look as he was doing it. But of course, how could I not look? I remember being told I was brave for not crying and I also remember worrying about the damage done to the bike, as it wasn't mine.

My mother told me I was a wilful child; I might have been difficult, growing up, but I used to reply, when I was older, that she should have set some boundaries and that she should have said 'no' occasionally. I think I used to try to test her, see how far I could go, what I could get up to. Which was altogether too far and too much. I never felt as if I fitted, retreating into books at a very young age. My favourite space was under the big dining table, my head resting on a chair-spell, reading a book, travelling to strange and wonderful places, meeting strange and wonderful people. I was a voracious reader and no book was denied me. Apparently my mother tried to limit my choices but my grandmother told her it didn't matter, for if I read something I didn't understand, it wouldn't hurt me. I'm not altogether in agreement with that sentiment, as one is likely to give wrong meanings, interpretations of a passage not fully grasped by a child's mind. But I suppose, having grown up, I managed to stay pretty close to the straight and narrow.

My conversations were contained within the books; I think I listened, absorbed others' conversations. Perhaps, as now, I've always been better at putting words on paper than out there, joining the general cacophony.

It was after we had arrived in Australia and my mother was expecting my younger brother in 1952, that I remember my mother being involved; my sister and I were fighting and my mother was most likely not feeling well – she picked up my older brother's cricket bat that happened to be resting in a handy corner and waved it about, telling us to be quiet. We looked at her and started to laugh; we had never seen her looking so…deranged. She had not told us there would be an addition to the family, though my sister and I vaguely thought that was the case. It would have been an excellent time for a lesson in human reproduction.

When I studied for social work, I realised my mother was the 'zoo mother' – keep the animals fed and clean, their cages clean and that was that. No emotional input. And these days that behaviour wouldn't be acceptable even in a zoo worker.

We had a pet rabbit, most likely my brother's responsibility, but it was never allowed in the house, as my sister was allergic to everything. My brother would probably have preferred a dog but that was out of the question. As the rabbit lived in the shed, I don't think it lasted very long.

My mother didn't know how to mother. My older brother had been a mistake and I, conceived on the eve of my father's departure for overseas service, was also a mistake. My mother should have been allowed to study, perhaps enter a profession or politics; my grandfather shouldn't have gambled but facilitated his family's place in society – but life happens and we can only deal with what we have been given. If we resent it, fight it, we are going to fail; if we accept it, mould it, build on it, we are more likely to succeed.

Looking back

We live in a world of reflections
and I wonder how many mirrors
we need to bounce image back
and back until we get to the beginning.

It must have started with Narcissus
who, in not loving Echo, caused
her death and who, in dying caught
our words which are thrown back at us
again and again bouncing back and
back softer and softer.

So Nemesis caused his undying death –
that too beautiful youth whose pining for
the unattainable, the love of self,
turned him into a flower.

The doomed lovers haunt us; we
find a place where Echo visits and
introduce her to our children while
we lose no chance to look at our
reflection in any shining surface –
the train window in a tunnel shop
or restaurant glass to spy on those
around behind, or to check the angle
of our hat.

First published in *The Eyes Have It*, Ginninderra Press 2012

Arrival – and after being nine

It was my birthday, 13 March 1950, a day as busy as that of six weeks before but this time we were getting off, not getting on. My father stoutly declared he had heard the captain wish me a happy day over the PA system, very early in the morning, as everything turned to hustle and bustle. My family was disembarking in Sydney from a ship that had started life as the luxury liner *Monarch of Bermuda*, gone through changes to become a troop carrier, a hospital ship and this, her penultimate voyage, as a migrant ship. I had thought it a big ship but at 22,000 tons it was, by today's standards, a cork on the ocean and of course it didn't have the stabilisers of the liners of today.

We'd left Southampton on a grey, drizzly day in February. I wouldn't move from the deck of the ship until I could no longer see the shadow of land I was leaving behind. Even at nearly nine, I knew this was a most momentous event and I wonder if a child of that age can feel bereft. I knew I felt sad, lost and alone. I don't know why. Certainly I was leaving familiarity behind and going to something of which I had no knowledge. I was angry, too, that no one had asked me if I wanted to go. My brother was given the option of staying behind with my maternal grandparents and finishing his education and, at nearly fourteen, I accept he was at a more critical stage than I, but I was angry at not being asked.

Although my parents had been assured of the excellent educational facilities in Australia, my brother found that he had been studying at a level far in advance of the form he was required to join once we were installed in schools. We've never discussed what he thought about that. Sixty and more years later, he would have been fast-tracked and soon entering university. In those days, it was a matter of age-related school years no matter if mentally a student was below or above it. Not a very good system.

The ship we travelled half the globe on was now named SS *Asturias*. We boarded on 8 February 1950. The colours I remember on that grey day are the green of my sister's outfit and my red. We each wore black shiny shoes, flesh-coloured stockings and knitted gloves. Everything else seemed enveloped in layers of fine grey muslin, a fabric light as air but impossible to escape if wrapped around like tight, steel bands.

Our vessel had been restored to something of its original splendour and was very comfortable. To accommodate maximum passengers, we were put into segregated cabins. My mother, sister and I were given room in an outer eight-berth on C deck – one of the best. It was above the waterline and had portholes through which we could see the ocean and, of course, they let in natural light. We were joined by three more women and two small children. Fortunately we all got on well, becoming close friends with 'Auntie M' and her family, friends with 'Mrs D' and hers, while 'Mrs T' was more of a loner. The corresponding husbands with respectively their one, one, and twin sons plus my dad and brother, occupied an inner eight-berth. The allocators of space got that right. The boys were thirteen, fourteen; I was the oldest child in our cabin, then my sister, Mrs D's David at six, and Auntie M's Elsa, about three.

Not all partnerings were as successful and had to be changed. I learned a few years later that some young travellers had played musical beds and some family groups, similar to ours, needed to be reorganised more than once.

I saw the film made from Margaret Humphrey's book *Oranges and Sunshine*, about the transportation, from children's homes in England to Australia, of allegedly orphaned or otherwise abandoned children. The children were lied to, not asked if they actually wanted to leave, just packed up and sent. Their treatment in Australia was, in the main, horrific, with forced labour, sexual abuse, no opportunity for a decent education. A group of these children was on the ship. I can't remember seeing large groups of children, presumably under supervision, on the deck.

The only compulsory thing we had to do was attend lifeboat practice, which might explain why I seek out the placement of life jackets every time I board a ferry.

The lore of the sea dictates a rough Bay of Biscay delivers a calm Great Australian Bight and vice versa. Our introduction to sea-life was one of *mal de mer*: our cabin luggage slid from one side to the other as we lay moaning in our beds, and members of the crew, feeling just as ill, kept checking on us, making us nibble on dry crackers and taking sips of water.

It's true that our bathroom was just next door but sometimes that was too far and the late parting gift to Auntie M of a beautiful crystal bowl was put into use as a receptacle for the contents of our stomachs. She told me later, she could never bring herself to use the bowl for anything other than flowers. With its beauty, it could have enhanced the taste of a salad or an old-fashioned English trifle.

Two sailors and a passenger died. My father and sister stayed well and took delight in describing their breakfasts of sausages, bacon, eggs, tomato, buttered toast. The burials were delayed until we reached calmer water. My sister and I disobeyed our parents for the first and sneaked to that part of the ship where the ceremony took place and the canvas-wrapped body was slid into the ocean. For the second and third, we went with permission.

The trip itself did not strike me, at the time, as being eventful; it was just another thing in my short, eventful life, circumscribed by war, its aftermath, meeting my father, and school. In retrospect, it was quite an education and perhaps gave birth to my wanderlust. A handful of young women, coming to Australia for a new life, volunteered to teach the children every second morning, and there were sporting activities, card games, a library. Concerts were also a feature, with performers gleaned from passengers and crew and adults and children had separate fancy dress parties, their dates announced at very short notice. I remember my sister going as the Queen of Hearts, in a skirt of netting with crêpe paper hearts sewn on, a big red heart covering the bodice, a gold paper crown and a tray, procured from the kitchen, with cardboard tarts stuck on. Mother attached ribbon to its handles so it could hang around my sister's neck. I was Little Miss Muppet in frilly dress with my bowl, empty of curds and whey, and a spoon, with a spider made from a cork blackened with shoe polish, and pipe-cleaner legs hanging from my bonnet. The captain shook every child's hand and we each received a bar of chocolate.

We had set tables for breakfast, not for lunch or dinner, but each morning we would have the same waiters. One serving us seemed to me to be elderly. He had grey hair. He was most concerned about my diet – I always seemed to be picky, didn't eat enough. This kindly man tried to tempt me with just about everything in the kitchen, bringing tiny assortments, nicely arranged on small plates, urging me to try. But I'd discovered puffed wheat and would eat nothing else. My sister, on the other hand, could eat huge amounts of anything when she was well. It had to sustain her for the many weeks at a time when she was unwell and ate nothing. Even water is hard to swallow when one can't breathe. Her love of food was shown in her ability to produce a Chinese banquet when she was maybe twelve.

On the suggestion of our part-time teachers, I made a diary, which my mother did not think important enough to keep. It survived the trip and our time in the rented house, and the last I remember was it being on the bottom of a deep drawer in my sister's and my shared chest of drawers. We had strictly separated space and my sister had even put a ruler down the halfway mark on the top. I was messy, she said, with all my bits and pieces. Last time I saw her kitchen, the benchtops were crowded with stuff, sauces, tools, whereas mine is clean and clear. Perhaps hers is the kitchen of a cook while my desk, dining table, coffee tables, are more often than not littered with books and papers.

After the extremely bad weather of the Bay of Biscay, we had calm waters take us past Portugal and through the Strait of Gibraltar but because we were behind schedule, no shore leave was allowed on the island, just time to take on supplies. No shore leave on Malta, either, but we did collect more passengers, men and boys going to make new lives in Australia or joining family already there. Fourteen-year-old George was going to meet his father, a man he did not know, had not seen for many years. He joined the band of boys already friends. He and Auntie M's son became extended members of our family. George died early, age forty-three, leaving behind a wife and two lovely children, the three soon returning to Malta. Auntie M's husband died eight months after our arrival, in an accident with a circular saw.

Valetta harbour offered some excitement in the form of the British aircraft carrier *Ark Royal*. My grandfather had been a Merchant Navy officer but we had never seen such a ship in action.

The political situation of the Suez Canal prevented our going ashore at Port Said and there was some doubt as to whether or not we would be allowed to sail through the canal at all. It was finally decided that we could. It took several hours to sail through and the whole ship seemed to take on the silence of the ancient lands on either side.

The scene was picture-postcard-perfect – blue water, golden sand, hot blue sky, pyramids, date palms and a caravan of about twenty camels with their burnoused masters walking or riding. Mother and I watched all afternoon and I wondered what treasures they carried. I thought of beautiful silks and jewels for a princess and what stories they would tell at night. There were no answers in that profound silence and suddenly, as if someone had flicked a switch, it was dark and night. As an adult, I have visited ancient caravanserai and brought them to life with those images.

Aden, and shore leave at last. But not until morning, the captain advised. Our parents told us next morning some had gone ashore and there had been one or two incidents. I can imagine now what they might have been.

As a former RAF man, Dad had arranged to visit the RAF base there. To see as much as we could, we took the long way round; the contrast between the moving blue sea, fast-moving colourful fish, flying fish, and the almost static sandy yellow scene couldn't have been greater. Cubed buildings, sky, roads, few people, fewer donkeys and the odd motor vehicle were all the same dun colour. Even the palms struggled to show any green through the golden haze. Suddenly we came across the colourful hustle and bustle of a market. My sister and I were petted and fussed over; my brother and parents were used to practise English on; but in those days of pre-tourist savvy, we were not pestered to buy. We strolled, looking, eventually buying small things.

We left the market and came to a jail, a rectangular concrete box with the front of vertical metal bars. It was dark and stank. Men and boys were crowded inside. As many as could crowded the front with arms outstretched begging for anything we chose to give. It was the first time we children had seen anything like it. We were definitely walking in areas that would not have been officially approved; we saw no other Europeans but felt perfectly safe.

We were in another world, arriving at the base in time for lunch – cool marble, green lawns, fountains and order. My sister was eating a chocolate bar while we were still in the vestibule. Suddenly a dark shadow flashed by, taking the chocolate bar with it. I remember my sister in that moment of surprised suspension, mouth open, hand now empty, eyes wide. The first concern was my sister's well-being and that being ascertained, the officer ordered the miscreant caught and punished.

My sister said 'No' most emphatically, continuing with 'he needs it more than I do.' Leaving the assembled adults rather open-mouthed. My sister was six-and-a-half years.

Late afternoon, we were driven back to the ship but didn't board immediately, watching instead local boys diving into the clear green water to retrieve the coins thrown in by some of the passengers. My brother and some of the other young passengers decided it looked like fun, stripped down to shorts and dived in. It might have been fun but I think they might have realised pretty quickly they were not going to make their fortunes that way. The locals beat them every time, even though the interlopers had succeeded in stirring up the sandy bottom.

Next stop Colombo in what is now Sri Lanka, then Ceylon. Here, the port was oil-slicked, floating with garbage, smelly. The one disappointment of the trip had been that the swimming pool had been used to store luggage instead of water, so here was another opportunity for hardy boys to splash in the sea. In they went. I'm sure my dad didn't believe it and I don't know if he actually thought it would get them out but he shouted down to them, 'Don't you know these waters are shark-infested?' It caused great laughter on deck, had no effect on the swimmers and came into the family lexicon for anything we weren't supposed to do.

No land between Colombo and Fremantle, but we did cross the equator. We were all asked if we felt the bump and had to prepare for the arrival of King Neptune. Even then, I preferred facts and considered the question silly.

Certain liberties were taken with the ancient Greek midsummer, 23 July, festival, but we had a lot of fun. Another party for the children, on deck, a bit like Christmas but at this we expected the King of the Sea. We saw some officers and sailors punished for some misdemeanour by being dunked in the ocean, which made some children wonder if we were to be similarly treated. Naturally, the party carried on into the night for the adults.

The weather stayed perfect as we sailed on to our first port of call in our new country.

It was a Sunday, that Fremantle day; the city was as quiet as a country graveyard. No open shops, not even a café. No museums, galleries, where we might be entertained or refreshed. My parents must have wondered what they had come to. We went back to the ship and prepared to sail around the Bight. We were told this would be pleasant, with calm waters. It was.

As I said, Sydney: a busy, confusing day that became a collage of images – the Woolloomooloo wharf café, dark, greasy, with dainty party food non-existent and where I celebrated my ninth birthday. The single worker, a big man, wore a singlet and long, dark trousers. The obligatory tea towel was slung over his shoulder and answered to every need.

All of the men, wharfies (waterside workers; one thing we were to notice very early on was the Australian leaning towards shortening names, or, if someone had a one-syllable first name, a 'y' or 'ie' would be added) twice the size of the Europeans from the ship, speaking a language we couldn't understand. The sooty train without a dining car that took many long hours to take us from Sydney to Brisbane.

We had to alight at designated stations to buy thick corned beef and relish sandwiches and tea in thick china cups. I remembered the train ride from London to Southampton, upholstered seats, a dining car complete with waiters, snacks ordered from and delivered to where we sat: I remembered the London hotel in which we'd stayed prior to our leaving – its order, its civility. I had been to London before, to see the ballet, and, war damage notwithstanding, it was a civilised city.

We saw wooden houses on stilts; miles of land with nothing on it, looking dead; barefooted children but looking healthy, well-fed; the ugly-looking grasshopper as big as a dinner plate; mosquitoes, sunburn; banana, papaya, mango trees in gardens; dry, brown grass, grey trees.

Brisbane city like a fairy tale with its size, cleanliness and quietness, no bomb-damaged buildings, a green sward in front of a Grecian-looking city hall, entered via a wide sweep of steps to the front portico; the nearby church spire the tallest structure in this surreal place. The area no longer looks like that. The soft green piazza was raised to the height of the steps and concreted. Underneath is car parking space. The look of the place changed a couple of times and now, with cafés, it is again at least people-friendly.

The first time my mother went shopping, she was overcome by the abundance of meat, butter, milk. She didn't dwell on the smaller variety of vegetables, cheeses, which might have been in scarce supply during the war but she had grown up with a wider variety than was now available. Over time that was remedied by the flow of migrants and refugees. I remember people going mad for Vietnamese bread after some of the refugees had set up bakeries when they came after the Vietnamese war. It was baked in the French style, as Vietnam had once been a French colony.

Auntie Flo had met us from the sooty train and it was she with whom we stayed until we found our feet. Our stay was short, three weeks. Auntie Flo was the official nominator as she was the only family member living in Brisbane. She had been married more than once, had several children but I remember only one still living at home. He might have been about twenty. Another cousin, Auntie Vi, and her husband Uncle Eddy, helped us find a house to rent and then move into it, minus, unfortunately, several pieces of silver. My mother's cousin's son found our silver cutlery useful for removing bicycle tyres from their rims and forgetting to return it. We saw them at family picnics and on other family occasions but very seldom otherwise.

Auntie Vi and Uncle Eddy had a farm at Rochdale and two children, a boy and a girl, a bit above and below me. They all became good friends with the parents being particularly helpful in all manner of ways.

Very soon after moving into the house, Aunt Dolly, another cousin of my mother, and Uncle Jack visited from Monto, where they had a dairy farm. The four cousins got together and exchanged family history as far as each knew it. Florence, Violet and Dorothy were daughters of Great Aunt Katie, my grandfather's fifth sibling. She had other children, two or four, but not living close or had died escaping Burma. They had joined the exodus as it walked from Rangoon to Mandalay to India.

My grandfather left Burma as a young man but World War II seemed to scatter the family. Another part of it came across from Perth, WA, to meet us. It was unfortunate we didn't stay in touch. Had I been a bit older, I might have taken the initiative. The Burmese family history is too sketchy, barely there. I have not discovered who or why the first Lonsdale went to Burma, or when – but my grandfather's mother was definitely Burmese. It was a highly respected family.

The owner of the house my parents rented was a bookmaker and lived opposite in what were two houses joined by a covered walkway. In 1950, one could not build a domestic house to the size required by this particular owner. It had many rooms, including one for music, as well as a tennis court and swimming pool. Rooms for the domestic staff were on the lowest level. Both houses were on the top of a hill, the owners' residence taking up rather more space and the bottom level tucked into the side of the hill.

They had eight children, and my sister and I made particular friends with those near our age. One of my last memories before we moved into our own home was of Margaret, a couple of years older than I, who needed to interrupt a conversation our respective mothers were having. Margaret was about to go out with friends and was asking her mother if she might have an advance on her pocket money as she had none of that week's left. Her mother asked how long Margaret had known she was going out that afternoon; a few weeks, came the reply. Her mother asked if she had thought about making sure she had sufficient funds to cover today's costs and Margaret saying, well no, she supposed she hadn't. Margaret would have been fourteen then, I twelve, and it would be quite a while before either of us would be out earning our own living but Margaret's mother pointed out that employers do not give advances on wages so no, she would not give any advance on pocket money. A strong lesson, obviously, that has stayed with me all these years.

The housekeeper, Nelly, lived in, in her own quarters. Shamefully, we followed the children of the house in addressing her as Smelly Nelly. I am truly sorry. Other staff also lived in, including the gardener, I think; others came when required.

Auntie Dolly and Uncle Jack had five sons, the youngest about my age. On our first meeting, they insisted on taking me back to Monto with them. I was a slight, shy little thing and terrified. I had to fit in with a dairy farm and horses, and while all the males certainly knew how to behave as gentlemen when the occasion demanded, around the farm they were boisterous, noisy, teasing.

For a few weeks, I was with a strange family that seemed to have casual manners, whose individuals would interrupt, shout, disagree, laugh, give hugs in passing, make fun of each other, but for the first time ever I felt I was with people who really liked each other. Loved would come later but I didn't know what that was then.

My mother didn't cuddle, didn't touch, except to help us dress and brush our hair. We didn't sit on her lap. My father wasn't there in the beginning but I was told my sister's father loved me, treated me as his own – in fact, he is named on my birth certificate as my stepfather. I was angry that my father was denied but if he was the normal, tactile, human, acting as my father, I am grateful.

I couldn't ride a horse, so I was put on the old grey mare and my young cousin once or twice removed was told to keep us in the kitchen paddock. He did not. He led us out and hit the horse's rump. I don't know how I stayed on – perhaps the old horse wasn't travelling very fast – but I was terrified. A little girl up on a horse is a long way from the ground. My young relation was severely reprimanded, I learned, but not in my hearing. I was, and am, a city girl, although I did ride on the horse later at Rochdale. Visits to Monto were more enjoyable when I was fifteen, sixteen, and being escorted to country dances and balls by the second youngest.

Of course I had to go to school. My parents had been advised that Roman Catholic run schools provided the best academic education. Three weeks seems to be the limit of things, as that is how long I managed there.

I lived in a totally non-religious house, I knew nothing of any religion, so the language and practices at a Roman Catholic school was like being in a foreign country. Well, we were, but the school was worse. Nuns must have still worn habits in England at that time but they weren't in public view. My brother and I might have gone to Sunday Mass about three times at my grandmother's urging but, knowing nothing about it, neither of us took it seriously. I probably knew more about what had happened to the Jewish people during the war. My Roman Catholic classmates crowded around me, many with a desire to poke me, see if I was real, wanting to know how I could exist if I didn't believe in Jesus Christ.

Next, a state school. I was still shy and on the first day I was sitting at my desk, looking down at it, trying to decipher all the teacher was saying. It seemed she was talking to some boy called Jacky and becoming very irate. I looked up and she was looking at me; she yelled, 'Yes, I'm talking to you!'

I had never been shouted at before and I was so taken aback I blurted out that wasn't my name. It's a wonder she didn't fall in a faint. My response didn't endear me to her but it did secure me a place with my fellow students. I didn't seem to be very long at that school, though, and I think Eagle Junction State School was next and where I thrived. I was a class monitor, a house captain and, for two years with the same teacher, placed in University Row with a dozen others whose IQ was a bit above the average. We were given more challenging work as well as learning French and Latin.

My first flight, alone, after I'd turned ten, and being invited to the cockpit to talk to the pilot. It was unusual for children to fly alone and the air hostesses, as they were named then, made a fuss of me. I arrived in a west Queensland town, St George, and was collected by people I didn't know with a long drive further west to their grazing property at Dirranbandi, and its strangeness.

I remember the dust and wondering how people stayed clean in it. I'd always been fussy about being clean. They had two children, Billy and Barbara, with whom I stayed friends for many years. When he was sixteen, Billy took on an apprenticeship in Brisbane so we would go dancing together, or see a film occasionally. Billy had given me my first boy–girl kiss behind one of the sheds on my first visit. I think our whole friendship stayed with that one kiss.

I just did, accepted, what my parents dictated in those early years.

I thought I didn't know these people but I never got around to asking my parents who, exactly, they were. I don't know why I was sent, either. Perhaps my mother was hoping someone would want to adopt me. My brother was becoming independent and my sister took a lot of her time and also money in medical costs. I don't know what Dad would have thought of that and I'm probably just being fanciful.

My new Australian brother arrived when I was eleven. As I had been, still was to a degree, a minder of my sister, so I became the carer of my young brother. His blood dyed my white shorts and shirt red when he fell while in my care, and I carried the toddler up the terraced garden, up the steps by the side of the house to reach our street-level frontage. My mother rang for the doctor. I didn't, and don't, panic. Our doctor was prompt in arriving. We laid towels and sheets on the dining table, put my brother on it, and I held him still while the doctor cleaned up the blood and inspected the damage.

My brother had cut his face across the outer corner of an eye, on the edge of a step. She said it needed stitching and gave my brother a local anaesthetic. The doctor specifically asked me to hold him still and quiet while she stitched. I felt wonderfully brave and trusted while the doctor talked of how easily toddlers, small children, can come to grief no matter how closely they were watched. It was all so gentle but she was letting my mother know it was not my fault. Our doctor was a very perspicacious woman. Eurasian, too, which was a rare racial mix in those days. Notwithstanding that was what ours was.

My dad liked to go to the races on Saturday afternoons. He allowed himself thirty shillings play money. He came home one such Saturday and my mother asked how he'd fared.

My father, looking very doleful, said, 'Well, you know how it is…'

My mother said she would put the kettle on for tea and I went with her to collect cups, plates, cake. We returned to the dining room and, in the middle of the same table my young brother had been operated on, was a pile of money. My dad had actually won. And quite a lot. It was usually a case of coming out even.

There was the twelve-year-old me running away, often but not far, because I felt unloved. My older brother coming after me and making me laugh while being piggybacked home.

I was still twelve when we moved into our Queenslander-style home. After all the expenses of buying and moving, the last purchase being a box of groceries, my dad said he had sixpence left.

Auntie M and Uncle B had bought an orchard in Stanthorpe where we went for holidays and my mother frequently was there at the busiest times, helping out. Every season we would be sent boxes of fruit – apples, delicious, sweet and dripping with juice when one bit into them; peaches like peaches are supposed to taste; and other fruits.

It was Auntie M who told me about the importance of cleaning one's ears, between one's toes and the secret bits. It had been Auntie M, too, who had overcome my mother's reluctance to allow my sister and me to share our huge bath on the ship with the other two children, David and Elsa.

My mother had been brought up by servants but did become a nurse and should have realised the value of mixed bathing; her lack of motherhood skills perhaps explained the gap in our educations. Auntie M kept on with the orchard after the death of her husband. Uncle B had been using a circular saw, fell on it and just about sliced himself in half. His son was witness to the horrible scene and ran three miles to get help.

It was also, during one of my sister's and my holidays there, when I discovered the taste thrill of peanut paste with apricot jam – the latter homemade, of course. I couldn't decide what to put on my toast so… I'd graduated from puffed wheat.

The house – and a farewell

Our Australian house on stilts was the sort of thing we saw from the train when we arrived in the country and laughed at. We came to understand the sense of such architecture, allowing air to circulate and help keep it cool. It was also supposed to deter snakes, rats and mice with the metal caps on top of the supporting poles.

Ours was double-storey height supported on its wooden stilts and what passed for a laundry under the back stairs. There was a copper, two concrete tubs and some contraption of heavy rollers operated by hand, that extracted water from the heavy wet garments. When it was possible, we upgraded to an automatic washing machine, automatic in that the body of the machine agitated the dirty laundry in hot, soapy water and then we had to guide the items through the rollers attached, into one tub of rinsing water, back through the rollers, swung around over the tubs, into the second tub of rinsing and then again before hanging out to dry. If you've never felt the weight of a wet sheet, you won't understand how we stayed fit and slim without the need of diets and gym fees.

From our rented home, we would sometimes go on picnics, taking our various bags of food, swimming costumes, towels et cetera, down the hill to the train station and going to the beach at Sandgate (or was it Shorncliffe?) and sometimes Redcliffe. Each carrying what one could.

One day, our mother asked us children about using the money the government gave us, then called child endowment, that went into the bank and would be used for our education or some such, to help in purchasing a second-hand car. It was stressed, it was really our money, to be used for our benefit; unanimously we agreed buying a car was to our benefit. It was a black Austin and served us well for several years.

So our under-the-house space was also home to the car. It rested on a concrete slab. The rest was dirt. Number 67 Cook Street, Northgate, wasn't the smartest house in the street, and the suburb, then, was considered an outer one. In the early days, it had been near impossible to persuade a taxi driver to drive my dad home from the city late at night. Now, it is the best street in a sought-after location, eleven minutes by train from the CBD. Dad had never wanted to drive so, while we might not have had the best house in the street, it was the only one where the lady of it had a motor car and regularly drove it. I used to catch a train to Eagle Junction station and a quick walk to Eagle Junction State School, and later, a train to the city and then a tram to Brisbane State High.

My parents hadn't had the house inspected by a builder or pest inspector before purchase; a foot of one of the furniture carriers went through the floorboards of the main bedroom. White ants. We'd already met, sort of accepted, the wildlife of grasshoppers, cockroaches, vicious ants, lizards, snakes, beetles of this subtropical clime while we'd lived in the rented house. White ants and borers were a new thing. And costly when encountered at such close quarters. Over the years, much of the house was refloored, the timber stilts, stumps replaced by concrete posts and more of the dirt floor concreted.

Another first for us was the outside lavatory. True, it looked pretty in the yard hidden behind a trellis of pink flowers but beyond the pale as far as my parents were concerned. A nuisance at night-time and an absolute pest during the wet season. My parents had been told, by the agent, that the sewerage system would be extended to this suburb in twelve months, two years at the most. It was a lie. Eventually, under the mayoralty of Clem Jones, the whole of Brisbane was sewered. Our new flushing toilet went on the back veranda. The bathroom, goodness knows where it was before, had been tucked into the end of the side veranda with a doorway made into the dining room.

Not counting the verandas, the dining and lounge rooms took up the length of the house, with a lovely carved arch separating the two spaces. The kitchen was large, the country house kind with room for a table and chairs at which we'd have breakfast and casual lunches and where Saturday's baked cakes, biscuits, slices, would cool before filling the many tins and which would be empty again by Friday. The kitchen table was circular and in my early teens, my mother and I would dance around it to some catchy music from the radio. As well as the chairs that went with the table, there was a stool which was my favourite place on which to perch.

The working part of the house was at the back, facing west. This home was built when all houses had their kitchen at the rear of the building regardless of where the hot tropical sun might be in the afternoons when the lady of the house was cooking a hot dinner! (My dad did actually cook sometimes but in those years it was usually the female who stayed home to look after it and its occupants. It was also before barbecues became so popular and where the men donned the aprons.)

I would have moved it to the front bedroom, east, and brought it up-to-date. Informal meals would have been eaten there. The kitchen would become the main bedroom with the veranda toilet expanded to become en suite. I might have added another room to the back.

The suburban bakery was diagonally opposite, behind a house just like ours. The yeasty aromas of bread were very enticing. One or other of us would go over to buy our loaf, invariably nibbling the fresh, crispy crust on the way back. The loaves and bread rolls were delivered further afield by way of a horse and cart. The horse had his stable on the same block of land. We could always get manure for the garden and in thanks we would often feed the horse a carrot. I still remember the sweaty, singleted baker scratching his back with the large knife he used to cut the dough into the desired lengths for baking. I was shocked by that unclean act and debated with myself about whether or not I should tell someone or allow for the fact the heat of the oven would kill any potential germs. I kept it to myself and obviously had not considered general cleanliness, hands, blowing noses, and the proximity of the stable. And we all stayed healthy.

One of the first things we did was plant a tree, a gift from Auntie Vi and Uncle Eddy. There's a photo of me next to the newly planted poinciana, my height then but which would grow taller than the house. I was becoming Australian in the house of my parents, not naturalised, I didn't do that until many years later, but fitting in, making friends, adapting to the rhythms of this country.

I suppose one begins being acculturised the minute one steps into a new environment. My mother was trying to maintain in us our Englishness, English manners, values, mores. Whatever the ethnicity, manners et cetera are mostly learned through osmosis so while we absorbed the good points of living, we might also have picked up mixed values. I fear I lacked graciousness. Much later in my life I had a dear friend, several years older than I, who was a gracious lady in every sense. She is no longer alive but I still aspire to her graciousness.

One day, still in the rented house, mother and I were walking down the hill to the rail station. A school friend was across a wide expanse of ground and shouted, 'Hey, Jacqueline, g'day, how're ya going?' I shouted back that I was fine, thanks. I was told I was being unladylike, I shouldn't shout and if I had to make a reply it should have been, 'I'm very well, thank you.' I told my mother I was not going to be rude and ignore him, I had to raise my voice if he were to hear me, and I was certainly not going to be so formal in my speech for a casual exchange. I was finding myself.

The Australian tongue can sound strangulated at times and even now, after sixty-six years of residency in this country, I can have difficulty in grasping a speaker's meaning. When my first son was still an infant, my mother had visited me in Sydney. We decided on afternoon tea at a pretty café by a lake. A waitress came for our order. We asked if there was a menu; no, so all right, what was available? The girl rattled off a list of treats to be had but neither my mother nor I could understand a word of what she said. We asked her to repeat, a bit more slowly, but still we could not grasp anything except the very last which sounded something like 'rossintos'. We hazarded it might be raisin toast so that was what we had, with tea.

It was there, in that house, I'd had a rapid growing up between the ages of twelve and nineteen, when I left for another state, another capital city, a different life. It was where, at moments of marital disharmony, my then husband arranged to send me and our son for an extended holiday! Until he sent the money for my return fare. For the approximate ten years we were married, my assertion that we lived under the same roof for about half of that was only half a joke.

It was where I first fell in love, and several times after that. But it's the first I remember and wonder about: the what ifs? What if mother hadn't been such a snob and lied, withheld information, confiscated mail when primary school ended and we went our separate ways…?

I would have been fourteen; the boy, whose schooling had been interrupted by polio, sixteen. He was gentle and gentlemanly; we were dancing partners. He came to my parties, I went to his. He didn't seem to have a father and I didn't know of any siblings. It was decided that he would leave school at the end of eighth grade, by which time students are usually fourteen and legally able to work. He became an apprentice mechanic. I was always destined for an academic life. My mother married my father but she wasn't going to have her children become tradespeople (or hotel porters) or even marry one! He ended up as chief mechanical engineer at the same place he started his apprenticeship, one of the largest processing businesses then in the south-east of the state.

The school had its centenary celebration not long after mother's death – our first contact for forty years. Oh, yes, our feelings were real but would they have survived the everyday trials and tribulations of living? At the dinner dance that night, I met two couples who had been ahead of me at school but who had been couples since the same age as I was at fourteen.

We were on opposite sides of the political fence, but he might not have been had he been exposed to my mother, our friends, knew the history. My mother had broken the mould in her family, which was, by accident of birth or nefarious dealings in the distant past, upper-crust and Conservative but my mother, from the age of fifteen, fought for the rights of the workers and joined the Labour Party. Her grandmother used to call her 'The Bolshevik'. But she insisted on living, as far as was possible, as the Conservatives of her day lived. Talk about confusion.

I learned, throughout that day and night, my friend had called in at my house on his way home from work to see me, leave a letter. His times didn't coincide with my arrival home, his letters were never delivered to me and his visits were never disclosed. After a few attempts, he said my mother told him I was not interested in knowing him, I was busy at school and living my life. I know I was very disappointed thinking he was no longer interested enough in me to want to keep contact. I wrote two letters to him but he didn't get those either. He was as disappointed as I. Why didn't my sister tell me? She was at home, would have known. And who knows, had we kept on being friends, dancing at Arthur Murrays and so on, I might not have become 'boy mad', as my mother claimed I did; I might not have fallen in love with the excitement of motorbikes, might not have had the accident. But the what-ifs are a waste of time; he married, had two daughters and said he was happy.

Sex and love – I'd always put them together, meaning the same thing. I desperately needed to be loved, so sexual intercourse started pretty early. At fifteen and still working the Saturday-morning job, I had begun to know a young man of twenty. We started going out and he introduced me to sex. He really did want to marry me; he had a very nice family that welcomed me but love or sex didn't take me so far as to accept his proposals. Once I'd started high school and joined the Royal Queensland Art Society, I went out with slightly younger, late teens, boys.

I formed a relationship with one of the artists, whose parents sent him to Canberra (he was still under age, which was twenty-one) rather than see a serious relationship develop. I have one of his Brisbane sketches. And then one night I was on my way to a school dance with a friend of my cousin.

At sixteen, my mother had been a motorbike rider; I was not new to them but did not have my own, but that night my mother did not want me to ride pillion on my friend's bike. Of course I told her she was being silly, but beware a mother's premonitions. And rethink the ties that bind.

The lights were not working properly but we'd managed to get to the other side of town and were not too far from the school. Our journey had taken longer than it would have had we been travelling at the usual speed, but my friend had been cautious. We had to go down a steep hill, our speed had picked up, the lights failed and we went into the side of a car making a right-hand turn. My friend's head went through the passenger-side window and I flew over the two vehicles, landing on my head, like an arrow, several metres away.

My cousin, being concerned about our late arrival, came looking for us. No mobile phones in those days. He arrived at the scene as the ambulance officer was putting me back on the ground saying it was too late, I was dead. My friend was most definitely not and he was attended to but both bodies, his and mine, were put into the ambulance. I don't know who or when it was decided I was not dead. I was in a very deep coma and I remember being in a lift and looking down at my body.

My parents were told I might not survive; if I did, the medicos didn't know what state I'd be in, vegetative, severely brain damaged. It was a case of expect anything. My friend was in hospital three days. He insisted on seeing me, as he could not believe I wasn't mangled. In fact, I looked perfectly normal, pale, no doubt, but no broken bones, no blood on the outside, it was leaking on the inside; if I did die, I was going to make a pretty corpse.

My mother's feelings about that particular trip not being safe were so strong she had even offered to pay for a taxi. It was a shock, though half-expected, when the police phoned to tell her the news – I think it was a phone call but she phoned my dad and then immediately drove to the hospital. Breaking the speed limit, she told me later.

In 1957 not so much was known about the brain as now. I have read extensively about the brain's plasticity and how it can repair itself.

Scarring shows on MRI scans; when I came out of the coma, I had amnesia, not knowing who I was or any members of my family. But I could think. When they visited, they called me by my name so when asked by doctors, psychiatrists, that is what I gave them. My family called each other by their names so I attached those appellations to those faces. That was easy; what was difficult was remembering the past. All the information I'd amassed at school and through daily experience had gone. I had been studying Maths A, the more complicated mathematics, but I couldn't and still can't go into the intricacies of it. Nor could I coherently explain the finer points of English grammar. But I get by. When friends talk about the books they read/had read to them, I am lost. I have none of that memory.

Sixteen and my brain was all but a clean slate. Events I could visualise gradually returned and I could build on those. It is amazing how many pictures one can store in one's brain.

My body did not escape injury, it just didn't show, and it can and does give me pain. My physiological age is older than that of a similar body that did not suffer such trauma. I learned, relearned, many things, although I did not return to school. I wouldn't have stood a chance. (I go more fully into my entering university in following chapters.) Studies have shown trauma has an effect on one's personality. I don't know in what ways I might have changed except I tire quickly, have little physical strength and stress can cause severe head pain and I become very vague, as if I am in a fog. I am less coherent, which must confuse those who know me.

That house saw my different psychological states and the efforts that went into making me whole again.

Some of my memory returned, I think, and I relearned; there were and still are, periods of fog. I don't know in what ways I might have changed but I do know, at least in retrospect, that I was not ready for marriage at age eighteen. I wasn't happy at home or within myself and marriage was the way out, the solution. My education had finished with the accident.

No bones had been broken but my spine was compressed by the force of my head hitting the ground. I was probably deeply bruised in places but those injuries were secondary to the state of my brain. It bled, was bruised, swollen. MRIs still show damage. At age seventy-six, my body is ageing and causing pain ahead of its time. But, as I floated above my allegedly dead body, I felt nothing except mild interest. No trumpets, no pearly gates.

The wide front veranda was where I had my first, full-blown, argument with my mother. Even here, in the warmer climate, my sister was not able to attend school. Anxiety could bring on an asthma attack and this might have been part of the reason. I had made snowmen for her, sat with her when she could hardly breathe, and, as Auntie M made clear, I spent more time keeping my sister company in our cabin or the ship's hospital than playing on deck with other children. I had also become her teacher. I'd taught her the alphabet, how to read, passed on my knowledge as it came to me and expanded. When I was invited to friends' birthday parties, I would ask if I might take my sister. An awful gall, when I think about it now, but somewhere in me I knew she needed socialisation. I had spent a lot of time with her, being her minder, teacher, socialiser.

I told my mother it was long past the time my sister should be having a proper education, through formal channels. She told me it was none of my business and I could do as I wished with my own children but what she did had nothing to do with me. I begged to differ, saying it was very much my business as I was the one buying her books, passing on the knowledge I gained in my own classes and also, when invited to a party, asking if I might take my sister as well. I shouted at her that it was my business when I was the one taking responsibility. I was twelve. My mother still did nothing.

My sister had a thirst for knowledge and would have done well had she had the opportunity to study; as it was, when we went to university parties, she was asked what she was reading and, depending on her mood, she would answer anything from archaeology to law to zoology. She was sufficiently knowledgeable to convince anyone of anything.

At thirteen, I had a Saturday-morning job and, as well as buying what I needed and saving what I could, I bought books, novels, biographies, history for my sister, who probably had a better mind than I. If she said she was doing law, she could convincingly argue black was white; archaeology, and you'd be itching to get away to a dig.

She never forgave our mother for her lack of responsibility and the fact she couldn't do maths.

Perhaps we all have a core of insularity and I do enjoy my own company. People would say I wasn't shy, and I could enjoy being the centre of attention, but I think it's like being a clown and wearing masks. I would always speak up against injustice and try to right a wrong but I felt, feel, shy. I was not encouraged in any of my interests and told continually that I wasn't good enough, not as clever as my older brother nor as intelligent as my sister. Yes, the same sister my mother refused to educate. I was also discouraged from having friends, Australian friends, as they were descendants of convicts and not up to our standard. I don't know what our standard was. We didn't have any money, getting by was a struggle, we no longer had those extended contacts, the network that connects like with like. And really, after the war, I don't know how secure any of those contacts might have been.

My mother had made a statement in marrying my father and probably closed many doors in the doing. After those first two and half years with my sister's father, I don't remember being read to and I seem to think I wasn't introduced to live opera until I was about fourteen and we had new neighbours. The divorced Mr Ladd had a daughter, my age, at boarding school. She went home during the holidays and for any long weekends. Often, during those times, Mr Ladd invited me to join him and his daughter for a visit to an opera or a concert. Mr Ladd spent all of his money on his daughter and I can remember her looking at me as if I were some strange insect.

There was the time we had arranged to meet in the city. I can't remember the occasion but I do remember the rain; it was pouring. In those days the top end of Queen Street was generally known as the Quay and the Prudential building took up the corner of Queen and George. I was there just ahead of time; there was no shelter, no awning, under which I could get some protection. But, horrors of horrors, I desperately needed to go to the toilet. There wasn't a public toilet handy; if I left to find one, I would be late meeting my companions. I thought I could hang on and use the toilets at the venue. They were late, I couldn't hang on and I was absolutely mortified as urine flowed down my legs. I couldn't blame a broken pipe on the building and I remember thinking that I would never again see all the passers-by who looked at me. But of course, my neighbours arrived. That might have been the last time we went anywhere together.

Mr Ladd knew a lot about opera, classical music, art and occasionally spent evenings at our place in discussion. From my observations and half-listening, they seemed to be equal conversations, each contributing, taking up in the middle of the other's sentences, but my mother never discussed such things with me. I don't know how well she understood the physics of osmosis but I think she firmly believed the child would absorb knowledge like a sponge soaking up water. She had said, at one time or another, that children shouldn't be born until they are sixteen and able to carry on an intelligent conversation.

The daughter, whose name I have quite forgotten, had become quite snobby at her girls' school and looked down her nose at me, in my very nice, well-made, but nonetheless home-sewn clothes. But for all my mother's wish that my sister and I behave like English ladies, in their company I felt gauche, untutored in the finer things, and my clothes were not stylish, sophisticated.

Internally, I was mortified by some of my clothes. In primary school, I was a pretty good sprinter and was about fourteen when I competed in some four-hundred-yard finals. My mother had made me a white blouse in some faux silk fabric. It was to serve a variety of occasions but the buttons were too small for the buttonholes. I was triumphantly jogging to a stop when I realised my blouse was completely undone. No vest, no bra for my as yet small but budding breasts. Of course I was embarrassed and I must have turned a brighter red than my recent exercise caused but there was nowhere to hide. I stopped, did up the buttons and carried on. On this occasion, I did know some of those who might have witnessed my embarrassment but it was the last meet of the season and I was about to go on to high school. The only one of my year to go to Brisbane State High, on the other side of town. The rest, who were going on to high school, were attending local schools or the industrial state high (boys) or the commercial college (girls).

Mother made my high school uniforms, so I didn't look quite the same as every other girl and my blazer was a particular embarrassment. It looked very home-made, not properly tailored, the shoulder pads not right, the maroon binding of cheap bias instead of grosgrain braid, but I had no choice. The winter jumper was navy blue for girls, grey for the boys. My older brother's grey was still serviceable so, yes, I wore that too. I suppose I should be thankful that my differences made me defiant, individual, when I could have curled up inside of myself. But it does take a lot of energy.

I must have been about fourteen, I think, when the couple on the other side had their first child. They didn't have a telephone so gave our number to the hospital, and one evening while mother was preparing dinner, a call came to say Betty had a boy. Mother asked me to pop over and tell her husband. He was sitting in his kitchen in the gloom, without his light on, and as I'd gone up the back steps he pulled me in. I stumbled and then I was on his lap with his hand inside my knickers. Not for very long, I assure you, but, shocked and upset, I flew home again. I told no one but surely my not wanting dinner, being obviously upset, should have alerted my mother to something, but she never did ask me what was wrong. I never spoke to him again.

Relations between parent and child are changing all the time and today (2016) I think there is more openness between them. Not in every family but more families are encouraging conversation and confidences.

More parents are actually prepared to believe their child when said child is accusing an adult of unacceptable behaviour. I couldn't talk to my mother and I would never have thought of going to Dad.

I hated her when a huge fuss was made when a stone catapulted through a pane of the neighbour's front veranda door and my young brother was blamed. Even if it were not he, it was one of his friends and I thought, all of this over a small pane of glass, nothing for the outrage done to me.

I felt outrage again when my aunt's second husband was teaching me to swim. He manoeuvred us away from the main group and groped. I kicked and screamed and that was the end of my forays into anything deeper than a bath. Mother thought I was having fun; Dad would come over and steer us back to the group. My son has told me I would find it very relaxing if I could just allow myself to float and he would help me, but my aversion to water because of that event is too strong.

There had been an earlier event, when I was ten and we were picnicking at Redcliffe; a friend of my brother, a big fifteen-year-old, had been sitting on one side of a rubber ring, me on the other. He threw himself off, which made me fall into the water too. I was dragged up, coughing and spluttering, and spent a little time on the beach but soon went back into the water. The friend did it again and that started my wariness, for it was not fear, about water.

I don't know how my brother, seven and a half then, and I survived at least some neglect. I suspect my brother shouldered more responsibility than a child of his age should have. And probably sooner than I was old enough I became a nursemaid, minder, for my sister. I have mentioned the bowls of fruit, as one remembers a beautiful still life painting, and knowing I could not eat any; they were for my sister. And also making snowmen outside a window so that my sister could see them from the warmth of inside the house. I don't remember my aunt or grandparents in those years but it was my sister who received all the attention; it was she who could blithely pick the heads off the flowers of my grandparents' garden while I was not allowed to pick a bloom. Always the outsider.

Before my early Australian school experience, I said I had never been shouted at; I had never been struck, either, but one day, sitting at the kitchen table talking to my dad, elbow on table, chin resting in my hand, my dad suddenly hit my forearm, telling me to get my elbows off the table. A small event but I can remember my astonishment; my father had hit me! I laugh about it now but at the time I was much aggrieved. I must have said something.

I was back in Brisbane for my twenty-first birthday, so it was celebrated in that house, as were the receptions of my two marriages. It was frequently a noisy house but it could also be quiet and still, such as at exam study time. It was political, hosting celebrations or wakes, depending on whether or not our party had won or lost. Indigenous students found solace, conversation, encouragement within its walls. Then there were the times we shopped for balloons and streamers in appropriate colours, made signs and danced to different music as several midnights witnessed various friends, Commonwealth scholarship students, graduate from being colonial subjects to proud, independent nationals. For the father of my middle child, I cross-stitched a bookmark with Uhuru, Freedom, worked down the centre.

The city stretch of the Brisbane River was the barrier separating the good side from the bad side. The south side of the river was the slum area. Those with little or no income congregated there. It was the Aboriginal side. Boarding houses were prolific, and just a little further upriver were factories. As people do, the Aborigines would have used the river as a conduit as did the early, and later, white settlers. It would have been the white settlers who despoiled the river with factory and human effluent.

Victoria Bridge connected the two sides but if an Aboriginal person was found to be crossing from south to north, the police wanted to know why. We met many First Australians through our connection with OPAL, One People of Australia League, started by a Mrs —, who owned a boarding house in Cordelia Street in South Brisbane. She housed many Aborigines and decided to form a sporting team with that name. She advertised asking for expressions of interest, donations of sporting equipment, money. My mother sat on the committee. Mrs — maintained she was Indian but, having since read some of the history, I am now not sure.

The first two full-blood trainee teachers resided there and liked to spend time at our house. They were always invited, never arriving unexpectedly. They would have to cross the bridge and catch a bus at North Quay. Invariably they would be stopped and interrogated by police. Where were they going? Why? Were they expected? What was the name of their alleged host? Did they have a phone? Frequently the police would ring us, saying that so-and-so claimed he was invited to our home, could we confirm that? Bus drivers got to know our house as new friends, from all over, would ask to be let down at the Cook Street stop. The driver would stop, blocking the road, and point out our house – third on the left.

We weren't the only crazy family in the street; a couple further up were medical missionaries in PNG. Frequently, when in residence at home, they had PNG people staying with them. Neither they nor we seemed to suffer any ostracism, anything negative, from the rest of the street's residents. Since white settlement, the Australian government has gone through many stages and different forms of managing the Aboriginal problem.

Early governors tried being friendly while at the same time giving away their land to settlers; the whites shot, caught, more wildlife than was needed for immediate use and knew nothing of which creatures represented the sacred totems of which tribes; genocide and slave labour have been practised and today, being a tiny fraction, 2.4% of the total population, manage to occupy more than half the space in jails and youth detention centres.

Successive governments have not tried to understand Aboriginal culture, these people who have been settled on this land for more than forty thousand years. No agreements were ever made, no treaties; they were lynched, shot, poisoned, not even counted as people, being classed as flora and fauna.

My young brother came in one day and in passing told us the

medical couple were back and had visitors. My sister wanted to know what kind of visitors, not explaining to eight-year-old brother she meant were they black or white. Our brother wanted to know what she did mean by what kind and when it was clearly stated he stormed, 'I don't know. They were just people.' Which is the way we should think.

Charlie Perkins's Freedom Ride took place in 1965 with a very mixed reception. On 27 May 1967, a referendum was held with about 90% of the people agreeing the Australian Aborigines and Torres Strait Islanders should be included in the next census. It took until 13 February 2008 before Prime Minister Kevin Rudd made an official apology to the People of the First Nations on behalf of a large proportion of the population who felt deeply about the wrongdoing inflicted upon them. It is referred to as the Sorry Speech.

The year 2017 marked the fiftieth anniversary of that referendum and in this twenty-first century, we are seriously discussing the Constitution and whether or not it should acknowledge Australian Aborigines. I have mentioned the forty-thousand-plus years they have inhabited this land, making them the longest-settled people on the planet. They had and have their music, art, architecture, many languages, belief systems, strict social and moral rules, which, if broken, met with appropriate punishment – which did not include the death penalty. I will venture to say they had a value system superior to that of the felons and most of their jailers who, on behalf of their government, appropriated this country. And many white Australians believe it is still a racist country.

Often, in my visits back to Brisbane, I would, with my mother and usually my sister, meet or bump into Faith Bandler and many more, during or after a mass meeting demanding rights for People of the First Nations. My first husband (Indian) and I were often verbally abused or at best looked at with incredulity, especially when I was obviously pregnant. The father of my second son (African) was frequently refused service in bars and elsewhere. As late as 1978, that son, as a boarder at Brisbane's leading private school, was picked out of a group of white friends by cruising police, and questioned. The boys had parental and school permission to attend a party of a day boy. Later, again with white friends, he would be barred from nightclubs until his friends realised what was happening and confronted the bouncer. They either all entered or none.

Often, my sister and I were the only white faces at the O'Connor Boathouse, where young Aboriginal people gathered to dance, play music. Indigenous 'Billy' was a special friend who was introduced to opera by way of *Carmen* being performed one day in the shell in the Botanical Gardens. He hadn't wanted to go, it being too highbrow, but he thoroughly enjoyed it and went on to listen and watch more. He proposed marriage to me when I was about sixteen and, while I was flattered, I knew I was too young.

Uncle Mac Petrie was an elder who visited sometimes; always dressed in suit and tie, he really was the perfect gentleman. He loved to have a collection of children around him and he would tell us stories. We usually knew when Uncle Mac was visiting but for some reason he came one day when we were out. He went to the churchgoing Christian family next door, where the man had molested me and whose front door pane had been broken, to leave a message. It was a boiling hot day; Uncle Mac told us later they had not even offered him a glass of water.

Expo 88 changed the south side of the river and, bit by bit, the north, city-side as well. The slum area was razed and the spectacle of Expo 88 was built, the decision afterwards to make all the river-side into parklands. Over time, it has evolved so that the performing arts centre (QPAC) is there, a ferris wheel has been erected, restaurants cater to almost every taste, the ABC has its headquarters as well as the administration of the Queensland Symphony Orchestra. Ferries take passengers up and down and across, the river. The University of Queensland has campuses on both sides. Over time, the slum of Brisbane changed to a prime location.

Mother's old treadle sewing machine lived here together with a work table bearing the indentations of stiletto heels made by the soon-to-be owner of a dress or skirt the hem of which needed to be meticulously measured. We weren't so snap happy in those days and now I only have a mental picture of the machine and its operator almost invisible in a cloud of white tulle. There is, of course, a photograph of the finished ball gown, and its wearer, posed, lacking the joyful tumult of its making. Ah, the stories of the outfits made on that machine would fill a book.

Very early on in our occupancy, my sister and I arranged backyard concerts, enrolling the local children to perform and sell tickets to their families and whoever else we and they could rope in. We were about ten and twelve then and had read about the work of the Endeavour Foundation and the hardships of the children they cared for. We wanted to help. There's a photo somewhere, from a paper, of us handing over a jar of money. I don't think our neighbours had before met anyone quite like us.

We bullied the local children into performing some sort of act but I think my sister and I were the main actors, although the only thing I do remember is my sister's opening performance. We were savvy enough to know we had to get the audience relaxed, and my sister was to start with a joke. She had a beautiful laugh, a pied piper of a thing that caught people up and made them laugh with her. She started, 'I have a joke…' and then a soft chuckle; a few more words and more laughter. People are smiling broadly at this. My sister remonstrates with herself, 'This is serious, I will tell you this joke but it…is…soo funny,' and her laugh built to a crescendo and uncontrollable. The audience was laughing, hankies wiping their eyes. I can't remember if she ever did have a joke to tell but the concert went on, the neighbourhood mums and some dads bought home-made lemonade and fairy cakes, as well as paying for their concert ticket, and went home happy.

Our fame would have helped consolidate the myth we concocted about ourselves, who we were – to wit, French princesses. When we told the boy opposite, the poor lad immediately went home, cleaned himself up and returned in a fresh set of clothes. Goodness knows what his poor mother thought. While I was told by my mother that, on the one hand, I wasn't good enough, our Australian contemporaries were not good enough to be my friends. If schizophrenia can be cultivated, I suppose my mother was going about it with determination. She didn't succeed.

It is with some chagrin that I remember some of our neighbours, one lot – a family of five children, mum, dad and grandma – who didn't own a thing, including the house, and borrowed all sorts of things often: soap powder (and horror of horrors, everything went into the washing machine together – whites, coloureds, and really dirty), milk, sugar and everything else they could run out of.

The father had a good job but drank excessively; frequent parties meant bottles thrown over our fence and sometimes breaking on the garden tap, but years after we'd all grown up I heard of the success the children had made of their lives.

A family of eight children up the street, one of whom, at the age of seventeen, had a baby which was passed off as one of her mother's – they all did well for themselves. I put it down to love and a belief in one's children, which, of course, we did not have. Standards had nothing to do with it.

For a lot of the time, the houses on either side of us were rented. When we first moved in, one side contained parents and three sons around the ages of my sister and me. Their bedroom window was opposite ours, so we rigged up a pulley between the two. The boys were horrified that we didn't eat lollies (sweets to us) or read comics and insisted on rectifying such a gap in our life. Lollies in a paper bag, the comics – pegged to our connecting line – were sent over. We lent them books and sent home-made biscuits across the space. We had to gauge the weight of whatever was being sent and attach it with an appropriate number of pegs. Not many items dropped to the ground en route. We didn't join them in their backyard games and the pulley was our secret, which of course was so obvious, we fooled no one.

Elsie and her husband rented the house on the other side when I was really into dating. Elsie really wasn't snoopy, she was just interested, and I never minded when I saw the lace curtain draw aside, whatever time it was, and her face appear behind the glass. She would remark on the niceness of my clothes, the presentability of my escort, the time I got home and whether or not my date kissed me. She and her husband had a baby, who was much loved, but Elsie had no finesse at all. The infant was picked up with no more care than a sack of potatoes, Elsie grabbing a bundle of clothing or wrapping, and straight up came the baby. The baby laughed much, much more than it cried.

In 1969 I was back living in Brisbane and by the end of 1971 I had bought my first house, in my name, making me solely responsible for the loan repayments.

In one way or another, women have been agitating for equal rights forever. At the beginning of the twentieth century, a man still owned his wife and children, and divorces were few. The 1960s had brought the Pill, giving women some control over becoming pregnant or not. More women went to, and stayed at, work. I was determined to have the security of owning my own home. The local bank manager was persuaded I was a good risk and I bought my house, quite literally on the wrong side of the tracks but affordable and mine.

I had a good job, a house, things were looking good. I think I have an itch to keep on wanting to know things, so I decided I'd learn to speak Italian at night classes at the University of Queensland. It fitted with my going straight from work, and the evenings coincided with the evenings my son went for football training.

It was arranged my son would go to my parents' house after training and, if my mother could put my son's dinner in the oven, to keep it warm, he would eat and I would be not too long after to collect him. She started complaining about his spoiling her evenings, her having to interrupt her television watching to get his dinner out of the oven et cetera. I told her he could do it himself; I said I'd stop going to my Italian class and I disliked her intensely.

She had never been a loving, supportive, parent. I wasn't encouraged to follow my dreams or act on whatever aptitude I might have had. She made my clothes and never stopped me from throwing a party but the words I remember her saying, over and over again, were that I wasn't good enough. Not as clever as my brother or as intelligent as my sister.

Several years before her death, I had said to my mother I would not allow her to die alone or in a strange place. That promise had come about because a great aunt or a cousin of mother's had been consigned to a nursing home – she had diabetes and had lost a leg – where she was miserably unhappy. There was a lack of any intellectual stimulation, no one she felt comfortable speaking to. She died alone. I had felt so terribly sorry for my great aunt, thinking she deserved more than that.

Such was the relationship between my mother and me that for the preceding twelve months, we had not exchanged one word. My son had happened, one day, to repeat something his grandmother had said.

Now, there is nothing my son doesn't know about me. I was a migraine sufferer, so he had seen me in extreme states of pain and distress, and undress, when I was both vomiting and involuntarily emptying my bowels. He knew about our finances because, as soon as he was allowed, he operated his own bankcard from my account. And not once did I ever have to pay interest on it. He knew about the casual lovers I had because, after all, we shared the same house.

So nothing my mother could have said to him should have been a surprise; what I objected to was that my mother would think it okay to discuss me, her daughter, with my son. I had told her that this time she had gone too far and I wanted nothing more to do with her.

It was Christmastime 1994 and my younger brother and his wife hosted the Christmas dinner and party. Of course my mother was there and there was no way I could not be. It was there I learned my mother was unwell. The diagnosis had not been given at that time but, just looking at her, I knew she was not well. She was not happy with her doctor but she did not have the strength to find another, so I arranged for her to have tests done at the local hospital. It was there the doctor told me the prognosis – six months. I had made a promise. I took leave from my job and moved back into the family home. We sacked her doctor with my telling him he was a useless old fool, and why.

When I was still not speaking to mother, in that year of 1994, my sister, who then lived in Townsville, had travelled down, stayed for a few weeks and went home again. This happened several times, my sister claiming to be acting as our mother's carer. My mother said she didn't want her there as she was always on the phone or out and was not a soothing person. She said she was badgering her about her parentage and my mother didn't want to talk about it. I can understand my sister's need to know about her father, but it was too late. My sister also said she wanted to build a relationship with our mother. I would have thought, living at home for all the years she did, that a relationship might have been forged.

That we none of us had the kind of relationship we would have liked was, nevertheless, the relationship we had to accept. She had not been my perfect parent but at this time I saw her as an old woman, dying. If it was in my power, she was going to do it in peace.

I went back into the blue room, the bedroom I'd shared with my sister, and dealt with the memories. We hadn't been a happy family but, as I subsequently told the young couple who bought the house, I really believed it had been happy. My sister travelled back and forth, several times. We did not share the blue room, though; she took our brother's room or lived elsewhere.

We are all, well ninety-nine per cent of us, complex, multifaceted, people. The one per cent, if that, I would say are the highly evolved, the truly good – the Dalai Lama, perhaps – but my mother was one of the ninety-nine per cent. She could be charming, witty, funny, was well-read and loved conversation. For most of the five months I shared with her – she died on 31 May 1995 – we had a good time.

In the early weeks of my return to the house, there was a lot of laughter. My mother took all the liqueurs out of the sideboard and ranged the bottles along the top. There might have been a dozen in varying stages of fullness – Crème de Menthe, Dubonnét, Tia Maria, Advocaat, Cognac, all you can think of, with the idea being we'd finish them before she died. Something every night, after dinner. I wish I'd kept the bottles. We finished off old wine and sat by the sea eating fish and chips from their wrappers.

During the course of my mother's decline, we spent much time on the front veranda. Always a favourite place to sit and often to host an afternoon tea. In the early days of my moving back in, Mother was still able to play bridge with her friends. They came to the house and I'd set up the table on the veranda. Afternoon tea was always served in the Royal Albert Country Roses china. Yes, shades of Mrs Bucket (pronounced as bouquet by the social-climbing television character). As she slowed, became weaker, Mother accepted more of my help and, finally, the wheelchair. It got to the point where I could carry her to the bathroom, where I would bathe her and then that, too, stopped and she was having bed baths.

She and I had discussed her care and we decided to ask a Buddhist-based palliative care organisation, Karuna, for assistance. Mother, her new doctor, the nurses and I decided I could manage all the medication. To begin, it was simply adjusting the doses of morphine but it graduated to more complex and personal treatment. As time and her illness progressed, the nurses worked out the aids that would help her, a different mattress, the hanging bar that would help her lift herself to a sitting position, a walker and, later, a wheelchair. When I needed, I could organise for a volunteer carer to look after her for a few hours.

She felt confident and comfortable enough to allow me to administer whatever medical assistance was required instead of calling for a Karuna nurse or the doctor every time. Obviously they trusted me to perform whatever necessary tasks there were, including the decisions on dosage of morphine. The nurses and doctor popped in, often unannounced, back from somewhere else, to have a chat, see how my mother was – and me, too, I realised later. They were lovely people.

While she had the energy, we went to a concert and saw a couple of films. The veranda outlook was superb, grassed footpaths with an avenue of poinciana trees that often met in the centre of the wide road. It could have been a bit southern American with the graciousness of the homes set back on their large blocks of land, predominantly green with splashes of wild tropical colour. These homes were not bought and sold, the owners stayed, grew old and died and that, with the feeling of space, gave a feeling of arrested time, and in my mother's time most of the owners were reaching their ends. A new cycle would begin, young families growing until, as it was at this time, their grandchildren would be back for visits. And, by the way, that area is zoned Residential A and no house will be demolished for units or anything else.

We spoke of the street and its slow changes, the gradual change of occupants. In this way, she made her farewells to those who'd been there as long as she, or longer. We tried to count the parties this house had hosted, the major events, and spoke of the minor ones, the impromptu Saturday night get-togethers and dancing on the veranda or singing around the piano. We spoke of the mammoth dinners at which it was nothing for there to be twenty friends and family seated around two tables put together – the regular dining table and the gateleg table, which I now have. My family kept its pain and sorrow, its bewilderment and unhappiness, truly hidden.

Late in the process, I was making my mother more comfortable in her bed. I was leaning over her to lift her further up the pillows and she had her arms around my neck. She looked at me and said, 'I really do love you, you know.'

I could look at her and reply that yes, I knew. I am glad we had made our peace.

It might have been three days before her death; her voice was reduced to barely a whisper and she wanted to say something to me. I leaned in, my ear close to my mother's mouth, and she told me a joke. I can't remember the joke but my explosion of laughter shattered the silence. We all of us shared a sense of humour and, while she had made me angry at times, disappointed in her as a mother, after she died there were many times when I heard something interesting or funny and my first thought would be, oh, I must tell Mum that.

All of the grandchildren had travelled from various parts of Australia to see her when she was still living. Between them, they follow and live Buddhist, Hindu, humanitarian philosophies and, as Mother neared the end, they variously wished her goodbye and suggested she was free to go. They didn't want her to suffer. They said they would live their own life as best they could and thanked her for the part she had played in it.

My sister and I have five sons between us and I remember thinking they were such nice young men. My younger brother's four children were very young at the time, twelve, ten, eight, six, or thereabouts, and my mother requested, and was permitted, to speak with them individually. My older brother's son and his partner of the time came with their baby, who went home with a new jacket knitted by mother.

As my mother's health deteriorated, my sister took every opportunity to try to establish a relationship and find out who her father was. It was the wrong time; Mother did not have the energy for the haranguing and was upset to the point of tears. I had seen her angry but I had never seen her cry. That was definitely not stiff upper lip and I was angry that she had been brought to tears now.

I sympathised with my sister's needs but I was not going to have an old woman's dying days spent in torment. Well, I don't know how tormented she might have been within herself, she certainly would not have had any torment over her impending death, but I was not going to see it happening in any other way either. I told my sister to leave.

She was staying somewhere else in Brisbane and found out that I would be out one evening and a carer would be in the house. She returned to the house and told the carer she was not needed, she would care for mother. The carer needed to check with the organisation on what she should do. It ended up with my mother in her bed, the carer, a staff member and my sister all waiting for my return. Apparently it was not the first time my sister had upset our mother on the few occasions in the early weeks that I went about my private business.

My sister ranted and raved about wanting to know the truth, establishing a relationship. The palliative care worker was counselling her about behaviour in the last days and weeks of her mother's life. My sister was told, if she could not try to help her mother to a peaceful end, she should stay away or they would have to withdraw their services. My two brothers saw more of her in those months and were surprised by how unbalanced she seemed.

While I don't believe in any heaven or hell, I do wonder what happens to the energy that we are. Our bodies decay, one way or another, but what happens to that life force that was us? Mind is not the same as brain, and some might call mind 'soul', but what is it? And if that energy that was the essence of us somehow stays somewhere, can that be how some people, more receptive, intuitive, pick up messages? Is this gene memory?

My older brother and I spoke at her cremation. She didn't have a large send-off – her children, some extended family, several close friends and the neighbours. Afterwards we assembled at her house eating the food prepared by the neighbours and drinking tea and coffee.

At the end and when I had time to think about it, I have said she had a good death. She didn't fight it, she didn't make strange noises and there were no emissions from the visible orifices. Her breathing was already very shallow and on that beautiful, sunny, last afternoon of May, I just stepped out of her bedroom for a moment as my sister just returned from the local shop.

She asked, 'How is she?' as she put her head around the bedroom door, then immediately followed it with 'I think she's gone.'

There are stories about people waiting for special moments in which to not take that next breath and Mother, being a private person, perhaps wanted that final privacy but it did seem as if she took a breath and then she didn't. As easy as that.

I went into the bedroom and for a few moments just looked down at her, then checked her carotid artery and felt nothing. She had enjoyed travel and I told her to enjoy her journey, wherever she was going.

We were a family of non-believers; my mother had been an atheist since the age of fifteen, or perhaps sooner, when the family priest, drunk every Sunday at her family's luncheons, couldn't answer my mother's questions. And she saw the total hypocrisy of religion. Her children were not inducted into any religion and the only religious instruction I ever received was what I read for myself. It was a quiet death, my mother just stopped breathing, but then the strangest thing – there was a sudden energy moving about the room, like a fast-kicked ball (round, of course) ricocheting off the walls. No noise, just movement. My sister said she felt it, too, like some force quickly moving around the room's space. Physically, my mother looked very much at peace; a change from the last weeks, when she'd resembled someone from Auschwitz. I made a note of the time of her dying but we were not in a rush to ring the doctor or anyone else.

The house hadn't taken long to sell. My siblings and I had put a modest price on it but I really wished I could have paid them their share of its value and kept it. I felt very strongly about it being the family home. I had lived in it for only seven years but it was the family house for forty-two.

The disposal of body, goods, chattels, the house, happened in due course, my own farewell to the house taking little steps along the way. My older brother thought the best way to deal with the contents was to have the four of us sit around the table and take it in turns to name one item at a time, starting with the big things. My sister and I agreed to do the same with the jewellery and some of the better china and glassware. It still left a lot of odds and sods. I was exhausted and when everything was done, went away for a week's holiday.

My older brother and I spoke at the cremation. Neither of the other siblings wanted to. My younger brother was the only one who cried; he had a better life than the rest of us, he was healthier, grew up in fresh air and space, had a pet and yet, when his mother-in-law died, he spoke, saying she was the best, the only mother he had. I had cried, once, when she was still alive and I was giving her a bed bath. The skin on her spine was peeling away; there was no flesh, and I thought, it's not fair. I should have given her an overdose.

On my return from my brief holiday (which turned out to be quite traumatic), I found my sister had cleaned out everything else – blankets, more china that actually had sentimental value, all sorts of little things. She had packed it all and left several boxes with the neighbour to pick up when convenient; she had already told us she wanted no more to do with us. I'm sorry she felt so alienated from what was left of a family that had changed its course for her. We haven't spoken since June 1995.

It was left to me to hand over the keys to the young new owners. I wanted them to be happy in this house so I told of the parties, the celebrations, the laughter, for they are the things I want to remember. I also spoke of the changes I would make and gave them the plans I had drawn. Passing on the house meant the end of an era, the beginning of another as I ceased being anyone's child and became a female elder of my little tribe. It had been the family home for forty-two years, though for the last seventeen it was more likely to be referred to as Mum's place. Dad had been its joint owner for twenty-five years, until his early death.

The death of my mother brought other endings – the total break initiated by my sister, the beginning of fracture lines with my brothers, the end of a friendship and the parting with a house that had been a home, albeit with all the imperfections of the relationships within it.

There appeared to be few changes made to the house in the times I went past, visiting my brother and his family. It changed from being white to mission brown, which looked awful, heavy and hot. More recently, I've been told, a swimming pool has been installed in the back garden and plumbers and carpenters have been working inside the house. Perhaps my plans of long ago are being used at last. I hope so; it keeps a bit of my heart in the place.

Work

My Saturday-morning job came by way of my aunt when I was thirteen. The job gave me some extra money and a feeling of independence. Well, it wasn't exactly extra money as I didn't have any to begin with but it was spending money. We didn't get pocket money but our needs were met. At that time, fourteen was the legal minimum age at which boys and girls could start earning a living but my aunt worked in the office of a department store called Penney's. In time it became Coles and now that particular store is no more.

This was in the days when department shops had separate counters for the various items. Each counter had its regular staff, its own till – cash register – and the senior of each counter was responsible for the cleanliness and satisfactory reconciliation of the cash takings each day. Staff did not leave until receipts and cash added up. I worked on haberdashery.

Ribbons, laces, buttons and elastic, hooks and eyes, sewing cotton – everything required for making a garment, from a simple child's playsuit to a lovely gown. Each Saturday morning when I arrived, I was faced with a neat, tidy counter, everything put in its place by one of the girls the evening before. It would be my job to restore it to that order before I left at close of business later that day. Closing time was one p.m. but we had to keep serving until the last customer left the shop. Then the counting and reconciliation of the cash, my tidying, sweeping and helping cover the counters with heavy cloths before any of us could think of leaving.

Of course there was pilfering, shoplifting, but it was minimal. This was mid-1950s and Australia was pretty much a working-class country; the people were basically honest. Children handed over their notes or recited their well-rehearsed request; husbands, sometimes a little sheepishly, acted pretty much the same way; and the women would look, browse, pull, poke, unravel this ribbon, that zigzag braid, wonder if lace would suit better, go back to the first, and so on. Sometimes she bought, sometimes she didn't. In a quiet moment, I or one of the other two on the counter tidied up.

I was already designing my own clothes, made up by my mother or occasionally myself – these more likely to be the slightly different, outrageous styles. If it was going to be a folly, it would be entirely my folly. My sense of colour, style, design served me well with the customers, though, as I would suggest changes to a pattern to better suit a figure or suggest various different ways of individualising a garment for a young girl. I liked the feeling it gave me, a thirteen/fourteen-year-old suggesting ideas to adults.

Years later, with three children in Sydney, I took in sewing at home. Chiffon was becoming a fashion fabric by then but it was difficult to cut and sew; I did a few sample pieces for a company and was given work. This was work I could do in odd moments and in the evenings when my husband was either working or studying. My sewing expanded as I started making things for friends who told their friends, and my supreme moments were when young women would travel from one side of Sydney to the other for me to make their wedding dresses.

A few years later, I made the three outfits my sister needed for her second wedding to a Chinese man. The first ceremony was at the Chinese temple, then the formal occasion of the register office and in the evening a reception at a Chinese restaurant. Her trousseau was largely designed and made by me.

I do little sewing these days, for myself or anyone else, but when I was a frequent visitor to the fabric shops, I could never resist engaging in conversation with other shoppers. Usually it would start as an exclamation on the quality or colour of the fabric and sometimes to tell someone the fabric she is holding to her face in the mirror just did not suit her. We two would then, usually, look for what did. Staff would tell me I should receive a commission but I couldn't help myself.

In those early days at the shop, pencil and paper were always near the till in case we needed to work out our sums on paper but it was a mark of pride to be able to do it in our head. Three and one half yards of ribbon at one shilling and ninepence per yard plus five buttons at sixpence each, the pattern at three shillings and sixpence. Elastic, and make sure you don't stretch it, we were admonished, might have been one and threepence a yard – one shilling and threepence for three feet.

My Friday afternoons at school – when the class was made to stand around the walls of the room, sitting down when one gave the wrong answer to a spelling or a mathematical question – stood me in good stead. In a class of nearly forty, I always remained as one of the last half-dozen, frequently one of two when the tussle for supremacy would last for some time, the questions becoming harder, the rest of the class either enjoying the contest or anxious for one to fail so that we might all go home for the weekend.

The money I earned on those Saturday mornings paid for fabric for clothes, personal books or other entertainment, and savings for Christmas and birthday presents. Often, walking home, I would buy an ice cream to lick along the way. It was all good training for future budgeting. As you've gathered, it was pre-decimal, the money in pounds, shillings and pence, halfpence, too, and inches, feet, yards. We even measured lengths in eighths – seven-eighths of a yard, please. Nothing multiplied by the same number as it does with decimal. Twelve pence made a shilling but twenty shillings made a pound. We had guineas, too, which were the same number of shillings as pounds so if something was one guinea, it was one pound one shilling; twenty guineas was twenty pounds twenty shillings, which really was twenty-one pounds but guineas were often used when pricing art or antique furniture, for example. The snobby way of pricing things. Length, weight, liquids all had quaint ways of measuring; twelve inches to a foot, three feet in a yard and a cricket pitch was twenty-two yards long and, I think, nine feet wide. We didn't have computers, calculators, just our heads and a knowledge of the times table.

Those were also the days of the customer always being right, never being ignored and, as I said, as long as one person was in a shop, having a right to be served. A few took a delight in lingering as long as possible but most were considerate of the long-suffering staff. I learned many things from my first job, not least that the old saying 'It's not what you know, but who' has a ring of truth in that my aunt wrangled my early and illegal entry into paid work. I maintained my position there until halfway through my sixteenth year, when I had the motorbike accident that changed my life.

For about two years, I was enveloped in a kind of fog. When overtired or stressed, it threatens to descend; there's a thick, black wall that seems to come down in my mind, like the portcullis guarding a castle. I used to think if I could identify the constituents of the wall, I'd have more mastery over it.

Sustained study was out of the question. Apparently, about six months later, I woke one day and told my mother I wanted to go to school. I thought I'd had an appendectomy. I did go; the teachers knew of my condition and I think my classmates must have been told to treat me as normally as possible and not to mention the accident. I floated about for a few days then decided I wasn't going any more. My class had given me a 45rpm record of 'Carousel' and a few other bits and pieces of pretty things when they were told I had woken from the coma.

My mother did not believe in idleness. No matter that my sister suffered with bronchial asthma and severe back problems, my mother found her a job in a dress-making factory, full of dust and lint, bent over a machine or hand-sewing. While my own life was still just a blur, she found me a job in a record shop in the city. It was an EMI outlet run by Bob Rogers. I don't think he was anything much then but became well-known as a DJ and radio announcer. And damn, I didn't get his autograph. Just like I didn't collect signatures from famous visiting conductors or musicians when I was volunteering with the long-since defunct Queensland Philharmonic Orchestra, or keep those things that become valuable antiques. I don't know how long I stayed working with Bob Rogers but I then found myself working as a clerical assistant in a government office.

Actually, I have remembered a job in an office, small, I think, with perhaps one other worker and the boss/owner. My colleague was sacked for something she denied and I believed her. I spoke up for her but the boss was adamant, so I got up and left as well. That would have been before I became a public servant.

I don't know if government positions are still gained through examination but they were then; I do not have any recollection of sitting such an exam but I remember getting out and putting back manila files in long rows of shelves. I worked in the basement of a city government building; it was dim, dusty and boring. Definitely, the more than two years immediately following the accident passed in a fog. There are moments of clarity but most of that life is behind an opaque curtain.

I have a very strong feeling that my older brother encouraged, persuaded, my parents to let me join the Brisbane Arts Theatre. That name no longer exists; it might have morphed into La Boite. We certainly have more theatre companies now than we did then. Again, this is something I didn't ever discuss with my brother – things just happened, but it would be interesting to know what went behind his thinking. Did he always see me as an extrovert and by joining a group of actors my true nature might return? On the other hand, perhaps he thought I needed drawing out. I used to draw and paint and I did some work on props; the only walk-on part I remember was as the maid in an adaptation of *Pygmalion* by George Bernard Shaw.

It was about this time we made the acquaintance of a group of Indian university students. I began going out with one of them and he would collect me from evening rehearsals with a hot supper of rice or chapatti, an Indian meal (curry), dhal, contained in the tiered stainless steel tiffin boxes. He wanted to marry me. I considered him nice enough and I really wanted to leave home; my vision was the beginning of a storybook happy family. We married in October 1959. Our son was born on 1 April 1960, two weeks after my nineteenth birthday. My husband couldn't get work in Brisbane and his younger brother in Sydney suggested he would have more luck there. He moved there before the birth of his son and my mother had insisted I stay home for the birth and six months after. This pretty much follows the Indian way, as it happens. I insisted on joining my husband when the baby was three months old. (My time in Sydney is detailed further on.)

I didn't ever realise how difficult writing a memoir could be. I have written other things, had things published but writing one's life story is something else again. The things I am attempting to cover now are my return to Brisbane in that agonising week between 1968 and 1969 and the variety of work I undertook in order to maintain my son and me.

Joining the Public Service in 1970 and buying my first house in 1971. The advent of Whitlam, the single mother's pension and then in 1976 my beginning university studies and my son starting high school. At the end of 1976, our Fijian holiday. Almost simultaneously near the beginning of 1978, my starting with Children's Services, the death of my father and meeting my second husband. Somewhere in-between I gained a TAFE teaching certificate and studied and gained entry to something akin to the Australian Psychological Association that, while a member, allowed me to instruct in various areas of human behaviour.

The whys and wherefores of my move are covered in later chapters but it does feel, and one would think quite contrary, that while I was suffering intense emotional pain, I was blossoming and proving myself as a worthwhile, capable, person. It is interesting to note, the lives I know about might (or might not) have started on an even keel but none then kept to a straight course, experiencing no squalls, cyclones or hurricanes. Those who claim to have had the happiest of lives can also list their share of tragedies and triumphs.

So, at the start of 1969, it was necessary that I find work. Nine years earlier my mother had been willing to look after me and my baby for at least six months. Now, after having gone through the trauma of losing two children, returning with one, my mother's welcome was such I managed two nights under my parents' roof. Fortunately my sister and future sister-in-law rented a house not far away and my son and I sought refuge there.

There was no government help then, so I plagued the shops and offices in the local shopping centre for part-time work. My first job was back on a counter, in Woolworths, selling cakes, bread, pastries at one end, small goods the other. Hard to think of the two food varieties now, being on the same counter. We didn't wear plastic gloves then or head covering, but tongs and other accoutrements were ranged up and down on the shelf along the back.

I was twenty-eight and my boss, the full-time worker, was younger, bigger, red-haired, bad-tempered and foul-mouthed, under-educated and someone my mother would call 'common'. And I hadn't had paid, outside, employment since before my marriage. I think you could say we didn't understand each other – different language, different manners, different everything. She was rude to me and I spoke to her as little as possible.

One day, I was searching for a pair of tongs to secure an item a customer wanted. I swear she had hidden them all. Finally she asked me if I'd lost something. I replied I was looking for a pair of tongs, to which she retorted, well, why didn't I ask, didn't I have a tongue in my head et cetera, to which I said that I wanted as little discourse with her as possible as she was so rude, ill-mannered and often stupid. All of this is in front of customers. Standards had changed since my teen experiences but still, not a good look. But it brought a turning point in our relationship and, from that time on, she couldn't have been more helpful.

It really is a good idea to keep a diary or a journal. I didn't and now only make occasional notes of events or thoughts, so my order of events then is probably not correct. It matters not. I do remember, this time, sitting the exam for government clerical work but about twelve months after my arrival in Brisbane. In the meantime, I still had to earn a living.

Another of my jobs was with a private medical fund. I have never belonged to one, believing in the public system, but my principles didn't extend to not working for one. It was still part-time, as my son was in primary school and in those early days of separation I felt he needed me to be at home when he was. My hours were slightly longer, though, and it was a sit-down job. It was in a different and larger shopping centre but still close to home and I shared a cubicle with a married woman, very pleasant, working for pin money.

We talked to prospective new members and signed them up if such was their decision and took the monthly payments from mostly older people who preferred to pay that way. So many elderly women, many widows, who had proudly never claimed in their lives, never been seriously ill, and all those years, catalogued in their little receipt books of monies received. Yes, the money that paid my wages, provided uniforms for the full-timers – my companion and I were both part-time, the cubicle opened between ten and three – and made sure the shareholders received good dividends. Yes, hypocritical being there, but there's something about putting a roof over one's child's head and food on the table.

Although my co-worker had been on the job much longer than I, she treated me as an equal. We each had keys to open up the cubicle and our own cash boxes. We took the cash boxes home each day but once or twice a week someone from the office would come to check our work and collect the takings. My fellow worker would chatter about her life, the husband in a good job, the two children, girls, both in school, her parents and how her mother would often cook a meal, a casserole or something else that could be reheated and left in her daughter's kitchen. So different from my own mother. My son liked fruit cake and I asked her one day if she would make him one if I bought the ingredients. She never did.

Sometimes she would turn up at closing time and offer to drive me home, which I readily accepted. But no sooner were we walking along a mall and she would say, 'Let's play bingo first.' By then, I'd missed a bus and she had me trapped. I should have learned that a lift home meant bingo first, a game I detest and will not play. Heaven help me if I end up in a nursing home!

Perhaps the other chain store work was before the one just described. I can't imagine changing my comfortable position for one standing up in a cold room packing meat for the chilled shelves on the other side of the wall, and especially as I was an almost vegetarian. I had never cared for meat and really didn't like to handle it. When I was married, I'd buy a side of lamb (nineteen pence per pound) already cut into sections, but it was my husband who sliced further and sorted it into the parcels that would be frozen for future use.

But a job is a job and I needed money. It must have been more than the previous position or there'd have been no reason for changing. All of my co-workers here were older, what I then would have called middle-aged. Now I am in my seventies and I see them in my mind's eye, they were probably late forties.

Most were English with working-class accents and constantly made fun of me and my rather different mode of speech and my smart clothes, not to mention my ignorance of various cuts of meat.

'We need more cuts of so-and-so out there. Can you start on that, luv?' with my agonised reply, 'Yes, but which is so-and-so?'

I always think I'm in the way in other people's kitchens and I think my colleagues must have thought that of me then. My clothes, of course, were soon hidden underneath the smallest but still too large white overall, the sleeve ends folded over several times. If I want meat for a particular meal, I still have to ask the butcher to suggest. My co-workers were, however, extremely helpful and showed me all the tricks of the trade. The styrofoam trays were packed so that the meat was displayed to best advantage, fatty ends tucked underneath, and sealed with plastic wrap through a machine, popping out the other end complete with identifying label and use-by date. 'Reduced' stickers were applied by hand as were new use-by dates when it was deemed the package that was about to reach its end date was still edible.

It was cold and hard work. I learned to give back some of the teasing, the jokes, but eventually something better came along, so, as with the other jobs, I left. My accent did change over the years but it was more acceptable in my next job. It seemed my accent could be a help or a hindrance, depending on where and with whom I was. As a nine-year-old child, a stranger in a strange country, my posh accent, my vocabulary, the books I had read and indeed, the ones I hadn't, were all points over which I could be tormented. Now, only few comment on my English beginnings as evidenced by my speech.

I contested the exam for entry into the public service, and received word to go in for an interview. I was offered a position with the Department of Army, Ordnance, at Victoria Barracks, Petrie Terrace. Of course I accepted and in due course signed all the Official Secrets Acts, and was told that promotion would likely be very slow. Meaning, that unless I requested an equal transfer, I would be doing the same work at the same level for several years. Five had been mentioned. Again, a job is a job and this was secure and the pay was good. I was surrounded by men but when I'd left Sydney I'd made up my mind there would be no romantic entanglements as I didn't think it fair on my son.

Half a dozen civilians dealt with the piles of paper generated by such a section of the army. Everything an army uses has to be provided, ordered, paid for, delivered, checked that all of that has happened and gone to where it was supposed to go. I was the granny of the group, the others young, not too long out of high school, at the beginning of their lives.

I was interested in them, what they did, thought, and we had many lively conversations. Part of our duties included making morning coffee for the officers, seven of them. They all had their particular likes, and ways they wanted their coffee made. I was instructed by my fellow workers into the intricacies of coffee making. We took it in turns. My younger colleagues didn't like doing it as they were always in awe of the officers. I had no such qualms. My grandfather had been a naval officer, I had met many people of high office and, while I appreciated the positions they held, they were still, at heart, just people.

Perhaps because of my natural attitude, whenever the officers had visitors, it was I who was asked to do the morning coffee. Or tea. So I would ask the visitors what they would like and on those occasions all of the coffees were made the same way; tea was tea, all served black with milk and sugar separate. I had hunted out a milk jug and sugar bowl in the rather messy kitchen and cleaned them up for such occasions. I still remember the surprised look on the face of one officer, who liked his coffee served with froth on top, made by mixing coffee, sugar and a little milk to a paste then slowly pouring the hot water over. Froth on top every time. And ordinarily, each officer was handed his particular brew. But really, I drew the line at doing anything special when I had to serve nine or a dozen men. And they were given biscuits. I think the 'frothy' officer, quite a dish actually, was surprised and bemused at my temerity. That first time, I smiled sweetly and said, as I withdrew, to let me know if anyone wanted anything else. And the next day each coffee was made as they each preferred.

I'd been in Ordnance about nine months when the colonel asked if I'd step into his office for a moment. Of course it was like being told to go the headmaster's office and my immediate thought was, what had I done? Ordinarily, if any of the officers wanted something extra or different, they came to us. In fact, the colonel wanted to sound me out about another job. Certainly a promotion, more money, but what would I have to do? It was in Public Relations, me and one colonel. The job description included typing and my heart sank. 'Oh,' I wailed, 'I'm not a typist.'

My current boss asked if I had ever used a typewriter. I had. 'Right', he said, 'that will be enough. The job doesn't require a lot of typing and there's no need for speed typing. Would you like to give it a go?'

In those days, Public Relations was housed across the road, Petrie Terrace, in two rooms on the first floor of an old building. Australia was involved in the Vietnam War; I was against our involvement but again, my private views were just that and I didn't allow them to interfere with my professional life. My new job meant I had direct interaction with the press, family of servicemen and the brigadier on my red phone if the need arose. It didn't, but how I wished it had.

I typed press releases and, each morning on my way in, I would collect all the daily papers and go through them, cutting out anything that related to the army. There were a couple of national service photographers who had a dark room in a part of the barracks proper. They would pop in to my office from time to time, with photos for the newspapers or often just to share coffee and have a chat.

My boss had the inner office but was rarely there, doing all those things that PR really is, which meant I was really in charge a lot of the time. I had an ordinary phone which was in use often, giving such information as I could to press inquiries and usually less to private individuals. It simply wouldn't do to give information to Jane Public before the papers had had time to print their exclusives. Family members would sometimes just come into the office, with queries, needing assurance about the safety of their family member at war (which of course had no answer; all I could give was the pat response that the army did its best for its members).

It was with some trepidation that I started that job, made even more acute when I first signed on. The sign-on, sign-off book was just an ordinary school exercise pad and I looked back to see what had happened to my predecessors. The book had half-a-dozen, at least, of different names but the date of the first entry was not very far back in time. The shortest incumbency had lasted three days, the longest thirteen.

In the beginning, each evening as I signed off, I counted, beaten that one, and that one, and so on until I matched the thirteen days, then fourteen days. Counting stopped after about a month, when I thought I should give myself a party. The colonel and I got along really well; he would take me to lunch sometimes in the officers' mess and often, on a slow Friday afternoon, we'd go down to the corner pub for a beer or two. I didn't wait until nine o'clock but started work as soon as I arrived at the office and I didn't leave at five if there was work still to be done, reports that had to go out. The barracks were not right in the city but if I needed to do something in town, I could take extra time at lunch. It all worked very well.

I'd met Stephen at a prom concert, held then in the City Hall, not long after starting that job. I was having a drink with someone else after the concert so hadn't taken a cushion or anything else to make sitting on the floor more comfortable. I sat in the choir stalls. They were not comfortable either, without a comfortable backrest. Stephen sat next to me and offered to share his blanket to make a soft backing. He asked me if I'd like to go for a drink later. I explained I could not and, as it turned out, he had no money on him and would have had to go home to get some. No 'holes in the wall' or credit cards then. We exchanged numbers. And I told him where I worked. A couple of days later, a huge bunch of flowers was delivered to my desk.

I was not out of step with a large proportion of the population in being against Australia's involvement in Vietnam. I had a friend, introduced by Stephen, who was a teacher, living in Sydney with his partner; he also was against it but his birthdate had been one of those picked out, the method of choosing conscripts then. As a teacher, he had gained a couple of deferments but his time was up; he had to front up to the authorities. He went on the run.

One night, late, there was a knock on my front door; it was he, needing shelter. There was no way I was not going to help my friend but he stayed only a few nights. He did not want to compromise me in any way. I also had to explain to my son, who had been taught the value of honesty, that on this occasion he could not say anything about our visitor. He was nine then and we lived in a house I'd managed to buy in my own name with no help from anyone. Almost unheard of in those days of the late 60s, 70s.

I have never hidden anything – my life, my values – from my son but there must have been times when his young mind had trouble sorting me out. Incidentally, my young brother's birthdate came up too but my mother had always said he would never go. The Labor party was in opposition but even so, knowing people at the top was helpful. It was the only time, as far as I know, that she pulled strings, and my brother was not called up.

I should say, here, that when I started my job with the Department of Army, my security rating was nil. There was a Liberal federal government at the time and my mother had been a lifelong member of the Labor party. And very vocal. I, too, had been a member and had marched for various causes. I had a brother-in-law who was born in mainland China, so in the late 60s early 70s we were suss. It would have to have risen when I moved over to PR. I don't know if I was walking a thin line or I was just an inconsequential little fish. I rather believe the latter.

That job was great, I really enjoyed it. I was left to get on with things, even the dusting (of course a cleaner came in every evening to empty the paper bins and vacuum the floor but she wasn't very good at dusting) and had not my boss, the colonel, been shifted to Canberra two years later, who knows that I wouldn't have been there many years later. He gave me a great reference before he went.

A major came in on a temporary basis. He was quite an okay chap, personable, and a ladies' man. He did little work but loved crosswords, so when he was in his office, which was most of the time except for his long lunches, my peace was frequently broken by queries such as 'What's a word for snow in six letters?' I would call back, 'There's a dictionary in your drawer and a thesaurus on the shelf,' and after a pause add, 'sir'.

One day he had an appointment with the brigadier in the early afternoon. As usual, the major went out for a long lunch, getting back just in time for the appointment. He rushed in to collect some papers and would have rushed out again, after a few words to me. He took up his favourite stance, arms akimbo on the door frame. I told him he'd be late, to which he replied okay, he was going. Then I told him he better get dressed first.

'What do you mean?' he said, looking quickly down at his pants.

'Belt,' I replied. He was minus his uniform belt.

'Oh shit! I know just where it is. Make excuses for me. Half an hour.'

Well, of course he knew where it was. Unfortunately, making excuses for him was made the harder because he didn't, as the colonel had, tell me the details of his work-related appointments. Or, in his case, his extracurricular appointments. However, I did make up some story for the brig's secretary but I rather think she and he knew the major well. I had no respect for him.

As I said, I had made the decision not to become involved with anyone until my son was much older. For other philosophical and political reasons, I would not allow myself to get close emotionally to a professional soldier. I refused many invitations but I respected those men and the jobs they did.

The two photo-lab boys were national servicemen, medevacked out of Vietnam and after treatment able to finish their service in a safe environment. I heard some of their stories. And I saw busloads of soldiers departing for overseas service, young, healthy, cheerful, joking; I saw many returned, old, the life gone from their eyes. I started writing this in 2011 when a friend of mine was still working with Vet Affairs, counselling Vietnam veterans.

The major eventually moved on and the new boss, another colonel, took over. He was much older and probably getting close to retirement. He did not like women; army women he had to tolerate, but civilian women! He shouldn't have to. He was not easy to work for and I became the strictly nine to five worker, keeping to what were my duties, nothing less but certainly nothing extra. I stuck it out for six or seven months before I requested a transfer.

There was a vacancy in the Public Service Inspector's Office so I took it. Right in the city and almost a regular desk job. I enjoy interacting with people and few liked the counter work, so I did that too. A different kind of public from that I'd met in Public Relations but a change from the desk nonetheless. Mostly it was people enquiring about entry into the Public Service, when the next examinations were being held.

Conversely, my boss sometimes discussed with me (I don't know why me) the pros and cons of sacking someone. There was actually one employee we discussed, his behaviour et cetera, and whether or not he should be dismissed. Of course the final decision, or several stages before that, was not mine. I felt a pang of pity for anyone losing his job, hoping he/she would change and be able to start over.

There were documents I had to sight, copy and sign – proof of age, citizenship, educational levels and receiving and signing for deliveries. Then sometimes I was an invigilator at the entrance exams. My desk was one of several in a large room. The fellow who sat behind me did very little work but was paid more than I because he had worked longer in the department. He seemed to know nothing as he was forever asking someone else. Often me, as I was closest. Public servants worked under an equal pay policy but that was not the rule elsewhere. Men were the breadwinners and therefore had to be paid more. No matter that a female, with the same qualifications, and say, single, widowed, through no fault of her own, with one or half-a-dozen children and a mortgage, would have to manage on significantly less. In 2016 females are still on an uneven playing field.

The typing pool was at the back of the room, behind an almost all-glass wall; every time the door opened, the loud hum of the typewriters escaped and I wondered how the girls inside could cope with that noise.

When I started that job in the PSIO, it was situated in an old building. Soon after, it was moved into the new government building in Ann Street. Everything to be moved had been packed into boxes, much of the furniture had gone and we were just sitting around waiting for the rest of the stuff to go. As always, I had a book with me, so I started to read it. I noticed some of the others with a file on their laps trying to look as if they were engaged in office work, which I thought the silliest sham ever, thinking why weren't people just honest?

This working life always had to accommodate the needs of my son and his safety. He was a 'latchkey kid', a phrase no longer used, I believe, but I hated the position I had put him in. My working had meant I could buy a house, which meant we both had a secure roof over our head, but it was an empty house my little boy went home to after school. Buying a house in 1970/71 was not wholly dependent on one's income and usually a female's income had nothing to do with it at all. In those days, a female had a father or a husband to take care of her needs, including shelter. We were not quite the commodities of the early 1900s but even in the 1950s we were expected to pretty-up for the return home of the husbands who had slaved all day earning our bread and butter.

Women did not buy houses in their own name but I'd always considered paying rent as dead money. I worked too hard for mine to give it away. It was my last landlord who had, inadvertently, spurred me on. He came on a Friday evening to collect the rent from the flats that had been fashioned from one very large house. It was in a good part of Brisbane and we had a lovely view of playing fields and the city on the horizon. On a particular Friday, he tried to give me a receipt showing an amount less than what I paid. For taxation purposes it was in his interests to show an income as little as possible. I told him that if I accepted that receipt, that was the amount of money he would receive. I was very angry.

Getting a loan to buy a house was not easy. I'd found a house I liked and could afford, if I could ever get the loan in the first place. It wasn't quite in the right area, working-class, but there were two schools nearby and by then I'd bought a car. The elderly owners were selling so they could move closer to one of their sons. They liked me and probably had taken pity on my plight; they virtually took the house off the market while I hunted for a loan. Finally, it was the manager of the ANZ local bank who decided to take a chance on me. I remember him well, his office, the friendly conversations about risk, my earnings and capacity to repay a loan. I became a homeowner, me, in my name, whoopee. I had twenty-five years to clear that loan; I paid it out in ten.

Labor came into power federally; Prime Minister Gough Whitlam brought in sweeping welfare benefits. Too many and too soon, many of us can say now in hindsight, but they did include a widow's pension which included single mothers. This was a chance for me to receive an income while staying home. I weighed the pros and cons, did my sums over and over again. The pension would be this much, my son's allowance that much; my expenses – mortgage, phone, electricity, school costs, clothes, food… I thought I could manage it. I handed in my notice.

Oh, my understanding boss. He tried to talk me out of resigning; take leave, he said, six months, twelve months, but don't resign. And did I listen? No. Did I ask him why he thought it not a good idea? No. Counsel had never been offered to me, even as a child. Every decision, every action, had always been mine alone. I thought I was making the right decision in wanting to be home for my child. It didn't occur to me that taking leave would have been a trial period and it didn't mean I was forced to go back at the end of that leave should I not want to. My idea was to give my son the rest of his primary school years and go back to work when he went to high school.

I've made a few wrong decisions in my life; leaving that job was one of them.

Money makes a difference. Lack of it can be the cause of tension, worry, anxiety, disputes, depression. Paying the mortgage and my son's needs came first. The bank didn't know my income had drastically dropped. I certainly wasn't going to tell its staff. I had no money left over for anything special, and certainly nothing for me – clothes, make-up, entertainment.

My son found himself a Saturday-morning job, collecting customers' fortnightly payments for their delivered newspapers, two routes alternating. He had a bicycle. I made some joke about his buying something for me; in his very serious way he looked at me and solemnly said he'd thought he'd buy some soccer boots. I wanted the earth to swallow me. Even forty years later, I cringe when I think of my utter selfishness.

In every other job, I believe I did well; in the most important of all, that of parenting, I think I failed. I'd rationalised that I could return to work when my son started high school. For a few months, we'd had the nephew of a friend staying with us, an Indian student enrolled at Brisbane Grammar School. Our young friend suffered no racial discrimination and his tales of masters sailing around in caps and gowns captured my son's imagination. He liked what he heard about the school and expressed a desire to go there.

I told him the only way was to win a scholarship. Even with the best job, I'd never be able to afford the fees, let alone the extras. With help and encouragement from his teacher, he applied for a scholarship, dependent on his academic achievements – no problem – and personal interview. Halfway through that same year, there was an advertisement inviting mature prospective students to apply for courses in teaching or social welfare. Could this be the realisation of my dream of becoming a teacher? I discussed the pros and cons with my son.

Part of the Whitlam legacy was providing free tertiary education; people were encouraged to study further and if necessary receive monetary aid while doing so. Years earlier, I had friends, university students, who worked at some of the hardest jobs in order to be able to pay the university fees required upfront. One of them died of malnutrition because by the time he'd paid fees and his rent, and bought his books at the beginning of each term, he had insufficient money for the necessary food. He did have dinner at our house, maybe once a week, and we'd joke about his voracious appetite and where did it all go, because he was as thin as a whippet. We did not know he ate very little for the rest of the week.

Becoming a student would mean a change in my income. We would still be poor but slightly less so. Could he cope with it for the next two years?

My son told me, 'Go for it, Mum,' but advised against becoming a teacher. He felt I'd be eaten alive by my students. (Was this another failure – buying our house in a working-class area and sending him to the 'wrong' school?) I applied to become a social welfare student. On application, it became so glaringly clear how very thin were my formal education qualifications. I'd passed the Queensland Scholarship exam, at age fourteen, giving me access to high school; the motorbike accident had prevented anything else. Surprising, really, I was invited to an interview.

Dear George, whose brainchild this fast-forward course was, and Ray, who interviewed me, must have seen some spark of intelligence in me but, to be on the safe side, suggested I delay this tertiary-level study and take a year, even two, to study English and Logic at matriculation level then reapply. I thought, if I delay even a year, I'll never do it. I enrolled to sit the Senior English exam as an independent student, collected a syllabus, the necessary books, and settled down to study. I had about ten weeks to cram what was then four years of high school study.

My son had become a coxswain for a group of law student rowers, and the wife of their coach became my mentor. One afternoon, I was busily writing an essay when my mother called. I went to answer her knock and told her I couldn't invite her in as I was writing. She didn't think that sounded important enough to bar her entry, so I had to explain what I was doing and that I hoped to be able to enter university on the strength of it. Very encouragingly she said, 'Well, I suppose pigs can fly.' She took offence at my lack of hospitality and stayed away for some time after that.

I passed, credits, but the only thing I remember about those days of exams was that the only quotable quote I could think of was 'Oh, let me not be mad' from King Lear. I like Shakespeare and see whatever plays of his I can but I didn't think that one pitiable quote was going to get me very far. I must have dredged up a bit more than that but, as I said, nothing stands out. Oh, my age as compared with the crowds of high school boys and girls.

I went to see George with my results and said, 'Will this do?' It sure would; I became a full-time student in the new year.

My son had passed his final primary school exams with flying colours and we were invited to an interview with the head of the grammar school. Although divorced, I had kept my Indian married name, which my son still has, but my son is actually Anglo-African, apparent when you see him. Don't forget, we were still only in the 1970s. Commonwealth students were just that, from the various nations that made up the Commonwealth. Many were Indian, many Chinese from Hong Kong, but there was a scattering of students from many other countries. My son's racial origins should have made no difference to his entry, on scholastic merit, to this private school. It was clear the head was taken aback.

The full scholarship suddenly changed to a half-scholarship. I'm sure this was an action meant to deter us from accepting. It was an hour or more of my having to read acute body language; my son's disappointment that he might not be able to attend was palpable. He was fully cognisant with my financial affairs and knew it would be difficult. I immediately made it clear that should my son want to attend, then he would.

His examination results also brought an invitation from the city's leading state high school, the one my older brother and I had attended. It had greater public schools (GPS) status, meaning it participated in events, had the status, of a private school. We did go for an interview but my son had his heart set on Grammar. Now, looking back, I think it was a mistake. I don't know my son's feelings. The state school had a mixed racial population and high academic achievements. My son did not have a happy time at Grammar; he became disenchanted with academe. He was bullied during the first term but, although I could sense something was wrong, he would not tell me.

Towards the end of term, he stopped one evening, on his way to the bathroom and said, 'There was something.'

Pressed to continue, he told me how five boys had ganged up on him; two would hold him, the other three bash him. Not where it was visible, obviously. I demanded to know their names, which he would not give, saying he had dealt with it. He elaborated by explaining that he had caught each fellow while on his own and given him a beating. He abhors violence but I had insisted he learn to box and he has always had excellent reflexes. Of course, I did make a complaint about it but it probably did nothing to improve the behaviour of those particular bullies. He didn't make any real friends but there were many boys who desired his company. He accepted many invitations for weekend sailing, country camping trips, bicycle excursions.

My income was stretched very thinly; it was fortunate I knew how to sew, and I still made most of our clothes. I made up my own label to put onto my son's clothes and I think my feeling was that of relief when he would return from a weekend excursion and tell me how his friends had pestered him to tell them where he bought his clothes because they wanted similar. They didn't look home-made and I always tried to make them just a little bit different, a little bit classier. I remembered my own high school time and the arrogant 'I dare to be different' mantle I wore in my brother's passed-on school pullover, the boys' grey while the girls had blue.

According to one of my passports, it was the end of 1976 when I decided to cash in a life policy so my son and I could go to Fiji for a holiday. It was my friend Stephen's idea. I had completed one year of study and my son his first year of high school. We arrived at the ending of Ramadan, the beginning of the festival of Eid. Somehow we became guests of honour of one of the large gatherings and were invited to attend the sacrifice of three bulls. We accepted but Stephen suggested I stand at the back in case the sight of killing upset me. I replied, no way was I not going to occupy the chair provided in the front and accept what was happening. My son was by my side and Stephen was to the side edge of the gathering. My son paled but managed to hold himself together while poor Stephen was most unwell.

I did well with my two years of full-time study. We completed more units in those two years than the students in the three or four year degree/honours course. I had friends doing the longer degree course but it was they who asked me questions about their study courses rather than my asking them. We had excellent course material but we had to work hard and long, almost five full days every week, starting early and finishing not before four in the afternoon. We had no time for campus recreation. Poor George took us for something called Community Welfare (which led to my joining various voluntary groups aimed at helping communities; one-time Queensland premier Anna Bligh at that time was also a member of some) and while my papers usually gained an A, they were invariably returned with the injunction that 'you must cite your sources, Jacqueline'.

George really was a sweetie, a bit of a teddy bear. He died, of cancer, still young, just a few years after I'd finished the course. He, and Ray who taught sociology, my first contacts at interview, gave me excellent references, with Ray urging me to go on to further study. I did, never stopped really, but part-time.

My maternal grandfather and his siblings, male and female, had degrees from various universities, none in the next generation, although my mother would have if her father had not been such an irresponsible gambler, and I am the only degreed person in my generation of the family. The paternal side had none at the corresponding level but there were several at the next, my great-nieces and nephews, after many generations of humble working-class origins. And my children and my sister's have a variety of degrees.

There was another lecturer, in family psychology, who read from one book and any questions asked had to have answers in that book. One paper I did for him came back with a C minus. I was used to getting As and A pluses. I asked him what he didn't like about my paper. Apparently, I had not agreed 100% with his lecture notes. I pointed out that my arguments were well-researched, my many sources cited, that psychology was not a black/white, right/wrong science, but I was expected to give him back, word for word, it seemed, what he doled out. I was older than he, had had children and was now bringing up a child on my own and had more experience of living than he would ever have. I asked him to reread my paper. He refused. I said I would take it to the head. He said if I made trouble he would bar me from his lectures. I told him he couldn't do that and that I'd also go to the student union. I can't remember what happened in the end with my paper, but he left soon after, for a job in the USA.

One of my student placements was with Immigration, where I spoke with new migrants having difficulties in adjusting, especially where children were concerned. These were almost exclusively families coming from cultures very different from those of Australia. Their school-age children wanted to be Aussies, eating bread and Vegemite sandwiches not the delicious Greek or Italian, Indian or Asian food, lovingly prepared and, horror of horrors, often delivered hot to the school gates at lunchtime. They wanted to wear similar clothes; older children wanted the freedoms Australian children had. For the parents, the change was too quick; they needed time to get used to all the changes on top of learning English and fitting in with workmates et cetera. I found that very interesting and challenging. Some of that would have been used to colour my book *The In-Between Man*.

Those problems are still with us but, interestingly, others I've had to deal with were very different – the technological revolution. Migrant parents often feel left behind because their children learn to speak English much more quickly, but with the rapid developments of IT many older people are feeling left behind. Parents were/are no longer able to help their children with advanced homework. On the other hand, if parents do not help with building their five-year-old's kindy project, instead of encouraging the child to be creative and think through what is required, then turn up with the child's creation, there are tears and tantrums because it isn't as sophisticated as those that mums and dads did with little or no input from the child.

Another placement was at a place called the Richmond Fellowship, which was originally meant to be a place for those with some mental instability and a stay there would hopefully bring them back to full or better functionality and prevent their commitment to a mental ward or hospital or prison. Unfortunately, it became a halfway house, looking after ex-patients and trying to rehabilitate them so they could return to living in the community. They were interesting people and just a little fey. Staff, which included me for the time of my placement, had shifts of overnight stays; someone in authority had to be there at all times. I knew I had to be on my guard, watch my movements and be careful in what I said. But one of them found out I could read tea leaves. They gave me no peace until I agreed to read theirs.

You might think, oh, easy, make something up; that's what I thought. It was not that easy. I know many of you are going to scoff at the whole notion (but go on, read the rest of the book) but when holding a cup and being bombarded by the messages it is transmitting, it is very difficult to maintain a sense of equilibrium. I felt as if I were being pelted by rocks and the words, strong, vile, bouncing hard on my brain. Trying to make up some nice, innocuous story while I felt as if my body was being taken over by demons was the hardest thing I've had to do. I don't think I fooled them for one minute. And, dear, gentle reader, none of this went into the report handed to my supervisor when I returned to college.

My grandma, I've said, was a deep, perceptive woman. Pragmatic but other-worldly. When she and Grandpa joined us in Australia, she took to reading tea cups in cafés, for fun more than anything else. She told me it was really just a matter of discerning people. Most clients are women, young girls who want to know if they already have the right man or are going to meet him any day now; are they outgoing, happy-looking or are they alone and look sad? Most young women attend in pairs. Older women often just want reassurance or whether or not someone close is going to recover some ailment. My grandmother just picked up on the body language. She could go further and tell them things that mattered more but that was not usually why they were there. She was more forthcoming with people she knew, family, but would never read mine, or do the tarot cards for me. Well, she would start but what she saw initially displeased her and fobbed me off with inanities. When she used the cards, I would see the death card and this was before my accident. She had the same difficulty with handling such a powerful message for me as I had with my Richmond residents.

We finished late in the second year, after the end of normal university times. I'd worked reasonably hard and was happy enough with my results – distinctions, credits, a couple of passes. My son and I had managed to get through on the income we had but it was essential I start earning real money. I started looking for a job but it was really pointless until the new year when all the uni results had been posted. My son boarded at school for the first term of my liberated time, his third year, so that I could travel to wherever I might be offered an interview. I was prepared to go anywhere I was offered a good job. Well, almost anywhere. I did have an interview at a central west New South Wales town but it was easy to pick up the racial prejudices evinced in the men who interviewed me. Neither my son nor I wanted him to board at school for an extended time but I sensed that he would not get a good education or a positive reception in that town. I was also offered a position in a north Queensland town but turned that down for its red-neck reputation.

As it happened, I was offered a job by the Department of Children's Services, Adoptions, in Brisbane city. Until my appointment, the section had been run by one social worker with a back office of half-a-dozen clerical assistants. There was no doubt there was a need for an extra pair of hands. We divided the work so that the already incumbent worker dealt with the relinquishing mothers and I would scour the files for suitable adoptive parents.

Nearly forty years ago, I was wary of would-be parents, or particularly would-be mothers, who were almost hysterical in their stated need to have a child. I wanted parents who were more balanced. Bringing up a child is not easy and I looked for parents who might be more resourceful, able to solve problems, cope with the ups and downs, the disappointments that do occur, as well as the joys of having a child. Not every woman is a natural mother but, more so in those days, women were expected to have children; that was their role in life. Today we accept women who have children and work but look askance at any who choose a career over motherhood. We also look down on those who choose to be full-time mothers. Can't get it right either way.

I don't think it is every woman's right to have children but have no bother with male or female homosexual couples adopting. I am not in favour of surrogacy or donor sperm; studies are showing us the psychological difficulties experienced by the resulting children. With donor sperm, I worry about the numbers of potential half-siblings, in most cases their fathers remaining unknown to them, and the possible attraction a couple might have for each other. After all, what attracts us to others are those traits that resemble our own. Adoptees, too, often suffer much angst at not knowing their parentage, even when they have been brought up in happy homes. It seems that connection between mother and child is difficult to erase.

We did try to get as much information on the fathers of the babes being given up for adoption but often not a lot was forthcoming. The girl might not have known who the father was, she might not have wanted him to know that she was pregnant so could not ask for his medical history or any genealogical details. And this is another area of concern for many adoptees added to their feelings of being given up by their mothers in the first place.

While I was in this section, I reintroduced the habit of showing to the back-room staff the baby about to be given away. The babies and children were brought to our city office by their foster-parent or a staff member of the institution in which they had been kept. The new parents came and, after the final signatures on this and that piece of paper, the child was handed over. A previous staff member had invariably taken the baby to the back office, where the clerks typed the necessary papers and did whatever else we needed of clerical staff cum secretaries. They knew the baby on paper and welcomed seeing the child in the flesh. My colleague had abandoned the practice. I saw no harm so reintroduced it.

The girls cooed and wanted to hold the baby; the couple of fellows tried to restrain their enthusiasm but never did less than allow the baby to hold tight to one of their fingers. They all delighted in making a baby laugh. And quite often a soft toy would appear as a parting gift or celebration of a new life.

My senior colleague thought I was being insubordinate and set about to make my life as miserable as possible. It got to the point of my handing in my notice. It did not occur to me that I could request a transfer. The head of the section I was then part of called me in, wanting to know why I wanted to resign. When pushed, I told him. He didn't seem very surprised but suggested I move into area work and a whole new chapter began. I moved to the building next door, joining a small band of workers with the nicest, kindest, most gentle of supervisors.

Very quickly I was part of an established, close circle of friends. I had been a single parent for nearly ten years by then and, while I hadn't exactly lived a nun's life, I refused to take any man seriously, as I believed my son needed my full attention. I was the only parent of the group and my son was a favourite with them all. He had a severe sixteen-year-old's crush on one of them, and really, she would not have been so very much older. Remember, because of my delayed studies I was older than my colleagues and my son had been born when I was only twenty-one, so my colleagues were not much older than my son.

Sometimes he would come in after school and my friends all came home for dinners at different times. He was often the subject of conversation at morning tea for while I was the only parent, the others were all very clever and learned so I poured out my uncertainties of my parenting skills. In the end, it was always summed up with 'He's fine, don't worry about him.' I'm sorry, my son; I should have done more.

However, these good friends decided I should at least have a boyfriend if not a spouse. In those days before internet dating, people placed advertisements in the personal column of the state's main newspaper. An ad was composed, listing all of my very good qualities, of course, which I duly placed and paid for, in return being given a collection box for the fortnight following the appearance of the ad in the Saturday's paper.

There must have been a lot of desperate men around, because I collected piles of mail two or three times each week. My friends and I amused ourselves when we gathered for morning tea or lunch, reading through these replies. It was they who decided who was 'in', who 'out' and who a 'maybe'. I arranged a lunchtime coffee with some of the 'ins', none of whom measured up. I had a few pleasant conversations but no desire to take things further, and some meetings from which I could not escape soon enough. It was in the very last collection that I read the letter from the man who became my second husband. It was ironic that my very best friend didn't like him but I didn't know that until after our divorce.

We'd arranged to meet one lunch hour. I had to postpone because of an emergency at work; we arranged another time. Again, I had to cancel, so we made an appointment to meet after work. And truly, nothing was contrived but I couldn't finish on time. We delayed the meeting for later that same evening. There were two lectures being given that evening, one starting at six, the other at eight, at different locations. I was interested in both and thought I'd go to whichever fitted in with the time spent meeting the latest and last would-be beau. I didn't get to either but stayed talking until well after midnight.

As I was working for the Department of Children's Services, our clients were children, mostly wards of the state. Most lived with their families, dysfunctional in as many ways as could be imagined. I heard language that had hitherto been foreign to me – in my home, we had not even used the mildest slang, let alone swear words. Our area was inner-city Brisbane and I discovered suburbs that would otherwise have remained just names to me. I was hearing first-hand of the cruelties inflicted upon my young charges by those who were supposed to be protecting them and the difficulties, as today, in finding emergency accommodation.

There was a fellow in charge of a particular refuge to whom I spoke often on the phone. His place was always my first port of call and through our conversations we learnt a lot about each other. We didn't actually meet for over a year and then we were both at the work's Christmas party.

'Goodness,' he said, 'you're not at all what I expected you'd look like.'

Intrigued, I enquired what he expected; I mean, I have the usual arms, legs, and all the other bits in their proper places. I also happen to be five feet nothing and, in those days, very slim. He said he thought I'd be six feet tall and, as he put it, 'carry more beef'.

It was my turn to say, 'Goodness gracious,' and enquire, 'Why, for goodness sake?'

He laughed, explaining that on the phone, when I wanted a bed for one of my charges, I sounded so authoritative, demanding, persuasive and older, and if he didn't produce a place at his refuge or some other, I would do an 'Auntie Jack and rip his bloody arms off' (from an ABC television comedy where Auntie Jack was a huge, and unlovely, transvestite who threatened to perform that action if one didn't tune in again the following week). He didn't expect a petite and softly spoken youngish woman like me. Interesting, isn't it, the images we conjure from voice and what those voices expect of us?

I would like to have called my supervisor my friend but, in truth, I was in awe of her. I did have one particular friend from among my group and through her was absorbed into a tight band of friends from different areas of the department. We were all on the same large floor but separated by positioning of furniture and the occasional partition. We are still friends many decades later. My adoption of crazy head wear began at this time. My hair then was long, thick and curly but on a bad-hair day looked untamed, messy. I owned several beautiful scarves and one or other of these could be wrapped around my head creating different 'hats'. My supervisor was amused and, when I wore one of them, used to say I looked like the Madonna.

I couldn't have been more different from anyone like her and I think it was partly due to my head's devout Catholicism and true goodness that kept me from approaching further. A lost opportunity, perhaps. (Several years later, we bumped into each other at a book launch; we now have infrequent lunches together, usually with two others who worked on our floor.)

It seems not much has changed in terms of social behaviour. I had to deal with eleven-year-old car thieves, shoplifters, drug addicts, single parents of thirteen to seventeen years old who insisted on keeping their babies who, in all likelihood, would come into foster care when they were two and trying to establish their own independence and selfhood – the time a child stops being the 'baby doll', albeit noisy and demanding but still more or less controllable.

We used government cars for making home visits or going to court and, being short, I always booked one of the smaller vehicles, but one time, an emergency arose and I had to take the only car available. It was large. Sitting comfortably, I couldn't reach the pedals or see out properly even when the seat was as far forward as it would go. Everything that could be used as a backrest was used but it was the most uncomfortable and probably dangerous driving I've ever done.

Another time, I was with a colleague, I driving, she passenger. I went through a red light and the inevitable happened – police sirens. Imagine, government car on government business, and you get a ticket. The explanations, the paperwork, the ignominy. We pleaded. I said the light had turned red only after I had started across, my friend batted her eyelashes over her brilliant green eyes and used her most charming American accent. The policeman was young and won over, admonishing me to be more careful in future.

Our clients were children and I argued for more time to be spent on the rest of the family, the parents or carers as they were pivotal in the rehabilitation of our young charges. I was told there was no time, no room, no money. I am happy to say, things have changed. Not enough, perhaps, and especially where abused children are being left in the care of the abuser. It truly sickens me when I have to remember, as now, the dreadful sexual abuses committed, but filled with wonder, amazement, admiration, for the ways the young women abused could transcend these acts. If I succeeded at anything, it would have to be the removal of these girls to permanent accommodation with relatives interstate. I was threatened with death on two occasions when I had removed daughters from the father's care.

Because the state was the legal guardian of these children, we workers the instruments, many parents simply surrendered any disciplinary role. Any misdemeanour was referred to us, usually claimed to be an emergency. Over the phone, we would try to instruct the parent in ways of dealing with the latest misbehaviour.

This led to my undertaking a course in behaviour management, concentrating on parent effectiveness training (PET). Once completed, I had to remain an active member of the institute in order to run ten-week courses consisting of three hours per week. I managed two evening courses per year and perhaps a weekend one spread over two full weekends, including Friday nights. I loved doing this. I had willing students and my yearnings to impart knowledge were being fulfilled. It was reasonably costly but I could, and did, reduce my charges if I thought an applicant really could not pay the full fee. Years later, I offered my services gratis to the Department of Social Security if the department would pay for the course materials. My offer was refused. Usually, the course attendants were already good parents, they just wanted to be better.

My years with DCS were ones of great drama, sadness, outrage, some success, and when I learned to swear. And fun, too. Somehow I had been roped in to join the Early Childhood group which was to set up a play area in one of the suburban shopping centres. We were provided with a large, depressed, tiled, circular space. The idea was the child would be entertained, amused, while a worker spoke to the parent about childcare and what was available to assist.

Someone had decided on the bright idea of providing bubble-blowing rings and solution. Someone knocked over a bottle of solution causing a wet, slippery floor upon which I slipped and twisted an ankle. A co-worker, French, handsome, gorgeous, picked me up and carried me through the centre, to a lift, up to a doctor's surgery where he waited with me and then helped me back with my strapped-up foot. It was the beginning of a brief, very friendly, affair.

My son finished high school but opted out of university – another story, his story – and my work experiences in the Solomon Islands are in that chapter. My next Australian work was some years later when I was again a divorced woman.

In a recent conversation with my son, he reminded me of my demo jobs: those mostly women in supermarkets, men in hardware stores, who try to attract the wandering public by showing off a new product or something that might have been slow to move off the shelves. My memory being thus jogged, I remember my first job well. A new brand of golden syrup had arrived, so in advertising that, I was required to make pikelets and serve them with the syrup. I had to promote the frying pan brand, the butter used and the pancake mix as well. I also had balloons to give to children. I could have done with an assistant. It was a lot of fun and by laughing at myself and my sometimes failed multitasking, I kept the crowds happy. I guess it's like busking – keep the crowd interested – and I did that by getting them on side. I do have only one pair of hands, so often I would recruit a watching woman to untie a balloon for a waiting child. No one ever refused; I think we're all actors at heart, as Shakespeare would have us.

Another time, I was to promote washing powder. Not nearly as much fun. I can't remember how many times I did it or exactly when but I did give away hot hot-cross buns with butter at Easter.

Of course some products sell themselves, others are harder but, for each one, the demonstrator has to think up a patter to attract customers in the beginning. And it can be the loneliest job in the world. Sometimes I felt like a lone shag on a rock, the tides of people ebbing and flowing, taking no notice of me at all. Some glances would be full of scorn; I was nobody, could not aspire to anything better, while others would scurry past, heads averted. These days I make a point of stopping when I see a demonstrator standing alone, trying to look busy and interesting. They are all just trying to make a needed dollar.

Just as I can't remember when I did the above, I also can't remember when I undertook a business course. It was during a time when I was unemployed, immediately after my second divorce, and the Department of Social Security, as it was then, required that I extend my skills base. I believed being able to type and know some office protocol would stand me in good stead. I attended classes in a very tall city building. My classes were held in the upper regions, requiring the use of a lift. The phase of the moon can't be blamed for my obvious madness at that time but going up and down in a lift with my po-faced fellow travellers just did something to me. Christmas was approaching; perhaps it was that but I'd get into an already well-filled little cubicle, all men (top jobs, top floors) facing towards the doors, not acknowledging anyone and I'd say, 'Right, gentlemen, I now call this meeting to order,' and not a flicker of emotion would stir the air. As we got closer to the festive season, I tried being a choirmaster with 'Okay, are we ready? Let's try "Jingle Bells",' and I'd wave my arm about. This did elicit the odd smile. But stuffy, so stuffy, and I couldn't help wondering where the joy of life was.

The lifts serviced many floors and many workers, so there was a bank of them arranged in a line. Just once, it might have been towards the end of my course, I came out of my room to wait for a lift and there, in front of me, was a long line of girls, and a few boys, all facing towards the closed shiny doors, looking at the floor, not even at the lights depicting the situation of the lifts. All quiet, all ignoring their neighbour, and it's quite likely they had all been in the same class just finished. They would have been in their early teens, not much older than my son. I just couldn't help myself; I started with the girl closest to me, stood in front of her, offered my hand and said in my poshest accent, 'How do you do? How good of you to come.' Surprised, she took my hand. I went the entire length, varying my words to the twenty or so girls and boys, and some actually bobbed as they took my proffered palm. I stayed very serious throughout but whenever I've thought of the occasion since, I've had to laugh. Maybe it was cruel of me but in those days people were not as free in speech and action or ideas as today. None of that would work now. There were so many people in that building and I was probably lucky that I didn't seem to cross paths with the same students or workers more than once.

I didn't become a good or even an averagely bad typist, just plain no good. My only saving grace after several weeks of tuition in office procedure and skills was to have an exercise in business planning added to that instructor's curriculum. And really, that was only a common-sense thing and maybe I thought a piece of cake because I was older and had to manage several grown-up areas of life.

These studies might have resulted in my being offered a one-off project of which details are very sketchy. Something to do with a government investigation into a business, its effectiveness and whether or not it should survive. The job lasted six months and I came to think that the small band of men I was working with had reached the end of their service, and their employer, the government, had not known what else to do with them.

After the Solomon Islands sojourn and back in my house – not the original; I had sold and bought twice or thrice by this time, I became one of the first batch to be trained as a telephone counsellor for Kids Helpline. During training, I turned fifty. The course had been going for some time by the time of my birthday and we participants knew other each pretty well. On that day, I arose from my desk and phone to join everyone in the kitchen for morning tea. A colleague waylaid me. His conversation no doubt started out being intelligent but soon turned to inane patter. I tried to suggest we make our way to the tea or coffee as we would soon be expected to return to our desks. I couldn't understand why he insisted on being so troublesome.

Suddenly he relented and I thought, at last, I must have a quick cup of tea. I entered the kitchen to be confronted by a room full of balloons, a banner proclaiming 'Happy Half Century Jacqueline', and a table spread with cakes and sandwiches. There was a birthday cake and I was presented with a beautiful armful of blooms. I didn't know whether to laugh or cry, so, in truth, I did both. My colleague apologised for his nonsensical patter but he had been designated to keep me out of the kitchen until signalled. I told him I was beginning to wonder if he was quite sane.

My son and his girlfriend took me to dinner that night, Chinese or Thai in Melbourne Street, South Brisbane, and gave me a hat. It's the blue one, in the hatbox, my dear son.

When the counselling programme began in proper, we worked four-hour shifts around the clock. I heard similar stories to those of my former DCS clients plus some who were intent on suicide. There was a particular case when a young person happened to get through to my phone. He was really in a bad way and we talked for a very long time. It took me over my four hours but one cannot leave the job because the time's up.

Supervisors could listen in to our calls and if we did get a suicidal caller, we were required to indicate by raising a flag we all had on our desks. The supervisor could, and would, suggest angles we might take. These were typed through to our personal computers. I could type questions or requests for water while maintaining voice contact with my caller. I had a few suicidal callers but this was the worst and our conversation went for over six hours. I was exhausted afterwards but hope the young person went on to live a fulfilled life. I had been asked, more than once, if I needed to hand over to someone else, but I didn't think that would be in my caller's interests. We were well looked after, received debriefing and however many cups of tea we needed after particularly difficult calls, and on that occasion asked if I would prefer a taxi home rather than drive my car.

The location was supposed to be secret, I'm not sure why; we were, after all, a telephone service. And I really don't know why anybody would want to harm us, but we did get calls to say a bomb had been planted or a fire started. There's nothing like standing out on the pavement at three in the morning in the middle of winter, but there you are, there's nothing like dedication.

After my positive beginning, this was the only job from which I was sacked. My friend, the son of Auntie M from our immigrant ship, had told me he thought his sixteen-year-old daughter was ringing the counsellors and was there any way I could find out something about it. The policy was, of course, strict confidentiality; we were not to discuss our calls with anyone but a supervisor who might have been listening in. I made the mistake of asking around to see if I could shed any light on my friend's daughter's problems. It was reported. I was summarily dismissed.

I joined an organisation whose aim was to care for the needs of those being turned out into community as the mental hospitals closed down. I had been tiring of the shift work at Kids Help Line but this was almost a case of jumping from the frying pan into the fire. It was a twenty-four/seven, hands-on job. The government of the day had not put any assistance programmes in place for these people. None of the social welfare agencies were equipped or had the staff to cope with this sudden influx of damaged people. The community was alarmed and didn't want these mad, bad people living anywhere near them.

The organisation I joined already ran workshops for those with intellectual disability. The new clients also suffered various psychoses such schizophrenia, pyromania, Down's syndrome and almost every other psychosis imaginable.

My clients were six in a group house, a married couple who managed to live in a flat (they were not ex-mental hospital patients but part of the original clientele), and several whom I'd recommended for single living with sufficient support. It wasn't easy work and I was on call twenty-four/seven; the aim was to give these people better lives than they'd experienced in a mental hospital where they were drugged, raped and had no voice.

Those we could, we got into jobs, helped them manage their money – I often used the old 'a jar for rent money, another for electricity, another for food and so on'. They came to understand how to use their pensions or earnings, probably better than many young people today who only see plastic cards and believe anything and everything can be done with it.

They'd had years of practice at learning what to say to please a psychiatrist, so I would sit in with them, listen to what they had to say and then, privately, give the doctor my analysis. Medications changed and usually reduced and while I knew my clients were always going to be limited in life choices, life did improve for them. I thought of the times there was no government support, no sheltered workplaces. Yes, often individuals would be locked up in back rooms or they'd be in jail or, before that, in the poorhouse. We've come a long way but still have a way to go.

My mother thought it a dreadful job and asked why didn't I do something else. I told her I could laugh with my clients, often. There was one woman who came into the group house, three times bigger than I, and fierce-looking. Her communication didn't go much beyond grunts, not because she couldn't speak but because she didn't want to. I have to admit, I was somewhat afraid of her. Had she wanted, she could have knocked me over by blowing at me. But I worked away with her until she trusted me and she did make me laugh. I don't know if she meant to be funny, knew she had said something amusing, but she certainly was a happier person.

One day I was driving her back to the house after a psychiatrist's appointment and we passed my old high school. I pointed it out to her, saying that was where I had been.

She said drily, 'Jeez, it must have been there a long time.'

She and I used to meet with her father sometimes, at a nice café somewhere, then one day at a staff meeting, the leader said someone wanted me sacked. My client's father thought I was unsuitable because 'I dressed too nice and spoke too posh'. Can't win 'em all.

Another member of the house, similar age and nearly as big, was very different. She had more mental ability and I got her into part-time protected work, but she was an unlovable person. Sneaky, greedy, mean. Soon after I'd had an operation on my right breast, a round-table meeting – a regular occurrence – was arranged. I happened to have a large, heavy book with me which I rested on the table. This young woman was a few chairs from me and not happy with the way the meeting was progressing. Suddenly, with all her bulk, she'd grabbed the book, gone to the end of the oval table and thrown it at me. It hit my left breast. I'd been told I must avoid severe knocks to either side of me; the pain was excruciating. The others were shocked. I took a deep breath, stood, told the miscreant her action was unacceptable and that I was leaving the house to take a walk while the rest considered what she had done and what should be done about it.

I had long considered this person would be better in a single-occupancy flat. Her parents thought not. If they had their way, she would be back behind some high-security fence. They had her institutionalised when she was in her early teens, probably as an uncontrollable girl, and she'd been abused sexually, physically, mentally there. With the backing of my supervisor, I did get her into a flat, where she managed beautifully. She remained my client but did not become any more loveable.

There was a forty-two-year-old man who couldn't or wouldn't speak. His label was Down's syndrome, which I did not agree with, and he'd been institutionalised since the age of two. He had spoken but some trauma in his teens had caused him to stop. He would have made a great engineer with proper training but we placed him in a position where he could assemble things. He loved putting things together. However, when upset, he had no control over his bowels. He carried spare clothing with him wherever he went. The driver who collected the workers and brought them back would often have David by himself as he stank and none of the others would share the minibus. He would have to strip off his clothes in the laundry, get a shower, and then wash his clothes in the tub. I wouldn't allow him to use the washing machine out of consideration of his fellow housemates. In the beginning, he was very resistant to this regimen but I insisted until he became upset less easily. I wasn't, of course, at the house all the time or even every day but David learned what I expected of him, and from the others, or a combination of sign language and showing by David, I was told he'd had an upset and behaved according to my wishes. Then he would receive my lavish praise.

I managed to get him to speak again. Limited and not everyone could understand him, but he was another with a wicked sense of humour and loved to play tricks. He was like a big, funny four-year-old sometimes. Other times, he would act more his age. They all did that, range between toddler behaviour to mature and back with no warning. But I was very fond of David. He had a sister who cared about him and who visited often and took him out at weekends. When I left, she wrote a wonderful letter to the organisation, thanking me for what I'd done. Not everyone wanted me sacked.

There was the young woman, tiny, shorter than I but with a vice-like grip. One day she had me held against a wall and wasn't going to let go. Of course I couldn't harm her in any way – I badly wanted to kick her – and it's very difficult trying to talk to someone who'd like to kill you and suffers with schizophrenia. We'd walked up to see her doctor one day and I was wearing a hat. In the waiting room, she suddenly grabbed my hat and started waving it about. Calmly I asked for it back. She decided to throw it around the waiting room, to my and the waiting patients annoyance. I said to them that she was behaving like a very naughty three-year-old today and left her to it.

Then there was the one who lived in a hostel and liked to set fire to it. Usually in the early hours of the morning. And another, whom we diagnosed as having Asperger's syndrome; she lived alone and was neat as a pin. She objected to the pavement rubbish bins outside a particular restaurant in her suburb. Frequently I would get a call from the local police, again late at night, to say my client had again set fire to the rubbish. She was the only client who ever went back into a closed institution. It was where she felt safe.

In a limited way, we gave our clients sex education. Although inmates could be raped within institutions, the rapists receiving neither education nor censure or the victims any instruction as to how to protect themselves, we were not, officially, supposed to discuss such intimate matters. In actual fact, my colleagues and I all felt they should see sex therapists and even have the services of a sex worker. They might have behaved like children sometimes but their adult hormones acted the same way as everyone else's.

There were others, during the six years I spent there, when I took extended leave to care for my mother. After her death, I didn't return to that or any other paid employment. Not all work is paid, of course, and I had/have my share of voluntary activities.

My most memorable, enjoyable, voluntary work was with the Queensland Philharmonic Orchestra. It would have been about 1990. There was a notice in the paper one day to say that before the next concert a meeting would be held to discuss the possibility of forming a Friends of the Orchestra. I thought it sounded interesting, so resolved to attend.

To cut a long story short, I was made the chairman of the steering committee. I maintain this happened simply because I suggested a placement of the chairs so that the bigger than expected number of attendees could actually see each other and thus make conversation easier. Which meant more ideas would flow. This carried over to my being president of the committee proper when it was correctly set up. I maintained that position for about seven years, until I went overseas. Again, I made some wonderful friends on the committee, and among the admin people and the people who came to our fund-raising events. We raised several thousand dollars each year and bought ancient baroque instruments, gave free or low-interest loans to musicians who wanted or needed to buy a particular instrument, and generally had a lot of fun.

The QPO's headquarters were in the Thomas Dixon Centre, the old shoe factory in West End, manufacturing the high-quality shoes of that name. But they had moved offshore and the premises were shared with the Queensland Ballet. The Ballet has it to itself now but we put on some wonderful events in the large room upstairs. We sold raffle tickets and seat prices were more or less set but I told my ticket sellers that if family with two or more children came, they were to use their discretion about the price of a family ticket. I wanted to fill the seats, make sure we got the children in and encourage them to come again.

We had Christmas concerts and dinners there and more concerts, including celebrating St Cecilia Day with a wine cart at St John's Church. I had concerts at my home, able to seat eighty or so, and a trio or quartet would play. I loved every minute of my time with the orchestra.

One memorable day, we had a fashion parade at Newstead House, by the river at Breakfast Creek. I made several outfits to fit the average size 12, which several of the female musicians modelled, escorted by some of the male members. The idea being, audience or models would buy, the money going into the QPO funds. It was a beautiful day and a great success.

John was a valuable committee member and he and I were just friends; we shared a similar sense of humour and I envied him his ability to quote poetry and Shakespeare, remember particular music and musicians. We'd have meals together, see films. I thought it was a friendship with no strings attached until one day I told him not to fall in love with me. His attitude towards me was changing and I sensed whatever it is that is the difference between friendship and something deeper. He said he'd fall in love with whomever he pleased but I told him that if I were the object of his desire, he would only get hurt. He was particularly helpful during my mother's last months, even being able to cook a dish of tripe and onions, which I could not do but which she had fancied.

I was exhausted after the cremation of my mother and at the house afterwards John and my brother decided I needed a holiday. John had a friend at Coffs Harbour whose home had spare rooms, so it was arranged and John would drive me down. When we arrived, the friend said he had prepared two rooms but if we wanted to use only one, that was fine by him. John said one was fine, I said we would use the two. I couldn't believe, after all I had been through, that he could be so insensitive and wondered what had made him think my feelings had changed. I had stressed I was not ever going to fall in love with him but I valued him as a friend. Well, of course, a beautiful friendship ended.

My love for teaching has never diminished. The courses I ran had a fee but while I was working as a social worker they satisfied my need to pass on information. After retirement, I became a volunteer tutor for U3A – University of the Third Age. This was a concept thought up by retired professors in France in 1972. To begin with, it was purely academically based. Some countries, England, for instance, are still academic and have close ties with a local university. Elsewhere, arts and crafts, health and fitness have been added, in some cases being the main features. Much depends on location and the demographic composition of the population.

Return visit: south to north

My mother had died in May 1995 but it took me until the beginning of 1997 to embark on my twelve months round-the-world travel. I had never wanted to return to England, preferring places I had never been to, but when I became an orphan with no one to whom I could refer, my feelings changed. I had no link above me. I was now an elder. I would get to the UK in three easy hops, staying first with friends in Singapore then my former in-laws who were, and are, still very much my family, in India, then London, where I would be met by the wife of a nephew briefly met on the recent visit to India.

    The family in Singapore was first met in India in 1984 when the two daughters were five years and maybe one and a half. I had seen my friends, the parents, since then, but not the children. I arrived at Changi airport mid-evening with, uncharacteristically, no welcome. My friends had not arrived. I waited. And waited until I thought I'd allowed for traffic snarls and such long enough; I rang the house. The elder daughter, now almost eighteen, answered. She knew nothing of my impending arrival and told me her parents and grandmother were out at dinner. I said I'd wait at the airport a bit longer and hopefully they would get home, be reminded, and come for me. That did not happen and I booked a night at what seemed to be the closest YMCA. Which happened to be opposite a mosque so a long quiet night I was not going to get.

    My mind was in a bit of a turmoil, tired and the enormity of what I was undertaking with my twelve months solo travel ahead of me, and already it was unravelling. After letting the daughter know where I was, I wondered what sort of holiday I was going to have if this mishap was a portent of what was to come. The question was, did I go on or did I give it all up and go home? Fortunately I carried on after I'd spent ten days with my friends, who arrived the next morning full of apology. It was never fully explained, but I think the female half of the couple had been given a negative medical diagnosis.

The elder daughter was due to travel to England for the beginning of the coming academic year to start university study. She asked if I would spend a day with her on one of the small islands. She picked my brains on Western male behaviour and general female things.

Before sending me on my way, my friend and I went to a Chinese temple and lit joss sticks to wish me a safe journey. As I have said, I have no religion but in Brisbane I had joined a craft group that was attached to a Christian church. My last meeting with the group was very moving as I had been asked if I minded the members praying for me, my safety and well-being. I was very touched and accepted their concern for me.

From Singapore I was on my way to India, landing in Chennai and enthusiastically met by a married couple, both children of two different siblings of my ex-second husband. Yes, first cousins; it was a love match, not arranged by the family and, as my ex-husband had married his niece several years before, a precedent had been set. The niece and nephew are still together; obviously my ex-husband and his niece did not last the distance. I have so many in-laws who all still regard me as one of the family; it is really lovely. I had thought of retiring in India, where I would probably have more family care than I do here.

It happened that I was there for the thirteenth day since the death of a family in-law. Hindu belief has it that the soul has had long enough to farewell the familiar and it is time for it to be on its way. Priests are invited to the departed person's home, a cow-dung fire is set up on bricks on the floor (Indian homes are mostly made of concrete) in the living room with all the family around in a circle on the floor. Chanting goes on all day, acrid smoke fills the room and one leaves the circle only for necessary visits to the toilet.

We partook of a grand feast at the end of the day. A young great-nephew, he was seventeen at the time, helped me out with some of the translations and, when action was required, I did what he did. My Hindi had been passable but much of what was sung was in Sanskrit. I was honoured, later, by being the first and only person to see my young relation's poetry. I answered his with some of mine.

My time in Chennai was enjoyable insofar as I was spending it with a niece and nephew, both in banking, and their two children, the elder son a keen student, his brother more mad keen on cricket. My niece wore traditional Indian clothes, saris or the Punjabi-style pants and long tops, and she rode a heavy black motorbike to and from work. It was an incongruous sight, especially when her helmet went on, this delicate young woman on that machine. I thought of Kafka's *Metamorphosis*.

Her aunt cum mother-in-law lived with them too and was showing early signs of dementia. She was also my sister-in-law, with whom I had got along well on previous visits. This visit, though, she made a fuss if I wanted to make a cup of tea, insisting I drink coffee at her times of choosing. She also made a fuss if I wanted to go out on my own. A few years later, my niece had to give up work to look after her full-time.

My few days came to an end and I had to move on. The train took me to Ernakulam and another nephew collected me on his motor scooter. He, his wife and two small children lived in the old family home with his father, my oldest brother-in-law, a lovely man whom I took for a brief holiday and respite from the heat, up to a guest house in Periyar National Park in the Western Ghats. I hired a car and driver. Neither comes with a guarantee but we did get to our destination with several stops to tie up another part of the engine with anything that happened to be handy – including vine.

There are always people walking somewhere and it was so on the mountain road. When we had broken down yet again, they stopped, offering advice, bits of wire, grease, whatever was thought would be useful for the job of getting us started. They were so incredibly generous; to them I was a wealthy Western woman and my brother-in-law an Indian of means, who, incidentally, advised against giving our helpers anything, but their willingness to help is a national trait.

My brother-in-law and I walked through the park with a guide and saw evidence of elephants and tigers being there. We also took a boat ride on the lake. Nearby was a spice garden providing retailers with some of the aromatic herbs that flavour that country's food.

Trivandrum has changed its name to Thiruvanandapuram or, more correctly, back to it. It is the capital of Kerala and I had friends there with whom I had to spend some time. The weather was extremely hot, dry and dusty, making me extremely ill. I saw an Ayurvedic doctor who advised I go to hospital. I declined. My friends took me to see a Molière play through which, I'm sorry to say, I coughed. My friends must have heaved a sigh of relief when they put me on the train to go back to Ernakulum, where my brother-in-law, nephew and his family did a wonderful job of caring for me.

Indians are very sociable, particularly when travelling on trains. They are quick to start a conversation and direct in asking one's business in India. They might have become more used to Western women travelling on their own but when I was there it was something to comment on. I didn't go into the matter of divorce but did say I had family in India. It makes for very interesting travel and I invariably picked up useful information.

My nephew's son was turning one, so a huge party was being organised. When their daughter turned one, she might have been given a pretty dress, flowers in her hair, but daughters have to wait for engagement and wedding parties and dowries. Sons are cosseted all their life. My nephew has never been a good business manager, money slips through his fingers like quicksilver and among the honoured guests at his son's party were the biggest moneylenders in town.

The cordiality between guests was as thick as syrup but if the moneylenders did not get their money, they would have no compunction in having a debtor killed. That young son is now in college and too much like his father. The daughter is doing very well, lives away from home, working in Bangalore. (In 2017, I received word of her engagement to a young man currently living in the USA. They met via the internet. She flew to the US and met him; the families in India had met.) She had asked her parents to find her a suitable mate; this must be the modern form of an arranged marriage.

My Indian family is educated, mostly forward-thinking; some marriages have followed the traditional arrangement; others have been straight-out love matches where boy meets girl; and this half-and-half style. I believe they all have the same chance of being successful.

Bangalore is an interesting city, a university town with almost all the inhabitants having PhDs. A very unhappily married niece lives there as well as other members of the family. I love the place; the very air seems to breathe knowledge and I love being at the university, but all good things must come to an end and I had to get to the next stage of my journey.

I was required to leave from the same city that welcomed me, so on my way back to Chennai I stopped at Mysore, where I have no relatives but the city has a beautiful palace museum. I had become a little lost and asked direction from two who appeared to be father and son. They had a little conversation, some of which I picked up, about which way I should go and then the father suggested the son take me on his motor scooter. The father would wait with their shopping. The son obviously weighed the pros and cons but eventually did ask if he could take me. I felt perfectly comfortable and safe in accepting. I took his name and address and, once in England, sent a letter and gift.

And in England I did eventually arrive. I think I had delayed my approach as long as possible, for what was I coming back to? Would this country of my birth disappoint me? And even here I was met by the wife of another nephew-in-law whom I had met briefly at the thirteenth-day ceremony. His wife had not gone; they were to be my London headquarters. It was where I left my main luggage when I took forays over the Channel to the Continent for several weeks at a time and similarly when I travelled around the UK. Through my London hosts, I met more Indian friends and relations.

My hosts were surprised on the days I said I was staying home to write letters or read a book; I knew my limitations. I did not have the stamina to be active every day. I still managed to travel the length and breadth of the UK – I swore I'd worn three inches off my legs. In Boston, I walked the Freedom Trail; in England, I walked the Roman roads.

Indians seem to hold on to their family members; their family trees have branches that stretch out to the furthest reaches and the thinnest little twig at the very edge is as important as the main trunk – even divorced in-laws stay attached!

I must have Lonsdale relatives in England but I don't know who or where they might be. I could have put an ad in *The Times* or something, asking for information about anybody related but I didn't. I did send a letter to the main newspaper in my home city of Grimsby for the Cuerton side, which prompted a reply from my dad's cousin. I knew Aunt Alice and her three daughters but knew nothing of this person who was the son of my dad's brother and his first wife. Alice was his stepmother but she all but kicked him out at a very young age. He went to sea, was self-taught and a really lovely, caring, intelligent, knowledgeable man.

My cousin welcomed me into his home in Cleethorpes, a pretty seaside town that has grown and now joins Grimsby. His wife, Marie, was not quite so effusive, suspecting I might be as hoity-toity as my mother was reputed to have been. I think we have become better friends at a distance and since the death of Maurice. We don't actually communicate directly – one of her sons, Mark, passes messages back and forth – but there is an understanding.

This situation gave me huge insights into how things had been for my mother many years earlier. She was the daughter of gentry, not rich by any means but with the background, the contacts, the manners and expectations of someone of her birth. My dad's side was working-class. Though really, what's the difference between marine engineer and plumber apart from a bit of gold braid?

As my mother had removed herself from my father's family, considering herself better, so the wife of my cousin was wary of me. It is true I really don't know how to cook a good, traditional English meal. I couldn't cook at all when I married and what I learned to make were all Indian dishes and I was good with them. Also, I am not a good housewife. My home is clean and relatively tidy but things are done when they obviously need doing – I see dust and think it's time for dusting. I remember one time when farewelling friends at the front door. We were standing talking and I noticed the thick dust on the door panelling; it came into my head, every flat surface collects dust. Not something that's taught in physics classes. It didn't help me to formulate any timetabling for cleaning house but I did remember to clean all surfaces when I got around to it. I had not seen any actual housework being done; I had not been invited to learn or help with cooking. My mother's reasoning being that, as she had grown up with servants, then I, too, must be shielded from the sordid details of running a house. My mother was an excellent housekeeper and cook. My sister, on the other hand, not well enough for school or work, was expected to help with the housework. I did not know this until I was quite a bit older.

I stayed with this newly found family three or four times and we became three tourists together. One of the places we went was from their home in Cleethorpes/Grimsby to Hull by bus. When I was a child, we had to take a ferry across the Humber River because there was no bridge. One of their sons lived in Hull, so we went a few times and later I stayed with him for a few days.

Cleethorpes is a seaside town where we would go for picnics and build sandcastles when I was a child. Hull and Grimsby are busy ports, though Hull has taken over as the main centre. The town centres of both are very attractive and I remember the blooming hanging baskets that gave both places a feeling of celebration.

Marie and I went together on a tour of the Netherlands. I made more extensive visits to the Continent on my own. These are recounted in *Around the World in Eighty Poems*.

Although I had made contact with Aunt Alice, long since a widow and living in a council flat, I couldn't pluck up the courage to actually visit her. I could walk to where she lived, from Maurice and Marie's home. I could not put it off any longer and I rang to arrange a suitable time.

Maurice and his family had, understandably, no contact with Aunt Alice, although Maurice had tried to establish a relationship with his half-sisters. He brought up his three sons to have ambition, get a good education. Maurice's own general knowledge was remarkable and his interests varied. I really admired him. We spent many evenings in his study computer room, discussing all manner of topics as well as family history while Marie watched soaps on TV.

The three sons have great respect for their mother. Mark, the middle one and the one I communicate with, takes her to his concerts and frequently on holidays. He has a full-time job with British Telecom and in his spare time leads a classical musical group that is professional in what they do, performing in major events; their Christmas performances are superb. My cousin-once-removed sends me the scores of new music and videos of Mozart's *Requiem*. He has a son in university, an ex-wife and a girlfriend who has a daughter of her own. A busy man but he loves his Mam. And this is my dad's ordinary side of the family.

It was a drizzly day the first time I went to visit Aunt Alice, and Maurice warned me to be careful on the wet pavement made slippery by the leaves. Without mishap, I found the flat, one in a huge block of very nice and large homes. I was warmly welcomed and Aunt Alice was keen to talk about Dad and his last weeks of life there. I visited a few times and we just chatted; I didn't learn anything new but again I was pleased I had managed to make very cordial contact. She gave me a set of a dozen crocheted coasters, which she had made, packed in a lovely fine-straw cylindrical box. The white coasters are beautiful.

Maurice was more adept with electronic technology than I and had done extensive research on the Cuerton family. He took us back to the 1500s. We were cordwainers, using the leather from special sheep or goats that grazed on a small patch of southern France. We made fine shoes and other goods for gentlemen and their ladies. I love good shoes. When I designed and made my own clothes, I could afford to have shoes to match each outfit. I often wore hats. Upon migration to England, our work became more diverse. Censuses show my father's great-grandfather described as a cordwainer and mariner, his grandfather a mariner and his father, as I have said, a plumber. Or a sawyer and journeyman.

I retraced my steps from what had been our English home to the market. It had changed with the times but still sold an assortment of cheap knick-knackery as well as the fruit and vegetables, meat and fish.

Maurice died a few years after I returned to Australia; I still miss him, the sense of humour that came through his letters, all the news and interesting chitchat. It is such a pity we were not friends for longer.

For several months, I travelled all over the UK and on the Continent, loving it all. I kissed the Blarney Stone and marvelled at everything in Turkey, but one couldn't talk modern politics. I threw a coin into the Trevi Fountain but it's not going to fulfil its promise of getting me back. Alas.

Greece was awesome but I found no humour. One time, I'd made a joke about the storks who liked to build their nests on top of chimneys, which made it handy for them to drop babies down. Maybe they don't know that's how babies arrive! I resisted buying souvenirs, except books, and a leather bag on the Ponte Vechio. It is sufficient for me to remember the sights and sounds and food of all I experienced and the feeling like a princess as I twirled around in the softest, silkiest-feeling leather cape, pale aqua with a white fur-lined hood with the sides clipped together around the wrists. The Italian salesmen didn't expect me to buy it, though they tried, but they did join in and encourage my joy in the beauty and luxury of that garment.

I went to the old Jewish quarter of Rome, and trod on ancient cobbled streets in many old European cities. They curve away, invite you along, and I wished I could hear the whispers that must have been passing even then from the tall leaning house on one side to the tall leaning house on the other. They would be stories of love, politics, intrigue. Some are joined by the clothes line on a pulley or a narrow bridge maybe four storeys up.

In Venice, I crossed a wrong bridge and tumbled into a wedding. Perhaps it means good fortune to have a stranger at your table, because they insisted on plying me with food and drink and I had to dance. During such activity, I managed to slip away over the same bridge.

Another nephew-in-law, his wife and their baby daughter lived in Norfolk. I had not met them but they insisted I spend some time with them. I am so glad I did, for they were lovely people. They called their daughter Brinda, an Indian name but close enough to the Anglo Brenda for the little one not to be teased or questioned about her funny name. I saw much of Norfolk and when the time came for me to move on I was really sad to be leaving my young friends. I did stay again and we kept in touch, irregularly, but I haven't heard from them for a long time. My ex-husband gets the occasional phone call. They are no longer in the UK; they were in US and Canada at different times. I don't know where they are now.

Every now and then when I needed company and ease of travel, I joined a bus tour. I did that in Ireland. Cosmos Tours were happy to put willing singles, of the same gender, in shared rooms, to save on the single supplement. I elected to do that. I met M. from Adelaide. We are still friends. In a recent email, we remembered the haunted room we had in one of the hotels, and what fun it was.

I was on my own, though, when I travelled on a bus to Warwick in England. Foolishly I had not made arrangements for anywhere to stay. It was getting late and I thought, I'm not going to make it to a tourist office and what do I do then? A heavily laden backpacker hailed the bus and sat next to me. We started to chat. She was Australian, visiting a chap to see if he was still her boyfriend or not. She asked me where I was going, where I was staying. I could answer the first, not the second. She said why not get off with her, not far from Warwick, and stay with her and maybe boyfriend. I certainly didn't want to get in the way but it would answer my dilemma as the sky darkened and I knew the tourist office would be closed. She insisted I accompany her and I wondered just how strong her relationship with the perhaps boyfriend might be. He met the bus, was quite unruffled at meeting two guests instead of just one, and I had a marvellous time for several days in a beautiful English manor.

My bus companion went on her way after a few days; I was invited to stay on, which I did, for a few more. My host was a wonderful travel guide. One morning at breakfast, I asked if he had heard the lute music during the night. He had not. There was not a lute in the house, he said. Another ghost. My bedroom window looked out over parkland through which the Avon flowed, and deer grazed on the grass.

No, my new friend was not the lord of the manor; he was the housekeeper. Which did not mean he did the dusting! The family was not in residence, no other domestic staff was there. My friend was caretaking.

Of course I visited the Shakespeare sites and followed Dickens routes, treading on the same cobbled streets their feet had trodden. In the Globe, I imagined I could hear snatches of Shakespeare's plays; similarly with Dickens's books in places such as The Olde Curiosity Shoppe. Italian music is kept alive by being sung in the streets by anyone with a song in his head. I criss-crossed the UK and the Channel, soaking up the culture of several centuries. I didn't want to leave, but after many months I had to use my ticket to the USA.

A few years before, on a visit to India with my second husband, we had met three young men, still boys really, from Tibet. They had won scholarships to study in Turkey, two in medicine, one to engineering. My husband and I were taking a bus tour of Delhi and we had stopped for lunch at a restaurant of the guide's choosing. It would have been moderately expensive for the pockets of our young students; we noticed they had ordered a meagre meal which they were sharing. My husband and I decided we would over-order and innocently invite the three to help us eat it.

At the end of the tour, the boys and I had exchanged names and I knew where they would be studying. They would all be together for a while as they had to learn the Turkish language, for, after all, that was the language of the lecturers. I said I would write when I arrived home. We irregularly kept in touch; I sympathised when they were down but also tried to buoy them up. I celebrated with their successes. And soon, it seemed, they were flying home, two qualified doctors, one qualified engineer. They were feted for a while but when it came to actually using their skills, they told me, the people turned against them; they trusted the old medicine, were doubtful of the newfangled engineering. The doctors ended up in South Africa, the engineer in the US, and it was he I was visiting.

There was much my young friend had omitted to tell me. He had acquired a wife but did not seem to be at all happy. He had a job but I didn't find out exactly what it was. He was less chatty and his English seemed to have deteriorated from the language he had in India many years before. In all the years they studied in Turkey, they had no home visits and they used to tell me of their homesickness. They had been so looking forward to helping their country, and that country's rejection of them had, I believe, deeply depressed my friend. He and his wife had a tiny flat in Boston, a city I love.

It was Christmas time; I had left the UK after many days of what seemed a total diet of Christmas dinners – but it hadn't snowed. In Boston it did. One whole floor of Macy's store was given over to telling the story of Dickens's *A Christmas Carol*, with tableaux in several rooms. With great clarity, I remember the carol singers, in period costume, performing from the back of a flat truck parked on the street, gentle snowflakes falling down. True Christmas card stuff. I had explored much of Boston on a previous visit but this time I went to the original home of Louisa May Alcott, the author of *Little Women* and other books.

It was closing time and I asked the person in charge if she could call a taxi for me. She asked where I was staying. I told her; she said she was passing there and could drop me off. I waited for her outside while she checked the building and put away the day's takings. It was cold, quietly snowing, and I thought I could not possibly go back to live in Brisbane. I would move to Tasmania. My house had been rented out for the year I was away, my goods and chattels were in storage, the ideal time to sell.

From Boston I was to fly to Toronto and have a fortnight with another nephew-in-law, his wife and their two small children. My husband's nephew was in insurance and the Indian head office had, at one time, sent him to Nauru to run that office. My husband and I had visited them there and I became good friends with them. Our correspondence had been thick and fast. It had been difficult reaching them on the phone from Boston to finalise details. Finally they told me it was not possible for me to stay with them. I was shattered; shades of the beginning.

At that time of the year, hotels were either closed or full. It would have cost me a lot to fly out of anywhere but Toronto, but I did, for a hefty fee, manage to bring forward my flight from the North American continent. From Boston I flew to Toronto and changed terminals, where I sat, wandered, ate, drank for many hours until my new flight took me to Honolulu, where I watched a sunrise, then to Sydney and on to Brisbane.

Neither my husband nor I was ever able to find out what had happened. Communication ceased. My former spouse and friends persuaded me Tasmania was too far away, so I settled on Mount Tamborine, in the Gold Coast hinterland.

Sun and snow

There were many things I liked living on Mount Tamborine. The climate was comfortable, including the morning mists through which I loved to walk and which inspired several poems. The house I bought was lovely, a very large brick cottage which occupied a quarter of a large square. The garage was attached to the house and I made it into another bedroom as I had taken one of the existing ones as my workroom. Where the roller door had been was made into a bay window to match the other. To house my car, I had another garage put around the corner, unattached. I still had a good-size mini-forest behind the garage and to the rear of the house, 18–22 Coleman Square. In the large space in front on the southern and eastern sides in front of the house, many native flowering trees and shrubs were planted. The wildlife was abundant.

I made friends, had very interesting political discussions, literary and artistic ones, learned about plants and gardens and the making of various foodstuffs. One not-yet-friend was out walking her mini-poodle, I was coming out of my gate. She stopped, introduced herself and asked me for whom I voted. I replied, she invited me to join her and a couple of friends for morning tea on the Saturday. These Saturdays were a regular thing; conversation was serious, very funny, covering everything. As well as these mornings, I graduated to her less frequent pre-dinner drinks gatherings with more people, different conversation. My new friend was nineteen years my senior and has since died. I miss her.

She had a true mountain garden with plants native to that area and everything was given its Latin name. She also educated me on bird and insect/reptile life. She would love my son. I loved her no-nonsense directness which, I know, can put some people off. My current doctor is direct, to the point; it suits me.

Another friend, more recently departed this mortal coil, was my severest literary critic and I valued her honesty. She also had likened my work to that of Margaret Atwood, an author I admire, so praise indeed – although I could never see a connection. She always left me in awe of how much she knew. Her second husband was a delightful man and a thorough gentleman.

It took ages for her to invite me to her home; her excuse, it was too messy. I told her I didn't mind mess, I wanted to see her in her own setting; I told her I frequently had to create a space on my own table in which to put my dinner; I said I like nothing better than to have to shift a pile of books in order to put down a cup of tea. I ended up spending a lot of time there and doing just that. Her son had someone read one of the poems I'd written about her at her Melbourne cremation. I was asked to read more at the Mount Tamborine Memorial.

One day, we three had gone to a Gold Coast cinema (to see *Snow Falling on Cedars*, based on the book of the same name by David Guterson) and I became the wheelchair pusher. I ran down ramps and around the car park like some demented speed-driver but we all laughed. It was also the day we had morning tea in the undercover car park. My friend had parked the car, opened the boot to get her husband's chair but, instead of closing the boot, began unpacking another box. Out came the mugs, the cake tin, the milk and sugar, hot water and teabags. So there we were, gathered at the rear of the car partaking of a delicious morning tea while cars drove slowly past looking for a parking spot and being surprised by our activity. It seemed so incongruous to me, I couldn't stop laughing. My friend couldn't really understand my humour; to her it was a perfectly ordinary and needful thing to be doing.

The two families, children from previous marriages, of the above couple were all brilliant, and keep on being brilliant, in music and art. Big minds. I used to accompany my friend to Jane Austen meetings, art exhibitions, concerts. Her husband died and she began to consider her son's suggestion of joining him and his family in Melbourne. (See *Ten Days of Normal*.)

Mary

I love her intellect and laughter
her wit is quick and sharp
her sense of fun is finely honed
she finds the joke where often
others can't. She suffers fools not
gladly, but unkind? Never
and I thought she didn't like me much
for she's reticent to ask me in;
she says she doesn't have the time
and her house is in a mess
but I love the book-strew clutter
where new titles pile the shelves
and she flits amongst possessions
both in the house – and out
like butterflies, both light
and bright
so I call her papillionatious
though she's tenacious as a bulldog
and things have to be just so.

But hurrah hurree today I'm
invited in for tea and what I'll see
is neatness and I wish she would
believe me when I say it's her, the
way she is that makes her so endearing;
and I want to see a pile of books,

make way for cup and cake
while she expounds on things beyond me
yet still depart with such a sense of fun
and hope there'll soon be another cup
with bun.

First published in *The Eyes Have It*, Ginninderra Press, 2012

Creativity was natural to me; I used to draw and had used oil and water paints. At this time, I was painting on silk and started making wall hangings which sold well. The ambience for writing wasn't there, but I could sew. I hadn't seriously made little girls' dresses, so at this time I started that as well as infants' clothes, which were sold through a lovely boutique. I was active in the Progress Association but the spirits of Tasmania kept whispering.

As I said, I was on the mountain four years until one morning in my beautiful, large bedroom, I sat up in bed and announced to its space that I was leaving. It went on the market that day and soon I was making my way to the southernmost state, by way of the long route. The furniture, soft goods, summer clothes, went into storage. My suitcase had enough to keep me going for a couple of months, the time I thought it would take to find a house.

The train trip to Melbourne was interrupted several times as I disembarked to spend a week here, another there, staying with friends along the way. From Melbourne, I boarded the ferry to Devonport and from there a bus to Launceston. It was always going to be that northern city that would furnish me with my next home; I don't know why Hobart had never entered my head as a possible place of domicile.

The idea was a nice house on a bus route, shops not too far away. None of the agents I contacted had anything that spoke to me. I was staying in a very nice B&B, although I had more of a bedsit with my own little kitchenette. Approaching the owners, I had explained my mission, that I needed somewhere until I had bought my house. We agreed on a price and I was a few steps away from the city centre. I could not, however, stay there forever and the situation was becoming desperate. One of the agents said he had one more place he could show me. He said it wasn't worth looking at and, indeed, was unliveable but it was on his books and I hadn't seen it.

We pulled up outside 22 Claremont Street, East Launceston, and I fell in love with the house – an old lady of a house, in need of a makeover, a good scrubbing. We went inside and I fell more deeply in love with its interior. It most definitely spoke to me, shouting loudly, 'I'm yours, I'm yours.'

It had been empty for some time, probably had squatters, and, before that, was rented. The owner, a very old woman, had looked after it when she had lived there. I bought it for $100,000. It was September 2002 and I used the rest of my money on bringing the old house back to life, twenty-first-century comfort with Victorian charm. If you've ever watched *Grand Design* with Kevin McCloud, in which hopeful owners set to work in bringing an old decrepit building to a comfortable living space, you will have an idea of the pitfalls. Whatever money is set aside for the job is never enough.

Sundays in Launceston were quiet days and on those I would explore. I walked up and down hills, along straight and curving roads, discovered the Gorge, historic buildings. When I had arrived, it was winter and the men all seemed to wear black. Invariably they would be bent into or away from, the wind, wringing their cold hands. Gloves didn't seem to be part of the fashion. This image against the architecture reminded me of a tiny patch of London's 1800s, miniaturised yet again. I could easily imagine the horses and carts, the noise, the ladies hurrying from shop to shop or taking tea in one of the cafés.

On one such day, just after I'd bought my house, I went into the Wood Museum, a collection of beautiful things from tiny thimbles to large pieces of furniture, made from Tasmanian timbers. The young woman sitting at the entrance desk asked where I was from and so struck up a conversation. I told her I was looking for workers to make my house into a home. She suggested I contact her brother. With nothing to lose, that is what I did. I didn't know anyone and if I wasn't impressed, I didn't have to employ him. It turned out beautifully.

He was a master builder and became the foreman of the small gang of workers, some chosen by him, some by me, to work on the plumbing, the electrics, the carpentry, tiling, cementing, roofing. All were artisans. The house was remade. I had two fireplaces and chimneys removed so the respective rooms would have more usable space, and from the bricks I kept twenty, all thumbprinted, convict-made, to share amongst my grandchildren. I have part of a chimney, too.

The fronts of the most attractive of the fireplaces were put in the original places against new wall in the drawing and dining rooms and a bedroom, with all remaining chimney places closed off. Central heating was installed via brass vents in strategic places along the edge of the floors. Some of the remaining bricks made a fan-shaped courtyard on one of the levels in the back garden.

The old claw-foot bath was restored, after it had been chucked out of the rotting bathroom and sat in the yard being the hold-all for all manner of rubbish. A huge shower was installed in a slightly enlarged already large bathroom and toilet. Another shower was installed in a small bathroom and toilet at the end of the laundry. Many thought the main bathroom was the *pièce de résistance*.

As soon as it was at least habitable, I moved in and my son came for a visit. I asked him to carve a name for the house, using one of the old, discarded pieces of wood.

He asked the name.

'Witzend,' I said.

'Are you sure?' he asked.

'Yes,' I replied. I brought the name with me.

In February 2003, friends I had made took me to the penny-farthing bicycle races, an annual event held at Evandale. A 1900 bicycle was leaning against a wall with a sign saying it was free to a good home. I asked my friends if we could take it with us. It was in beautiful condition. I attached baskets front and back, the front filled with artificial flowers, the rear with what appeared to be a picnic including the bottle of wine – well, a corked bottle – and a book. It leaned against the wall under the name of the house. Many people walked past, exercising, as I was two-thirds up a hill, or taking children to or from the private school at the base of it. The little tableau attracted the gaze and as I sat at my desk, in front of the drawing room window, I would see the smiles appear, the discreetly pointed finger or nod of the head, the happy words exchanged. I loved it.

Early in my residence, friends came down from the mainland and one evening we went to a restaurant on the pier. It looked modern, nice decor. We were not approached and shown to a table, so we organised ourselves and soon a girl came to take our order. We asked for menus and the wine list. The restaurant had the menus but not a wine list, so we asked what they had to drink. It was a licensed establishment. Our waitress replied there was tea, coffee, wine. Yes, we said, what kind of wine and after a slight hesitation the girl told us they had red and white. The male of our party went to have a look at some bottles and chose one. Other friends, travelling around the tiny state, told me of the lack of facilities, the take-it-or-leave-it attitude of many caravan and B&B sites. Things had vastly improved by the time I left.

On the first anniversary of my being in Launceston, I held a garden party. Eighty friends and neighbours came, some meeting old friends they had not met with for some years. Apart from the foreman of the renovations, and his family and sister, my first friend said she picked me up at a little café. I had gone down into town for lunch, the house being worked on, heading for a place I had found and liked, Red Pepper.

On this day, there were no spare tables but Marjorie and her visiting Hobart friend were at the only circular table that seated four. She saw my head checking space and then withdrawing. She very quickly told the owner to let me know I could share her table so Janie chased after me – not very far. I would have been content to order, eat, mind my own business, but Marjorie was having none of that; she wanted to know who I was, what I was doing, and promised to give me details of the local U3A, in Launceston called School for Seniors. I gave her my phone number. She did ring, which surprised me as, frequently on the mainland, chance encounters promise many things but don't follow through. She is a dear, dear person. I was the only non-family member at a dinner when one of her sons, a reader at Warwick University, UK, was on a brief visit. That inclusion touched me deeply. She is a name-dropper of the first order and on 'kissy-kissy' terms with Jacki Weaver,

Graeme Murphy, Paul Mercurio and several other 'names'. I tease her about it. Marjorie was ninety-five in 2017.

One day I was at the café by myself. I noticed another woman looking for a spare table and, none being available, indicated she might join mine. We talked; she learned I liked to write and said she would pass my name on to another friend, a member of an established writers' group. That person rang, we arranged to meet, I was invited to a meeting. Normally, new members to the group were invited to at least two meetings and invited to read something they had written then formally invited to join – or not, as the case might be. I was unanimously invited that first evening and so I became a Launceston Tatler.

For that first meeting, I was taken to the large and beautiful home of a member living just out from the city. I was offered champagne and canapés. The meeting began, two members did readings which were discussed, and then we had supper. A sumptuous offering. I thought, if this was the standard set, I could not match it. The next meeting was held in a tiny worker's cottage on the edge of the city. The dozen or so of us sat where we could, we ate and drank more simple food, laughed a lot, readings were presented followed by coffee. I was much more relaxed for when it was my turn. Both of these hostesses and another woman and I became closer friends and frequently met at my place for lunches. Conversation flowed and we decided we should write a book based on the subjects we covered. We tried.

That third person mentioned called me Jacki at the first meeting. I said my name was Jacqueline. Her first thought, she told me later, was 'Humpff! Uppity female' but she saw something in me that made her persist; we became very close, laughed at the same things, saw the ridiculousness of various situations and often had to make sure we didn't catch the other's eye or we'd dissolve into unstoppable laughter. She moved house as often as I did but made all of hers into B&Bs.

One day we were talking on the phone and she suddenly shouted, 'Have to go. My young men are leaving and they haven't paid me.' The picture conjured was hilarious. Her cleaner had to climb down the ladder for fear of falling off it. My friend then was the grandmother of teenage children and had been a London East-ender.

Another guest had caused some concern. He was Chinese with not much English and had several visitors who, to my friend, seemed unsavoury, suspicious. Although he had paid for several nights, he was away for some of them. My friend and I were due at a luncheon and she told me she had gone through the guest's room and belongings and taken his passport – so he couldn't run away! It was at that moment hidden in the boot of her car. As writers, my friend and I aided and abetted each other in expanded imaginations, but the funny side of her story fought with the possible serious side. I told her she had to return his passport, hopefully before he found it was missing; she managed to speak with the sinister friends when they returned him to the house and her guest didn't look as if he had been beaten up and all was satisfactorily explained.

My own writing became serious and I managed to write the novel *The In-Between Man*. It had been brewing in my head for many years. The mayor at the time, Ivan Dean, launched it. That he had actually read it was proved by the bits he chose to quote and quite embarrassed me. It was a great afternoon and I sold many copies. Many more subsequently sold with the help of the local independent booksellers. The next book was an account of my round-the-world travels written in rhyming verse. Very bad poetry but fun, if difficult at times, to do. Life was full and fun.

As well as attending U3A classes, I became a tutor offering various courses but always one in creative writing. Currently, in Redcliffe, my most active class consists of a group (that can be as large as twenty-six people if all registered members attend) designed to discuss current issues. It is very popular because, I think, many of us live alone and don't get the opportunity to discuss what matters. A second class is required.

In Tasmania, I was dubbed the senior writing tutor while a fellow tutor had the beginners. There wasn't any difference in our skills but my friend had more patience than I and was more gentle with fragile egos. And another class I enjoyed with a fellow tutor was titled France, French and the Beauty of Grandmothers. This was popular and repeated for several terms.

The School for Seniors was housed in what had been a school and become redundant. To have so much space, so many rooms, meant many classes could be held. It was a short walk from my home; I was very happy there.

Had I stayed in the house, I might never have left Tasmania. It is a creative little state, stronger in some areas of creativity than others. That spot and my house must have been in the centre of one such zone, but the house needed more work, I'd run out of money and I didn't want it to look shabby. It had been on and off the market for a while with no decent offers. It was off the market when I came home one afternoon and a couple were looking at the house next door that had just gone on the market. They were not over keen on it and discussing it on the footpath.

If you can have a sotto voce nudge, my friend was giving me lots of sotto voce nudges with similar sotto voce urgings to speak to them. If only to end the pantomime, I told the couple my place could be for sale and asked if they would like to have a look. They did and loved it immediately. They wanted the same things for the house that I would want. We shook hands on the deal over a cup of tea.

I bought a villa, one of six, out of town and never really settled into it. I was there two years.

Student life

Simple rooms, dinner a side-
dish for friends whose jeans-clad
legs entwined those of the table
bruised and chipped;
candles and wine were the entrée
to conversation
which became meatier
as the meal progressed
ending in sixties cigarette haze,
the chequered cloth
absorbing drips and spills
the odd burn
the fabric becoming thinner
and worn
but heavy with laughter, words
and memory.

From *An Australian Poem*, Witzend publishing, 2013

And yet again

It is possible I misheard, or interpreted to my satisfaction, the words of my sons in regard to my playing a part in the lives of their children, my grandchildren. My siblings are on the mainland and the Pollyanna in me thought family mattered.

Whatever I thought, it was wrong. My two Sydney sons didn't want me to live too close to them, as I might become too needy. When I heard that, I was very angry, as I've never relied on other people for anything. My middle son was in Alice Springs, so wherever I lived was going to be a good distance from him. My first son didn't want me to bump into his father, especially if such a contretemps should occur at his home; I think he felt traitorous by having anything to do with me.

I thought the northern NSW coast might suit and my second ex-husband invited me to stay with him in Tweed Heads while I made my search. That was a disaster, too, as he wouldn't let me borrow his car; he was a terrible driver and every day we went out we hit something. It might have been the gatepost, scraping a kerb, a gentle knock on an already parked car, but whatever it was didn't make for good moods. We didn't get started until nearly eleven, as he had to meditate then eat, and we had to be back home by four o'clock so he could meditate again and have his dinner at six. He wouldn't allow me to cook or eat meat in the house and if I brought anything in, I wasn't allowed to use his cutlery or china. I made a too-hasty decision on what I did purchase.

One drives into these over-fifties resorts which present an attractive view. The managers have their spiel of attractions, all the activities and bonhomie, the benefits. The houses are cheaper than out in the open market and I didn't have a lot of cash. We finally drove into Sapphire

Gardens, Eagleby, and looked at four or five vacant homes. The houses themselves are very nice, large, three bedrooms, two toilets, though only one bathroom and huge open-plan living area. My ex-spouse was quite taken with one and, while I was doubtful, I made an offer on it. I really needed to get into my own place. Eagleby is next to Beenleigh and I should have remembered it as a not very nice place to live. I dismissed those thoughts, believing the community within would provide the friendship, stimulation that I needed.

How wrong I was. As a single woman, the married ones were afraid I wanted to steal their husbands (this was borne out by another single woman who felt the same way) and so were not friendly; the overall IQ was low, so there were no activities that appealed to me; the highlight of their week seemed to be the meal at one of the local services clubs that cost $6.95 for two courses. I kid you not. The house went on the market almost immediately. It took four years to sell. My lifesaving activities were the Logan Hyperdome library and its book group, which led to my being invited to join a second book group, which in turn introduced me to a Redcliffe resident. My diagonally opposite neighbour, who is still my friend, introduced me to another.

After I'd had time to think about my Sydney sons' attitudes, I could see their point. They don't know me at all and while I have police clearances in two states for voluntary work that might involve children, they didn't know that either. Not long before one of the rare phone conversations with my oldest son, I'd had a trip to Canberra to see a particular art exhibition. Floriade was on at the same time. From that, I thought it might be nice to have the odd weekend with my granddaughter, then fifteen, to share something special in the country's capital or anywhere else. My son flatly refused; it was a preposterous idea.

My sister didn't resume speaking to me or, at that time, our brothers (she had cut contact with the three siblings at the end of my mother's cremation). After what I thought had been a good relationship with my younger brother and his wife, my brother severed contact. Apparently he saw me as being too negative.

My longest-serving friend, known since 1978, put it down to my being intelligent, questioning, not accepting everything on face value. I like to discuss the pros and cons. At that time, too, I might have been going through a period of depression; such periods happen too often.

It's a pity my brother or sister-in-law did not think to discuss with me anything they thought to be amiss. We don't expect repayment for past action but perhaps some understanding. Although my income was always a fraction of that of my brothers, I helped them both out at different times with cash and shelter.

My older brother and his second wife had the use of my house for some of the time I was overseas, rent-free, and never did pay for the damage they did to it. When my younger brother returned from England with his girlfriend soon-to-be-wife, and my mother refused to have anything to do with her (she wasn't good enough for my brother), she came to me. She stayed with me for some time.

Recently, my older brother did not invite me to his eightieth birthday celebrations because he thought I wouldn't want to go. I probably wouldn't. I have little to contribute when he has a group of his friends around. I know nothing of their sport, I don't drink and while I might be vaguely aware of names in the world of popular entertainment, I don't care who is sleeping with whom or what their latest antics amount to. But he might have allowed me to make my decision about attending or not. In the past, I had stayed with them on my visits and I suppose they thought that would be the case this time. He might have had friends staying or, if not, probably saw me as a dampener. Whatever. We have enjoyed jokes, repartee in the past. At one time, relations with both brothers was good, although we have never been really close. Our mother was a divide-and-rule sort of person.

So I moved to the mainland for nothing. I don't like the heat – I have joked that while we came to Australia to give my sister warmth and life, it will kill me. I left behind a full, busy life and friends mostly in the writing fraternity and I miss my place in that. But here I am and here I shall stay.

After four years of being on the market, the house sold and I bought an apartment in Redcliffe, a coastal town on the northern border of Brisbane. I have been relatively happy here, tutor and attend classes at the local U3A and am close enough to Brisbane, albeit requiring a bus and train, to go in for daytime orchestral concerts or anything else, including meeting with old friends and attending meetings of a couple of writers' groups.

There is a saying, 'the past is a foreign country', and one cannot – at least so I have found to my cost – go back. My brothers, the friends I had when I worked here, have all moved on and they too have their close groups of friends who have kept up with the nuances of each other's daily life. Yes, we have all kept in touch but letters and emails are very superficial; one needs the conversations that cover the deep and profound as well as the inconsequential. Again, I find I don't fit in. So I find myself in a strange place without a passport, a displaced person.

The family

Lonsdale grandparents

That I grew up in a dysfunctional family has been demonstrated, but as a social worker I wonder whose isn't. My parents didn't like each other, making for an uncomfortable atmosphere. It had been a case of two lonely people being in the same place at the same time. My mother probably also saw it as snubbing her nose at her parents but they had not done anything to further the social standing of their daughter. My grandfather had been a compulsive gambler, losing, in the end, all. I don't know at what point the first Lonsdale went to Burma (Myanmar) but they were a settled and respected family at the time of my grandfather.

He was the eldest of thirteen children; at least six left Burma and settled elsewhere. Some, direct or extended family, trekked from Rangoon to Moulmein and some to India during World War II as both British and Japanese bombs rained down. Many hundreds of Burmese citizens attempted to leave their country and many died along the way.

After the war, some members of the surviving family scattered to England and Australia, and probably USA and Canada. As the émigrés would marry 'white' and become paler, whatever family stayed in Burma would have married Burmese and become 'browner'.

And history is divided, lost. All the children had university educations and they included concert pianist, artists, nursing sister, teachers, commerce graduates, engineers. Richard, son of my grandfather's cousin, Dr Hugh Lonsdale-Hans, designed aircraft engines for Rolls Royce. Through Hugh, they were friends of the Attlees (Clement, 1st Earl Attlee of Walthamstow, Viscount Prestwood). He was the British Labour Party leader from 1935 to 1955 and prime minister between 26 July 1945 and 26 October 1951. He presided over the establishment of the welfare state in Great Britain and the granting of independence to India. Long before she was allowed to vote, my mother was a Labour Party supporter. It would be interesting to know how much she was influenced by Clement Attlee.

Hugh's daughter, Richard's sister, Evelyne, married 1st Viscount Montgomery. (Or his son. That needs clarification.)

My mother's social set, especially when she was living in London, would have consisted of people such as the above.

It would seem my grandfather was the only one – then and since, touch wood – afflicted with the gambling bug. My mother and sister were/are both painters; my mother won prizes for some of hers: I don't know if my sister ever entered any competitions. There are several Lonsdale authors. I find it fascinating that a family with some of the same recent antecedents can take such diverse trajectories.

Frederick Gordon Lonsdale was born in Burma, Rangoon or Moulmein in 1876 and died in Brisbane in 1959. My meagre information describes him as a marine engineer, First Officer Merchant Navy, gambler, wool classer. He left Burma at age nineteen and, as far as I am aware, never returned. Family folklore has it that he worked for a time for his uncle who owned the newspaper *The Rangoon Gazette*, but when it was discovered he had been embezzling funds, he was summarily sacked. That might have resulted in his being sent to Australia where he became a jackaroo and then wool classer.

In Burma, he would have been the sahib, the boss, master. There's a photograph I saw of him when, as a young man, he had been on a tiger shoot. The photo shows him as successful in killing one of the beautiful animals as he is pictured rifle in one hand and a foot resting on the animal's flank. The tiger, however, wasn't giving up without a fight; he wasn't quite dead at the time of the picture and managed to scrape his claws down the side of my grandfather's leg. It left a lifelong scar.

He really was a handsome man and a gentleman. He was charming and I used to think of him as a roué in the nicest possible way (like Clark Gable as Rhett Butler in *Gone with the Wind*). He had that facility of being able to keep people in their place without giving offence. My older brother had it. I don't think it's a manner one can cultivate; one either has it or one doesn't.

At some point, Grandfather enrolled in an English university to study medicine. His family, of course, gave him an allowance, paid his fees et cetera. After two years, he decided engineering was more to his liking, so he switched courses. This happens often, actually, medicine to engineering. The story goes that he neglected to inform his family of the change as medical fees were more than engineering fees and he pocketed the difference. My understanding is that he joined the Merchant Navy before or at the outset of World War I. He was also a very competent artist and painted many pictures of war on the sea, none of which we have.

He married my grandmother, Mary Katherine Jones, born 1893, in about 1911. Katie, as she was known, had a brother who was a photographer and apparently it was through him that the two met. He had a photograph of his sister in the front window of his studio. My grandfather, struck by her beauty, went in and engaged my great-uncle in conversation. A friendship began and very soon an invitation to dine with the family. (My great-uncle fought in World War I and suffered various injuries, including the effects of inhaling mustard gas. He never returned to any kind of normal life and when I knew him he had a cottage out in the country surrounded by the sounds of nature and no neighbours. I stayed there once and I had to draw water from a well. I couldn't have been very old but I know it was summer and I remember the colours and the feeling of peace.)

My grandfather decided on first meeting that Katie was going to be his wife. He lied about his age, which was twice that of my grandmother – he was thirty-six to her eighteen, but said he was twenty-eight. In all other respects he appeared a perfect gentleman, very handsome and youthful-looking, and had the family history. He had the fine-boned stature of the Burmese and the pale burnt-honey colour of the mixed race. My mother was officially their second child, born 13 December 1913, the first, a girl, having been born nine or ten months after the marriage. My mother's birth certificate states her birth as 14 December 1913 because my grandfather didn't like the two thirteens. It was celebrated on the thirteenth and stated as that when asked. It caused confusion when her birth certificate had to be produced for verification.

Life is not fair; we are not always rational. With all the fuss of my mother's birth, someone had neglected to securely close the front door of the house and the little girl went out into the snow. She was found some time later and died of pneumonia. In that very subtle way, my mother, her birth, was blamed for the accident.

Another daughter was born eighteen months or two years later and then, finally, a son, Gordon, upon whom his father doted. Unfortunately, Gordon contracted meningitis at age four and died. My grandfather, I was told, was inconsolable and never recovered from the loss. All of the stories point to Gordon being a very clever child; so was my mother but she was a girl and lived.

My mother had described the unknowingness of day-to-day living, whether there'd be a house to go home to; whether or not it would have its servants; what pieces of valuable furniture might be missing. There would be no jewellery to pass down; no glassware or paintings, not even those by my grandfather. Not even beautiful clothes; my mother was ten and needed a new dress but apparently there was no money. She took a pair of her father's trousers, wide-legged in those days, unpicked the stitching and made herself a dress, a pinafore, which she then wore to school. All hand-sewn, of course.

Grandpa would have cut a dashing figure in his uniform. It is surprising there are no photographs. My grandmother's family would have considered him quite a catch, good family, family money and my grandfather in a respected position. I know he was respected by his men and fellow officers. He would not countenance bad language, at home or at sea. I grew up speaking correct English *sans* slang and swear words. He used to say the use of either displayed a poor grasp of the English language. He would have spoken Burmese and Hindi in Burma but once he married my grandmother it was nothing but English. One of his sisters was visiting one time and started speaking in Burmese to her brother; he stopped her to say it was rude to use another language when not everyone within the house could understand it, so English only please. He never lost his accent, however.

My grandmother quickly discovered her husband's gambling habits which, on occasion, meant losing servants, house, furniture. She and the two children would be taken in by her mother until her husband won back what he had lost and they moved back again. But she was no wilting female. She understood the money to be had in the sale of food and drink. Even in the worst of times, men will gather in the local pub and buy however many pints they could afford. She knew there would always be money coming in from such an enterprise, so she bought at least one pub, possibly two. The only one I know about was in Whitby in Yorkshire. I don't know when or with what, where, the money came from.

Whitby is in the jet-mining area. Jet is a beautiful stone but alas, we did not inherit any pieces of jewellery or *objets d'art*. My grandmother's clothing, though, was always of the highest quality. There is a Whitby Castle and Bram Stoker set part of his book *Dracula* in the area, incorporating pieces of local folklore, including the beaching of the Russian ship *Dimitri*.

At the end of one of his home leaves and preparing to return to his ship, my grandmother asked him to call in at a couple of businesses to pay some bills for her. She gave him cash with which to do it. Sometime later when he was on the high seas, my grandmother received letters requesting the payment of the overdue bills – yes, my grandfather had found the temptation to gamble with the money given him stronger than the security of his family. Grandmother phoned my mother, telling her she had to return to help with the pub because there was no money to pay staff. There was no mention of my aunt in the telling of this part of the story so I don't know where she was or what she was doing. She was not helping out in the pub.

That my grandmother was a strong woman is evidenced in her buying and operating a pub, even a nice, friendly, family, English pub. Self-preservation and protection for one's children are strong motivators. She could be hard, didn't suffer fools and expected everyone to earn their slice of bread. My grandmother was a sensible woman in many ways but had a quick temper and was as hard and critical of my mother as she was with her servants, who, if or when they displeased her, could be on the receiving end of her rolled-up whalebone corset. My mother had also been at the end of this weapon and said it really did hurt. The maids would have been the primary carers of my mother and aunt and probably took out on them the frustrations and anger that should have been directed at my grandmother. Had they, of course, they would have been sacked. As my grandmother, I remember her clearing a pathway through shopping crowds with her folded umbrella.

As we are all complex, my grandmother had her complexities and is something of a mystery. She was a storyteller and storytellers, as you know, you cannot entirely believe. She was fair and very good-looking in her younger years. Strength of character showed in her mature years. I blame my itchy feet on my grandmother. She always maintained she was a Romany, a Gypsy. I think she was joking but she had perceptions, insights, most of us do not.

Her father was born in Dublin; the story has it he had been a doctor. My grandmother used to tell us of their collecting herbs in the fields – were doctors their own apothecaries in those days? I don't know where my grandmother was born. She was a wise woman, someone who might have been called a shaman in a different culture. She used to say I had 'the gift' but my mother would have none of it and forbade her to teach me any of her skills. I might have been wiser had she been allowed, but teaching or not could not prevent the unusual experiences I have had.

On the other hand, my peripatetic life might be due to the fact that I was born on a Thursday, not that I might have Romany blood. You know, the nursery rhyme about the days of the week and in the version I knew, Thursday's child has far to go. Then again, it might be that I am just rootless, a will-o'-the-wisp, no fixed address.

My grandmother told us the story of one day sitting in her front room and looking up to see my grandfather walking past the window. She was surprised because he wasn't expected. The Great War was being raged. She said she jumped up and went to open the front door but the street was totally empty. She learned later that at that precise time, Grandpa was going hand over hand on a rope from his ship to a nearby disabled one. He fell. Into the icy Atlantic Ocean. The details of how he was saved were either not given or I've forgotten, but saved he was and no doubt he fixed the disabled ship. How strong are the thought waves at such times.

That my grandfather did not like to be idle is evidenced in the work he did at the local swimming baths, maintaining the machinery. He would have been about seventy-four when my family left England in 1950. I have a vision of him in his overalls, a small, slightly bent elderly gentleman. My mother inherited her father's need to be busy. She did not, thank goodness, inherit his fastidious tidiness, at least to the same degree. My mother used to tell how, if she left a book on a side table to go to the toilet, it would be back on the bookshelf by the time she came back; knitting left on a settee while she went to make herself a cup of tea would have been tidied away into a cupboard during her brief absence.

When these grandparents joined us in Australia, Grandma took a job in a city café reading tea cups. She said that was more for entertainment than actual enlightenment. Her clientele was 99.9% female and she just picked up on their body language. She had her regulars, however, so she must have struck a chord with at least some. My grandparents would sometimes have dinner with us when we had visitors, mostly the overseas postgraduate and doctoral students. They invariably wanted my grandmother to read the cards for them and were amazed by the personal histories she could see in them. So they would take seriously the things she said of the future.

She would also read the cards for all the family, except me. She would begin with my having had a good life and then claim she couldn't see any more or she was tired. That was before my accident.

Me, metaphysics and things

Even through the war years, I had some sort of birthday celebration every year. Even as an adult, not many birthdays pass unmarked. For my fourteenth, I invited a Dutch boy. He had arrived in Australia not long before; his English was very limited but, as seems to be my habit, I wanted him to feel welcome. His birthday present to me was a bit late but he had taken time to cut out of timber a Dutch farmer and his wife. They are flat, not sculpted, but their features and clothing are beautifully drawn and painted. He wrote on the back of them and signed his name. They have travelled with me since then and adorn my wall now.

It would be very remiss of me to not mention my Arzburg china. Friends of my friend Stephen, a young newly married couple, gave me a dinner setting for four of this high quality tableware. It is perfectly plain, white, with a narrow edge of fine ridges. Over a reasonably short time I added to it so it became a breakfast, luncheon and dinner setting for eight. It also has a coffee set for six. The coffee cups are demitasse and apart from the sugar bowl and milk jug, the coffee pot and cups have not been used as much as the lunch/dinner ware, which has been used a lot. I cannot remember that generous young couple but I do remember their kindness, and my friend Stephen.

And speaking of china, I had given my mother a tea set of Royal Albert Old Country Roses, which she used when her bridge ladies came around. After my mother's death, my sister took it against my wishes – I was hoping to have it back. My firstborn son bought me a set of Royal Albert Satin Roses. It is less flamboyant, blue and silver, more elegant, though I do have a lot more of the other.

The few fun times my sister and I had together stand out in my mind as events. There are photographs of us being active at picnics, another of the time we went to the Brisbane 'Ekka' – the annual country, industrial, fashion and fun fair. Fears of polio, changes in weather, lack of interest, prevented further visits.

When I was in my late teens and older, Mother wanted to be part of the parties, acted like one of us, flirted with and monopolised our boyfriends. There was an occasion when I was seventeen and she and I were visiting an art gallery. I was a member of the Royal Queensland Art Society then and had had some of my work exhibited along with my fellow members. We were discussing a particular painting, as I no doubt thought I knew something of the merits or otherwise of it, when another visitor to the gallery came to examine the same painting. He engaged my mother in conversation, reiterating and refuting some of the things I had said. He suggested we discuss the exhibition over a cup of tea; I already thought he was a sleaze.

Over the course of afternoon tea, he asked me if I would have dinner with him at his flat. He fancied himself a cook. By this time, we had ascertained that he was thirty-four, exactly twice my age. I looked to my mother to back me in refusing but she said how lovely that would be and, between them, a date and time was arranged. I was to make my way there.

Today, a girl would just say no but I remember thinking then that my mother had failed me and if that was what she thought of me, I felt she was sending me out to be a whore, and that was what she'd get. As it happened, on the appointed date and in his flat, he made my skin crawl and I was not cooperative. He tried to get hold of me, threatening rape and worse, and then to leave me in the bush on Mt Coot-tha, one of Brisbane's tourist centres. I did manage to escape and caught a tram to its terminus at Clayfield, from whence I took a taxi the rest of the way. I had insufficient funds to pay for it, so Mother had to.

If I wanted a new dress, though, my own design or something sketched from a model in a boutique window, she would make it. She would stay up all night to finish it if it was needed in a hurry. If I announced that a few friends were coming over the following night, she would cater. I think, sometimes, I did as much as I could in trying to force her to force some discipline on me. I do say I brought myself up because I had to work out what was right, what was wrong, and it is not easy.

I experienced that enveloping light again, as when I was a very young child, when I was outdoors on the Lincolnshire Dales in my home county on the visit back in 1997. As far as I have been able to work out, it didn't change my life, I had no great enlightenment. I feel a bit cheated, there should have been a message; other people report near-death experiences and have an epiphany – me, I just thought, wow, what was that? Perhaps the page was torn out. I've stayed just as nondescript as ninety-nine per cent of the population. After the motorbike accident and being pronounced dead, I did look down at myself, and registered interest at seeing a dead body but no light tunnel, no great message. I just get told my life signs disappeared for a time.

In the Solomon Island section, I tell of my preparedness for death when I was just so peaceful and giving up. That I didn't die is perhaps due to the act of giving up, not fighting, and thus giving my body the chance of fighting for itself. But no epiphany. I've also had out-of-body experiences.

My sister, at a critical time in her fight for life, later reported seeing all the people whom she knew loved her, standing around her bed telling her to come back. She had been travelling at extreme speed down a brightly lit passage. At the time of my experiences and my sister's, had we reported them more widely than a very few trusted friends, we would have been considered crackpots at least, mentally unstable at worst. At the beginning of the twenty-first century, doctors and scientists are beginning to pay attention. But she was in hospital at the time, in an oxygen tent. Lights, movement and possibly being told by medical staff to 'come back, don't leave us' need to be taken into account.

I cannot explain how, when I lived in Sydney and my sister lived in Brisbane, in a disastrous marriage and with two small children, I suddenly heard the voice of my long-deceased grandfather. All his life he had not lost the accent he had; his pronunciation of certain words, as a result of his growing up speaking Burmese and Hindi – there was no doubt it was my grandfather's voice. His message was that my sister was suffering a very low period; she was fed-up, he said. It was so strong that I had to phone her.

In those days, telephones were not the addiction they seem to be today and we used them when we needed to, so making a call from Sydney to Brisbane for no tangible reason was an event. It was the middle of the afternoon and fortunately she did answer the ringing. She told me she had taped up the doors and windows, sealing herself and her sons into the flat, and was about to turn on the gas elements. Her doctor husband was abusive, mentally and physically, the children then about twelve and twenty-four months old.

Later, she moved to Cairns and for a while we chose a time in the evening when we would have mental conversations and write down what we believed those conversations were. Our interests ranged over many topics, so there was no reason that on any particular evening, our thoughts would be on any particular subject. It is interesting that on checking our notes, we really did have a conversation.

Does this sort of thing happen only between people who are close? I think not. Perhaps it is just intuition but there are times when I just know things. I've known where there'd be a parking space on a busy Saturday night in the city and perhaps it's just my reading of fashion, but I've been ahead of that, too, in my designs. Many times I have woken to see a person by my bed, looking down on me. I was never afraid and never felt these presences to be malignant. I used also to find myself floating outside of my body. I could never take a trip on my own volition but I did wish I could and travel long distances, visit foreign places, as others have reported doing.

A friend of mine suggests this other-worldly knowledge or extra dimension might be genetic memory. Some believe it is memories of past lives. I believe everyone had those skills at one time but we have civilised them out of our system. Some of us still have vestiges.

After I had bought my first house as a single female, the elderly wife of the couple who had sold it, died. Often, when I was cooking dinner I would feel someone approaching along the hallway but when I turned to see who it was, a shadow disappeared. I knew it was the old woman and one evening I didn't turn but said that it was quite all right for her to visit, it had been her home for a long time. I didn't feel her visit any more after that.

The lute music in the English manor has been mentioned. My host insisted there was not a lute on the premises and had not been one according to his knowledge.

My second husband worked in Fiji for a time and I travelled back and forth. I knew his wardrobe and that men rarely wore ties. When we were in separate countries, he would ring me. We treated it as a sort of game as I told him where he was in his office, what he was wearing, that he had a new shirt and asked why he was wearing a tie.

Time and place have always been important to me. I am not alone in having to find the right place in a house in which to set up one's creative tools. I did have an office in my Victorian Launceston house, complete with corner desk, printer and bookcases with reference books and I intended to write there. But it just didn't feel right; a desk in the open-plan kitchen-dining-living-room did. I never knew what to do with the drawing room; I tried several uses for it but in the end it was just a room. Beautiful but always cold, unwelcoming. I only felt really safe in it when it was full of friends. The rest of the house was just lovely, comfortable and a joy to live in. I have a friend whose writing is stalled because, owing to circumstances and not living where she would like, simply can't find the right spot in which to create.

I have tried having a conversation with the images that appeared by my bed but when I spoke the image faded away. I have never felt afraid. On my visit back to the UK, I went to the site of the last battle of Bonnie Prince Charlie; I left this dimension, was transported back to the actual battle. I saw, smelt, heard, felt the action. But I wasn't on either side, just a neutral observer. Things came to life when I visited the Roman baths in Bath. Sulphur smells, wet, naked bodies, wet footprints on stone – when I came back to the present, I thought it might have been a clever sound/light show. Circumlocutorally, I asked others about their experiences; no one seemed to go where I did.

Mother

Had my mother been someone else, not related to me, I have wondered if we might have been friends, as her friend Auntie M and I became friends as I matured. Mother was intelligent in many ways, reasonably well-read, a fierce Laborite, although I accused her of not moving with the times – her Labor was fifty years in the past. We were both strong women but when I think about it, there was not enough on which we could agree and I could be a devil's advocate, whereas she could never be. For her, things were black or white; for me, there are many shades of grey. And every colour of the rainbow. For example, she was an atheist, whereas I chose to be agnostic; she despised my sitting on the fence. It's likely I chose agnosticism just because it did annoy her. If asked now, I say atheist. I did forgive her shortcomings; one needs to examine her background, her upbringing.

While my mother's Labor values might have been a bit old-fashioned, she was very active in the party. She acted as campaign manager for Frank Doyle and Clem Jones and it was she, at branch level, who brought up the subject of no-fault divorce. She was a state representative and took her proposal to Canberra, where it was embraced, and work began to see the law changed from there having to be a guilty party – usually the husband photographed in a compromising situation with another woman – to irreconcilable differences. She also was instrumental in having the kerb cut-outs, making it easier for people pushing prams and people in wheelchairs to cross roads.

Only in Australia could my mother and Auntie M have become friends. Auntie M had gone into service at age thirteen, the kind of person my grandmother would have employed. There's a certain irony in that I considered her more of a mother, and then friend, to me. We didn't agree on everything, either, but we could discuss. As so many working-class people were, she and her family had voted Conservative in UK then Liberal here. The general belief was that those with the money would look after those without. My mother's message had always been that it was they, the workers, providing that money through their labour.

Both parents had good minds, which we all seemed to inherit, and some of the best times were when the family sat around the dining table, replete after a good meal, and the repartee would dart back and forth, very clever, subtle, mixed messages that not all of our visitors understood. We could find something hilarious while it bewildered friends not used to our humour.

Circumstances contribute to making us what we become. My mother was strong, independent; she had a strong intellect and wanted to learn; boys' games were more interesting than the girly pursuits of the day, and she never liked frilly dresses, though she did have ballet and piano lessons. One Christmas time she was given a valuable porcelain doll when she had repeatedly said she wanted a cricket set. Her story was that she dragged it along the front hall and from the front door hurled it down the tessellated pathway.

She was a top student at school but when she was fourteen her father declined to pay for any further study, despite urgings from her teachers, the head, and friends, to let her continue her education. He said she would have to go to work. It is interesting that her younger sister, not bright, was never required to work. I don't know what kind of jobs my mother had, except she did work in an office and told us how she had stood on a desk to tell her fellow workers to stand up for their rights, insist on proper conditions and pay, and shorter hours. And vote Labor. Her maternal grandmother used to call her a Bolshevist.

She was dismissed from that job. She continued her education by going to night school and had managed to buy herself a bicycle on time payment. One morning, setting off for work, the bike was missing. Her father had sold it for gambling money. He didn't recompense my mother in any way and she had to walk to work and at night to night school – still paying off the absent bike. When she had reached the required educational level and was old enough, she applied for nursing training and went to London. I can understand the bitterness she would have felt.

Mother was well into her training and doing well, as she did with anything she set her mind to. For perhaps the first time in her life, she was having a good time, in London. She was one of the new women, certainly not totally independent, as she was required to live in at the nurses' quarters of the hospital, but she did have days off. She danced, played tennis, went to night clubs with the young men and women of her set.

And more than once she was late back at the home, after curfew, and had to climb over the wall. Also in those days, hair had to be completely hidden under their caps. My mother's was thick, curly, unruly and keeping it contained required many hairgrips. It also pulled the skin tight over the temples and some patients thought she looked Chinese; one refused to be treated by her.

She fell in love with an Indian man (a doctor?) and they wanted to marry. My mother's parents were willing to give permission but the young man's family was not. I don't know how much or for how long the fellow tried to persuade his family to change its mind.

When her mother phoned to say she had to return home, it must have been with a great deal of reluctance that my mother gave up that independence, working towards a totally independent life, to return to the confines of the family and work she did not want to do. A high price to pay for her father's addiction. (When he'd gambled away the money meant for bill paying.)

I don't know if my father worked in my grandmother's hotel or one nearby but they met. I think it was a case of two lonely people, and angry, and possibly heartbroken, in my mother's case, coming together and finding some sort of solace. They were married on 26 January 1936 and my brother was born in June of the same year. They were described as 'waiter' and 'waitress' on their marriage certificate. I think my mother might have been grinding her teeth when she gave that information of herself. When one is tracing one's genealogy, the listed work description of an individual might not give a full picture, if any, of that individual.

My mother said she realised very early on she'd made a mistake in marrying my father. She wanted a divorce. My grandparents would not countenance it. Later, with war looming and Dad having joined up, my mother broached the topic again. This time, my grandmother is alleged to have told her to stay married, the chances being that he would be killed (casualties in the air force were high), and the air force pension would be generous. I suppose circumstances can kill any sentiment.

It was a mistake for both of them; there was no meeting of minds, no shared philosophical or social understanding. Mother removed herself as much as she could from having anything to do with any of Dad's family. And from Dad, too, if I'm not mistaken.

We used to joke that Mum and Dad had had sex four times, resulting in the four children. Of course we had to amend that to three when we allowed full cognisance to the circumstances of my sister. In those days of the 1930s, social differences were marked and even in the twenty-first century, when people like to pretend England is more egalitarian, it never will be truly so.

She had received proposals of marriage from young men of her social standing and I remember one reason for refusing was that the chap wasn't tall enough, but obviously none of them were right for her. Perhaps with the loss of her Indian, she set her mind on a career. When her chance at independence was snatched away, I think she might have crumpled a bit and Dad was handy. I think she might have married him in the end as an act of defiance. Neither of her parents wanted it.

As a married woman and mother, I don't think she would have been accepted into any of the women's corps but she could drive ambulances for the duration of World War II. Her parents refused to look after my brother, saying he was my mother's responsibility. I can imagine my mother being resentful of her circumstances, resentful of the people she saw as causing them, resenting the accident of her child. She must have resented me, too, arriving four and half years after my brother, when she might have started to look forward to having more time to herself. And most likely leaving Dad.

I have referred to myself as 'the last shot' arriving, as I did, exactly nine months after my father's overseas' departure. And if we believe any of our childish, ill-thought theory, it was ten years later that my parents again had conjugal relations, resulting in my Australian brother. My sister believed she was resented, too, being poor compensation for the loss of our mother's lover. Not to mention the time and sacrifices given to keep her alive. We all experienced that. And had my grandparents been prepared to look after my older brother and Mother had become an ambulance driver, the story would undoubtedly be very different.

Very soon after my father left on overseas service, mid-1940, and was away for the entire war, my mother took up, as she said, with an old beau. She would have been pregnant with me at the time, the dates, as I said, fitting, and Dad's 'last shot' hitting the target. My birthday is 13 March. The former beau was held back in England, on essential services, but I don't know in what nature his work was essential. He passed me off as his daughter so I feel blessed, in a way, to have had the love of a father-figure for my first two-and-a-half years.

However, on my birth certificate he is listed as my 'adoptive father' and, for the time he was in my life, I didn't lack the love of a father, but I was angry that my own father was denied. His place of work received a direct hit and he was killed. As I have said, life did not seem fair for my mother. It is not surprising she became a bitter and somewhat selfish person. She told me that her lover would read to me, loved poetry, opera, and music. I found amongst her papers, after she died, some pieces of poetry written by her. Had her father not been the man he was, she could have entered one of many professions.

My mother, foolishly really, because we could all do maths, denied my sister's paternity and we were supposed to believe she was my dad's daughter. My sister was always angry at not knowing who her father was. She was also angry at being ill most of the time. It was because of her needing a warmer climate that we migrated to Australia but she was never well enough to attend school or work and our mother did nothing to attend to her educational needs or any socialisation. She resented my being free, having new dresses and doing all the things I did.

Mother worked in her mother's pub during some of those war years. Being near an airfield, it was frequented by airmen. They had their own individual beer mugs or tankards and when an airman was lost, his drinking vessel stayed on the shelf, placed right side up. A very sad reminder of the price of war. My mother said that often a returning airman would raise his tankard to a fallen mate, a silent prayer of thanks for his survival.

The war ended, my father returned at last from his middle Eastern post and met me, the almost six-year-old daughter he hadn't seen at all and trying to get to know a son who was not much more than three when he left, nearly ten when he returned. And the infant who wasn't his at all. Strangers, all. They set up house again and I can't imagine what kind of life they had. As I grew older, I became aware of the tensions, my mother's constant belittling of my father.

Dad continued with hotels, working up to management. It suited him, and probably Mother, to work at night, sleep in the day. It meant that I saw very little of him and, as a child will, I believed my mother, took her side and, I'm ashamed to say, contributed my share of sneering at what my mother saw as my father's shortcomings. It was many years later that I saw the kindness, the gentleness, his unselfishness and the mathematical skills that had earned him a job in a broker's office.

Mother became a waitress again some time after our arrival in

Australia. I can't remember if it was when we were still in the rented house; quite possibly it was. She did a luncheon shift in the Asturia, or some name like that – I remember thinking it was very like the name of our ship – a nice city café. The waitresses had their particular section of tables to look after and there was a man who regularly chose a table in my mother's part. In the beginning he gave his order, which my mother found unintelligible and she had to ask him to repeat it. On the third try, she asked him to point to it in the menu. This went on for three weeks, by which time mother had picked up on Australian pronunciation and ways of speech and the customer no longer was required to point to his order. On his way out as he paid his bill, he remarked to the owner, who was of Greek origin, how remarkably quickly these New Australians picked up the English language.

When she died and I was cleaning out the house, I was surprised by some of the things she kept. The lamb made from pipe cleaners had not been given to her; I had just fashioned it one day and it had sat on the low picture rail of the bedroom shared with my sister. I might have been about fourteen when I made that. The two small blue china dogs my sister and I had jointly given her one Christmas in England. One had a chipped ear. We had bought them in the summer when my sister could walk to the market with me. There were letters, pieces of poetry she had written, nylon stockings and hair adornments. Perhaps they were just there because she hadn't thrown them out.

On the other hand, she didn't keep the diary I'd written and drawn in during the six weeks of our crossing hemispheres. That had more value as it described the sights and sounds seen and heard in the sea and the ports we visited as written by an almost nine-year-old. She didn't keep any of my paintings or early writings; indeed, they were dismissed as a waste of time. I was never encouraged in those pursuits, which is strange, as I found her poems and indications she had wished for a writing life as a journalist or novelist. She would have made a good investigative reporter.

She was asked to stand for politics, in England and Australia, but the ill-health of my sister meant she didn't have the time. Later, when she took up painting, she won several prizes. She also made a lovely coffee table at a night class she went to. I wonder if anyone in the family kept it.

I keep thinking of the detritus that fills my cupboards and drawers, that means nothing to anyone but me. I could clean it all out, make life easier for whoever is to tidy up after I'm gone. If I have time.

I have to accept my mother had excuse enough for being bitter, angry, twisted, confused. If anyone could say life is unfair, she could. We say we all have choices but sometimes those choices are limited, as were mine when deciding what was best for my sons.

My mother grew up in a time when women were only just beginning to step out on their own; she would have been torn by her mother's plight and her having been treated badly by her husband, so shouldn't she stand in solidarity with her mother? And her mother had, after all, acted radically. Marrying my father was perhaps foolish – she would have had a choice of suitors from her social level – but I am not her, and the distance is too far for me to accurately see or feel her terrain.

Father

My father was just a few months older than my mother, born 3 July 1913. His beginnings were most unhappy ones. Henri, which became mostly Harry, was two years old when his mother left him, his brother Sydney, and their father, in 1915. My father's brother was seven at the time. My father had been left strapped in his high chair when his mother walked out. I'm hoping it was close enough to the time of his brother and/or father returning to the house. My paternal grandfather was a plumber, I think, though on my father's birth certificate he is described as 'Wood Sawyer (Journeyman)'. He could look after the more independent older child but not the still dependent younger.

The infant, my father, was taken in by his aunt, Lillian, and her husband, Henry Alfred Metcalfe, who I understand was a Methodist lay minister. I think there were no children from the marriage but I'm under the impression his two spinster sisters lived with them. They were a headmistress and a teacher and a few years later came to know my mother in the capacity of student. The two sisters were among those who tried to persuade my grandfather to let my mother continue her education. It was never mentioned if my parents ever met as children. There would be no reason for their ever being in the same place.

Dad's brother's first marriage produced Maurice, Dad's nephew and my cousin, but the marriage didn't last, or the wife died, and Maurice and the second wife did not get along. At a very young age, he joined the navy and pretty much lost contact with the immediate and extended family. My Uncle Sydney and Alice had three daughters who were close in age to my sister and me. We didn't socialise very often; I remember the few picnics we shared but my mother tried to minimise as much as possible the time spent in their company. In her mind, marrying my dad was bad enough and she was stuck with him – she didn't have to have anything to do with his family as well. I was always afraid of Aunt Alice; she was big, blowsy, loud, someone my mother would call common. The daughters were physically bigger, meatier than my sister and me and played more boisterous games.

I don't know if my mother even knew of the existence of Maurice. Had they met, I'm sure she would have liked him. He was a self-educated man. Obviously he had travelled with the navy and was keenly interested in the places, people, they came across, and their politics. Over the years, he'd collected friends around the globe and kept in touch via the latest technology. His general knowledge was extensive and his reading interests broad. I am sorry we didn't meet many years earlier. I would have had a compatible cousin.

Dad didn't talk about his family. Mother didn't either but with hers, we had more handles from which to hang questions. There were other members of her family within close proximity whom we could ask, too. Dad was isolated. His father, my paternal grandfather, did remarry, to a lovely woman called Nell (Ellen Jemima Whittle). I don't know when or how long they were together but I do remember staying with them and calling up the stairs when my grandfather asked me to tell my grandmother that tea was made, and I called, 'Nell, tea's made', which became a family story. It might have been that my grandfather referred to his wife as Nell not Grandma, as she was not my blood relation. I have a postcard they had sent me of the Cleethorpes pier, soon after our arrival in Australia. I don't know how much mail they might have sent but that seems to be the only piece I have. I do remember them with great fondness; they were a gentle pair.

Dad died, in England on holiday, in 1978 and I was the only one handy to go through his papers and attend to those things that are necessary. Things like notices in the paper, informing his boss, his insurance company, the airline company to let them know he would not be using his return ticket. I came across his war medals, the glowing letters of appreciation written by superior RAF officers, the two times he'd been reported missing presumed dead. I was glad I was my father's daughter. He'd been staying with his brother and Aunt Alice. The local paper did a feature on him. His Brisbane employer said lovely things about him and that his sense of humour would be missed around the office. He and his secretary took me to lunch when I finally went into town to collect the bits and pieces Dad had left in his desk. They had also offered to help in whatever way I needed in settling Dad's affairs.

His letters written to me while on his holiday back home were alive with the things he'd done, the people he'd met and how good they all were; the scenery, familiar buildings, sounds, the English taste of beer and sausages, fish and chips.

My mother, at the time, was sailing around the world with a male friend. He and my mother were very good ballroom dancers and my mother's letters were full of the praise they received, how they became the focus as other, lesser dancers stopped to watch them, the praise for my mother's dresses – all me, me, me. Even the famous statue of Christ, in Brazil, managed to take second place when my mother visited it. I have to admit, when I radio-telephoned the ship to have the news of Dad's death relayed to her, I was very blunt in the telling.

My younger brother, still in his twenties, and his not-yet wife – who were in England for five years, working and touring – had to arrange for the cremation of his dad. It was March, a couple of days before my birthday, and in the northern hemisphere, a cold and miserable beginning of spring. I never grieved his death, though. He wasn't old, sixty-five, but he'd had enough of his life; he wanted to stay where he was, in his home town and with his brother and his family. I felt sad for him. He'd never really wanted to leave England but now he was back.

Dad had diabetes, neglected to take his medication, neglected to tell anyone he was. He caught a chill in the cold, damp spring of England. It developed into pneumonia, he went into a coma and died. His diabetes was caused by wrong diet – too much rich food, too much alcohol. My assessment was that with the lack of love in his life, his emotional needs unfulfilled, he fed his stomach instead. Until he fell asleep, he was a happy drunk. He could cook and it was Dad's job to set the table for any special occasion. It's a long time since I've sat at a table with such gleaming silver and glassware.

At one of his last Christmases at the house, where we had all gathered from various parts of the country, Dad, through a combination of tiredness from work and preparing for the day, and over-imbibing from the bottle, kept dozing off at the table. Whoever happened to be handy would straighten him up and he'd sort of wake. Then we weren't quick enough and he fell off his chair. We helped him back up but suggested he lie down. No. But he fell again and again we helped him back up. The third time we tidied him up a bit on the floor, a cushion under his head, and walked around him. Poor Dad.

My dad had always been in the hospitality industry and had become manager of the National Hotel that used to sit at the end of Queen Street where it met Ann Street. I think that area was generally called Petrie Bight. It might have been owned by a Sister Jaeger at that time. There was a Christmas party put on for staff's families and there'd be games, pantomimes, a clown, Christmas food and, of course, Father Christmas with presents. There were other years, other presents, all of which I've forgotten, but just this one when I received a small, round, woven, sewing basket. I still have it, minus its lid.

A few years later the National became notorious as news of the prostitution that was carried on there, and police corruption, became known. By then, my dad might have been employed by the Hotel Cecil. That end of town, the Botanical Gardens end of George Street, was notorious as being the red-light district. The Cecil, I remember, employed Japanese war brides, as Japanese wives of former servicemen were known. They performed the tea ceremony in their beautiful kimonos.

These lovely old hotels were destroyed, the Bellevue disappearing overnight, with no warning whatsoever, thanks to premier Joh Bjelke Petersen. Then, as now, the leaders had no concept of future and the importance of history. Petersen destroyed the beautiful Cloudland Ballroom, too. That and the Brisbane City Hall were places I danced in. School speech nights were held in the City Hall.

I think I was angry at the way mother had always treated Dad, denigrating him to us children so we grew up treating him very offhandedly. As I said, I didn't grieve his death, he died where he wanted to be, but he was too young. I wished I'd had more time to really get to know him. Of course I replied to his letters and I hope he knew I loved him. He was a kind, unselfish man and everything he did was for his family.

The ship my mother was on was heading towards Southampton, where she disembarked and travelled to London to be with my brother. I think they travelled to Cleethorpes before she flew back to Australia. She didn't meet Maurice but she most likely met her brother-in-law Sydney and Alice. Briefly.

I can't remember whether it was my mother or brother who brought back the gifts my dad had bought for us. I have a little thermometer with a Cleethorpes pixie sitting hugging his knees in front of the litmus paper that indicates wet or dry. It sits on my bookshelf and there's no way I would part with it. He'd also bought Cleethorpes rock, a length of sugary sweet with the name of the town written through its centre.

It was wrapped in plastic and I kept it in the freezer for years. My second husband threw it out one day when cleaning the refrigerator. I was most upset. I was never going to eat it; I just wanted to keep it.

Uncle Sydney died not very long after my dad. Aunt Alice lived a much longer life.

What history of the Cuertons we have has been mentioned, thanks to cousin Maurice. There is no doubt there were artisans amongst them and today many professionals.

Two brothers were consigned to the poorhouse when their father's life was lost in the Battle of Balaclava in the Crimean war, about 1854. They must have been very young or they would have been expected to find work. Or become soldiers. Today we have Legacy, the RSL, Commonwealth pensions, to care for bereaved families.

After my cousin died, his son Mark drew a pruned family tree going back to my great-great-grandparents; three greats for Mark.

Siblings and Shep

My younger brother had a dog, a luxury denied my older brother because of my sister's allergies, the war – just different circumstances, climate. I don't know how many dogs he had while still at home; Rusty, though, was the first and so named because of the colour. The two, with or without other friends, could be gone for the most part of a day. He might have had just two, given the life span of Border collies. Shep was the one still living in the house when my son and I returned to Brisbane. The house I shared with my sister was close to the family home and Shep would spend a lot of his time with us and the three children. I never minded where my son was if Shep was with him. He was a great protector. When he was looking after three small children, he would round them up like sheep. And look very worried with the responsibility of it all. When my brother left home, Shep stayed behind.

My older brother had become a chartered accountant. I don't know if he'd ever had any burning desire to do anything else. In England, aged thirteen, he was studying human biology, as were other students that age, that wasn't even started as a subject until form six in Queensland. He would have had to start over, with plants, frogs et cetera. In those days, university fees had to be paid upfront, no time payment scheme, so without a scholarship, university students or their parents needed to be wealthy. Unless my brother had secured a scholarship, there was no money to pay fees. But as I say, I don't know what his leanings were.

My brother seemed to accept life as it was, and just got on with living it. He married at the then accepted age of twenty-three or four to a woman I didn't much care for. Or rather, I didn't think it was a suitable match. He wanted children, she did not. She was tall and stylish but lacked a sense of humour. She was of German descent, and age brought on the heaviness of that race.

Nine years into the marriage, my brother was having an affair. My sister-in-law stopped taking the pill she had secretly been taking and became pregnant. Too late; the marriage was finished. My nephew was sent gifts for birthdays and Christmas but had minimal contact with his father. My brother was good at sending gifts; my mother used to get a beautiful bunch of roses, one bunch, to cover her birthday and Christmas, and my mother thought he was the best in the world. His philosophy seems to be acceptance, to be happy, and he was always full of bonhomie. He might be still, I haven't seen him for a year or two. I admired the way he could talk to a man sitting in the gutter in the same way he would address a titled gentleman; perfectly natural. When we have been together, as adults, we have shared the same sense of humour, understand each other's nuances.

My younger brother, eleven years my junior and fifteen years younger than his brother, was the healthiest, tallest, of us all. While being pregnant with him, our mother had eaten better food, and more of it, than she'd been able to do with the rest of us. This Australian member of the family was born into sunshine and a free, outdoor life. He knew both his parents from the beginning and both parents had more time to give him. Our parents had more disposable income by then so there was nothing, within reason, he lacked. He and our dad used to meet other fathers and sons at the pub once a week to discuss whatever boys and men discuss.

He did not want an office job; he wanted to be a carpenter. Our mother's sensibilities kicked in; she was not having a tradesman in the family. This attitude might have been the cause of the deep rift that developed between them. The younger brother followed the elder into accountancy. He worked for a while, met a girl and they went to England to work and travel for five years.

When they knew they were returning to Australia, my brother asked me if I could help him find an apprenticeship in some form of carpentry. Unfortunately, everywhere I tried, employers had closed their books but, once back, he found a plumber who would take him on. He was twenty-nine, the oldest apprentice. And we all laughed and laughed because as soon as he had finished his training he set up on his own. His name and profession went into the phone book, immediately underneath my mother's. He has done well, is still married to the same girl and has four children – two plumbers, one electrician and one daughter who went into magazine advertising.

My sister-in-law's original home had been in Sydney. She and my brother met on a ship returning from trips to New Zealand. By the time they returned from the UK, they had quite decided they were going to stay together and my brother expected she would stay in the family home until they found a place of their own. She and my mother did not get along; I invited her to stay with me. She was always a lovely person, hard-working, and would take any job that paid well; their home is always bright and polished, full of flowers – I always felt a peace within it. It was where all the children's friends congregated and dutifully obeyed my sister-in-law's rules on language, manners, fairness. It was noisy and fun. Neither my brother nor my sister-in-law speak to me now as, some five or six years ago, my brother considered me negative. He didn't bring it up with me but told my son when asked about the rift.

My sister, I have come to realise, resented us all, me more than our brothers. It is true none of us was encouraged to follow our dreams but three of us fought for what we wanted. My sister was trapped by ill-health and lacked the street smarts we three had picked up in our daily living. And of course, we are all different.

I was mercurial, dramatic, falling in love for a fortnight then getting over it for the next. When she was seventeen, she met a chap who definitely loved her but she thought what she felt would pass in time. With me as a model, how could she not? She did not talk to me at all about how she felt, which was a pity because she really did love him. They went out together for many months, he finished his university course and had to return home to Penang. He wanted to marry her. None of us knew. I would have been in Sydney at that time. He was probably the love of her life. Years later, her children grown and she single, they met again, in Penang. As had happened with my young man of sixteen, he had married, had children, was settled. But it was a love lost. And I don't believe it is better to have loved and lost…one is forever going to wish.

She had other proposals and at twenty-one married a doctor whom she eventually divorced on the grounds of mental and physical cruelty. On one occasion when my husband and I were visiting Brisbane with our children, my sister looked so ill, like someone just released from a concentration camp; we insisted she and her two little boys come back with us. She put on weight, slept, regained her health, but we told her she must take steps to divorce him. Her doctor had documented her condition over the years she was married.

While still with us, she soon was well enough to dress up, leave her sons with me and go off to the city. She picked up a chap while waiting to buy a cinema ticket and her evening outings began. Which is how she managed to see Sarah Vaughan at Chequers. It was while she was with me then that I learned about her first love.

After several months, the three went back to Brisbane; she and her husband separated, leading to divorce. Reports were, he was a really good doctor.

Years later, I was visiting my mother one evening and caught Shep in my car lights, lying on the road. He wouldn't move, so I parked and went to investigate. He was old; I thought he might have been hit by a car but he was so well-known and loved in the neighbourhood, I couldn't believe anyone would just leave him there. I couldn't see any blood but clearly he was not well. He couldn't get up to follow me in and I knew he was close to death. I went inside, told my mother and said she should ring the vet. She wouldn't do that so I said we at least had to get him off the road and hopefully up to the veranda. I really had to insist. Finally we got a blanket, managed to get it under the dog and between us carry him upstairs. I gave him water and talked to him. He'd been such a beautiful, clever, intuitive animal.

There was the time I was trying to make a point and happened to have my hairbrush in my hand; I was waving it about and my son happened to be in the general direction if it were meant as a weapon. (My son says I was, in fact, trying to hit him with it. There was the time I was baking and doing something with a wooden spoon; my son was being annoying and I raised the spoon with warning words. He caught hold of my wrist and said, 'There, there, Mum, settle down,' while he patted the top of my head with his other hand. And we both laughed. I don't think he was ever hit by me in anger.) Back to the hairbrush: Shep bounded up and snarled at me. I was astonished. Putting the hairbrush down, I held out both hands to the dog, showing them empty and telling him I would never harm my child.

Another time, a visiting dog, a lovely golden retriever, was given one of Shep's biscuits. Later in the day, my mother's neighbour said she had seen Shep carry something down the back steps and bury it behind the banana trees. She went to investigate. It was Shep's bag of biscuits, loosely hidden under leaves and branches. To open the cupboard door where they were kept was tricky, meant to be childproof, but Shep was not going to share his biscuits with that showy dog.

He knew when I wasn't well, and would sit with me, his head on my lap, his eyes asking, 'What can I do for you?' He died that night I'd found him on the road.

He'd very definitely been a house dog but he wasn't allowed in with dirty paws. His coat had to be reasonably clean too. He'd sit on the back veranda, studiously getting all the grit and dirt from between his toes. When he'd finished, he'd give a little bark to say, 'Let me in, please', and there'd be a neat pile of dirt where he had worked. He particularly loved chocolate biscuits, even, it was shown, more than people.

Guests were being farewelled one afternoon and while Shep had done the gentlemanly thing and risen and shaken his tail, he didn't accompany the group to the front steps where more conversation would take place before they finally left. When we did go back inside, the remaining biscuits had disappeared, the plate was spotless and we faced one guilty-looking dog.

Another time, when Shep was visiting us at our rented house, he decided to chase the cat. The house had verandas, so the two could race around the entire house. Furniture fell, the goldfish bowl upended, and there was nothing we could do until they tired of their game. When they did, Cat sat looking very regal, preening, and Shep clearly thought it had been jolly good fun. We tried to retrieve as many fish as possible, neither animal having any interest in them whatsoever, and generally put the house to rights. He hadn't been my dog but I did love him.

There seemed to be no emotional connection within the family. In age, I was closer to my sister, with almost two and one half years separating us; we should have been friends but she was always ill and our relationship consisted of my being her carer or teacher or in my way, making some sort of social life for her. She was never well enough to go to school, even in Australia; she used to say our mother was purposefully not allowing her to have a proper education or anything else so she would be the old maid and stay home to look after her mother. Who knows?

As well as the health-giving climate, I think my mother might have considered Australia, with its alleged classless society, a more congenial place to be. She had cut her husband, and therefore all of us, from his family because it was working-class. She was no longer part of the society to which she felt she belonged but of which my father could never be a part. My mother's growing up had certainly not been what might have been expected. My mother's cousins did well, but my mother's life did not take that path. The shift to the Antipodes was, I think, to remove herself and her family from a social situation she found distasteful and unavoidable, to a new, young country where she hoped my father might be inspired to something more than he was. (I should write another novel titled *The Nowhere Girl* after the Anglo-Indian *The In-Between Man*).

First marriage

My first husband was a very good-looking, fun-loving, kind man. For all the reasons imaginable, it is a pity our marriage did not survive. We were too young, inexperienced, and suffered a lack of money, which places a strain on the best of relationships. Had parents on either side been willing and able to offer counsel, it might have helped. And any relationship takes two to make, two to break; we neither of us was perfect.

Most certainly, I have long since realised, I was not in a healthy psychological state when I insisted on marrying. My dad was against it but always lost an argument with my mother. I just wanted to leave home, create a happy, loving nest of my own and live happily ever after. The physical and psychological damage sustained in the accident has stayed with me, no doubt affecting my thinking. However, as I said earlier, I managed to do, achieve, reach, several milestones in spite of it. Just not a perfect marriage.

Neither my husband nor I was interested in cricket but two of his housemates were. My parents were attending an international match at the Brisbane cricket ground, commonly known as the Gabba, situated in the suburb of Wooloongabba. A short space along the bench sat two young Indian men whom my mother engaged in conversation.

Initially, she mildly rebuked them for taking time off school; a rebuke delivered most charmingly it would not have felt like one. My mother was petite, pretty with black curly hair and, yes, charming. The young men laughed and said they were university students and on holiday, their year having ended. Conversation included an invitation to our Christmas dinner. They declined, describing their living arrangements with three others and that other Indian students would be joining them for that day which can be very quiet if one is alone. However, it happened that my parents and family were invited to visit them, which we did sometime in January 1959.

They were all Fijian Indians; four were diligent students of dentistry, two of commerce, one of engineering, and then the one who became my husband…he was studying science but was not a good student and spent more time on entertainment. It was not that he was not clever, far from it, but, it happens, he simply was not good with bookwork. He knew in his head what he needed to know, he just couldn't successfully write it down when questioned. The other four considered him the playboy. An image he enjoyed playing up to. We became a couple. I became pregnant.

Later, he told me of his (mis)adventures in Fiji when he would visit girlfriends; something would alert the members of the house that the girl was not alone and, usually, the father would try to get into his daughter's room to investigate. The girl would say yes, yes, she would unlock the door, while her beau, later my husband, jumped out of the window, generally leaving behind some article of clothing.

The day before the wedding, my mother asked my intended if he was quite sure he wanted to go ahead with the marriage. The groom insisted he wanted to marry me. I just wanted to get married and thus be able to leave home with my visions of happy-ever-after. My parents were entirely the wrong combination and there was always a tension in the home. It turned out that my husband and I were also the wrong combination.

Money was short and we rented a room, with use of a kitchen, in a large house in Glebe. My life as a single parent started then and my fantasy started to crumble. My father, bless him, had not wanted to give his permission for the marriage, necessary then until the age of twenty-one. He had nothing against my intended but I think knew I was not emotionally ready. My mother and brother wore down his resistance. At its end, I returned to Brisbane with one son, thinking I would be returning to the bosom of my family.

To be fair, my mother did discuss all the options with me – abortion, adoption, keeping the baby and bringing it up as a single mother – none of which was acceptable to me.

So I married and my son was born a fortnight after my nineteenth birthday. My Indian husband dropped out of university but could not get a job in Brisbane. It was 1960 and the colour bar was very much in place. He had a brother in Sydney who advised that he would get work there. He went before the baby was born and I joined him three months after the birth. I have to say, my mother insisted I stay at home at least that long, by which time I would have my strength back and hopefully know how to care for a baby.

My marriage ceremony and reception, if that was what it was, couldn't have been more different from that my husband would have had with an Indian wife. Registry wedding and just the family at home to celebrate. Indian weddings can last a week, the guest list is huge and they cost a fortune. And of course, the cost is borne by the bride's family.

Going to Sydney and looking after home, husband and baby was an entirely new experience and I had no one on whom to call, ask for help. I guess I muddled through. The only jobs I remember my husband having were one in a factory assembling television sets, which were still new on the market, and another working at the University of Sydney, where he stayed until retirement.

He was in the physics department and that was how my sons met the famous Julius Sumner Miller. We shared several meals together. My husband was away all day and several evenings, doing something at night school; I was alone with a baby. I lapsed into deep depression. Even at the weekends, I was often left alone, as my husband went to spend time with his friends. I think he was one of the instigators of SBS radio.

My mother visited a few times and tried to explain to my husband that I needed more time with him and other adults, that I needed to go out somewhere at the weekends, have a change from the house, have some fun. I tried to book myself into evening courses but my husband always managed to be not at home on those nights.

The only proper outing I remember was when we went to see a stage performance of the opera *Porgy and Bess*. We were still living in the house divided into flatettes and the older, single women volunteered as babysitters. We arrived at the theatre and my husband couldn't find the tickets. I thought, if I didn't get in to see this, after all the anticipation, I would die. I remembered the seat numbers; the manager said to wait until the doors closed and if no one had claimed the seats with tickets he would let us use them. Of course no one else had the tickets and we did see the opera. When we arrived back at our flat, my husband found the tickets in the inside pocket of his suit. I wrote to the manager and sent them.

Life must have been hard for my husband too. He had to work, he had responsibilities. I'm sure he must have wished, at times, that he had given a different answer to my mother's question the night before the wedding. He had no idea of how to be a husband, how I might need company, conversation, being taken out of the house sometimes. I looked after our baby, cleaned our room, did the endless washing, cooked in the communal kitchen. Our bickering started the impromptu visits back to the family home. He really didn't know what else to do. We had a few house moves, he changed jobs and, as I said, at some point he was employed in the Physics Department of Sydney University. We met many interesting physicists.

My husband was clever, he just didn't have the bits of paper that said so. The university recognised his talents. For friends, he mended clocks clockmakers said were unfixable, and any kind of watch; he repaired our shoes, improved the house we eventually bought, repaired and made better the children's toys. If he couldn't buy spare parts, he made them. He would find a way to do almost anything. His first son takes after him in that. In fact, they are all pretty handy with whatever they set their minds to.

But, like many men, he was a baby when it came to pain. One

day he was pruning a climbing rose in the back garden; I was in the laundry. He came in, in an agitated state, saying a branch had fallen on him and asking if his face was bleeding. I told him that if he kept squeezing the area, it soon would be but it wasn't at that moment.

Interestingly, before leaving Sydney all those years ago, I contested an examination for possible employment as a computer programmer. If any friends of today are reading this, I know you have snorted with incredulity, laughed with derision and otherwise don't believe me. But, friends, it is true. Computers were still relatively new then. My husband knew them intimately but, I admit, I was so far removed from anything technical, my husband even dismantled, cleaned and oiled my sewing machine. However, I sat for that exam. And guess what? I was amongst the top scorers and would I start training in the next batch? One of life's 'ifs'; what would have become of my life had I followed that path? I didn't and this is my story now. And for those of you who don't know me, I do not like working on a computer. It cannot be denied, though, that being offered a place certainly boosted my self-confidence.

We had several house moves until we were able to put a deposit on our own, between second and third child.
 I remember I became as Indian as I possibly could. My hair remained long; it was dark and curly. I wore saris, which I managed well. I was fascinated with the history of India and went back to something like 3000BCE in my studies. In many ways, I knew more than my husband. But I am not Indian, was not living in India or Fiji, and didn't have the benefits of Indian family life whose maternal and sisterly help would have been forthcoming.
 After the birth of my third son, I was unwell and my hair became lank, looked dull and was more than I could cope with. One of my friends called in one day and I asked her if she would look after the children while I went up the street to the hairdressers. I had my hair

cut short. Before my husband was due home, I showered and prettied up as best I could but his greeting, after taking in my shorn locks, was 'What the bloody hell have you done?' I expected some understanding of the drain my heavy hair was having on my health. I think I was suffering three births' worth of post-natal depression.

From when I was a small child, books, I have said, were my refuge. They were still my refuge. We had friends, I spent time with the female half of the racially mixed couples we knew, but I was not being challenged by intellectual debate, so books were what I escaped to. I remember the day I was cooking dinner, stirring a pot of curry, the wooden spoon in my right hand, my youngest son cradled in my left arm and a book held open by my left hand. I remember the day because I became conscious of the picture I made and the fact it was not really safe. Something had to give; I had to cook, I couldn't ignore the children, so I switched to *Reader's Digest*s.

My husband would talk to me while I attended to household chores but if I handed him a tea towel he would find he had to be somewhere else. But he taught me to drive. He bought big, imported American cars which were almost akin to a fourth son. I made a left-hand turn one time and scraped the kerb; I thought he'd be furious but he wasn't. Another time on a college night when he would get home from work, have an early dinner and then go to his lectures, I totally forgot what day it was. I was so sorry but he said not to worry and made do with a sandwich. He bore no resentment at all.

We could have made things work had we had more understanding of each other's needs and expectations. Our sex life suffered; with no change of scenery, interesting conversation, nothing but children and housework, and as I said, my husband looking on as I bathed the boys, served dinner, cleaned up afterwards, the last thing I wanted was sex.

His younger brother came to live with us. I can't remember the house but it was double-storeyed. One Saturday morning he came downstairs about 10.30; I was in the middle of baking biscuits and slices, as my mother had done, for the week. My brother-in-law expected me to get his breakfast. I told him he was too late, he would have to get it himself. He turned to my husband and asked in Gujerati what was the matter with me. I had a passable knowledge of Hindi by then but still understood the question. I answered back that there was nothing the matter with me, I was just not his slave. His shocked surprise was my reward.

Nor can I remember where we were when the two brothers were working on the car. They were away from the house and had my first son with them. Suddenly there was great commotion, with the three of them bursting in, my son spouting blood from the top of his head. Some piece of the car, not properly secured, had fallen on the child's head. He wouldn't have been more than two years old. In order to see what had happened, I needed to wash the blood away, so we both went into the shower; I saw a hole in his head. Me still wet, my son wrapped in a towel, I asked my husband if he was capable of driving us to the hospital. Both men were panicking. My son was kept in overnight, head patched and no lasting damage. It wasn't until I returned home, knowing all was safe, that my knees turned to water.

My sister-in-law stayed with us for a time; she never disguised her dislike of me. It might have been a mix of envy of her brother in that he had a life very different from that he would have in Fiji and that I had removed her brother from the closeness of the family. She might have wished to have a life as independent as the one I seemed to have.

I have said I don't panic, and there was another occasion – we might have been in our own home by then, quietly watching television in the evening – when there was a commotion going on outside and then a banging on our door. By the time we opened it, a Greek couple up the street were fighting in the middle of the road.

They had obviously had an argument and the husband had attacked his wife with a knife. She had run, he chased. Blood was pouring from a deep gash in her arm. The wife had fallen to the ground. I ran to her, the husband tried to wrest me away and I shouted at him to get away. Surprisingly he did. I told my husband to ring the police and ambulance while I was tying a tourniquet around the woman's arm. A few more (male) neighbours had come out by this time and joined my husband in keeping the man away. I stayed on the ground holding the woman until the ambulance crew took over. I don't know what the end result was for them but for me it was another shower and change of clothing.

My husband's resolution to an argument was to ring the airline company and book me a seat back to Brisbane. One memorable arrival happened very late at night. The taxi driver was unpacking my stuff and my infant son's from the boot, creating some noise and alerting my father.

His head came out of the front bedroom window. 'Well,' he said, 'it's our Jacqueline.'

During these visits home, I would resume my social life and my sister and I could sometimes be found at university dances.

My first husband always maintained I was smarter than he; he felt inadequate, I know, when we had visitors from the UK and conversation might cover history, books, politics. I tried to tell him he knew more than I in things Indian and scientific. What I did regret was his lack of knowledge of Hindu philosophy, that he could have passed on to the children. These are the reasons I use when I defend arranged marriages. When properly arranged, a couple comes together one complementing the other in knowledge and skills; they come from a similar philosophical base, not necessarily believing in the same things but being able to appreciate the differences and see an equality in their different selves.

We had bought our own home in Broughton Street, Drummoyne, before I was pregnant with my third son. On a hill, it had a street level entrance with the ground falling to the rear, so it had downstairs space which we never did anything with. I don't know why we didn't rent it out. There was a veranda along the back from which we could see yachts sailing on the harbour and, if we leaned over, catch sight of the bridge.

The boys had a sandpit, tricycles, a pedal car. We wouldn't buy them weapon-type toys so they fashioned their own from whatever was suitable. The boys wanted to jump from the veranda so my husband taught them how to land. There were never any broken bones. Not from that activity, at least. And I remember my flying down the steps one day when my oldest son was screaming. It really was blood-curdling. He had trodden on a fallen peach and a bee stung his foot. Between sobs, he said it wasn't the bee's fault, he shouldn't have trodden on its peach. He knew the bee would die.

I couldn't go out to work but I could work at home. I did sewing. Chiffon was the new fabric, difficult to cut and sew, but I had the knack and secured a job of sewing pieces for a company. I also started making clothes for my friends and word spread. I was very proud of having customers coming to me from the other side of Sydney for me to make a wedding dress. I might not have made much money but I was trying to make a contribution. The chiffon rep and my customers were bright gems in my very lonely life. It (usually) gave me the opportunity to talk about what was happening in the world, particularly with the rep, as he was male with a male view of things.

My grandmother used to send me what she would describe as 'an old skirt' with suggestions I might be able to make my son some winter clothes from it. She was an ample woman, so the skirts had plenty of usable fabric. Sometimes I would make a skirt for myself. You could say this remaking was becoming a family tradition.

We were in the swinging 60s; wife-swapping was in vogue. Note, it wasn't called husband-swapping! My husband and his best friend decided it sounded like fun so, after one evening dinner, my husband took his friend's wife home and his friend stayed with me. I don't know what happened in the other home but nothing happened in mine. This must indicate the extent of our unhappiness.

There was the time my husband had bought many plants and had them treated for sending to Fiji. They were kept in an alcove in the house waiting to be transported to the airport. My oldest son wanted to know why his daddy was buying me flowers when he didn't love me. My heart broke for my son.

Even when it was the norm for women to stay home to look after it and the children, we were still second-class citizens. Surveys then were conducted on street corners or door-to-door. One day I answered the door to a survey-taker.

Basic details, occupation?

Before I could reply, my questioner answered herself, 'Just a housewife.'

I quickly interposed with 'No, I'm a research student looking at the psychological aspects of domestic economy and child behavioural management.'

She was most impressed, stood taller and certainly addressed me with more respect.

And I was angry. I managed a house on very little money, had three young boys with hugely inquisitive minds whose questions I answered truthfully and as fully as was warranted. Frequently, even before they could properly read, we resorted to the encyclopædia, so they quickly became accustomed to research.

Part of my husband's control of me was to keep me short of money. One national voting day, I thought I might like to buy one of the women's magazines on my way back. I asked for a shilling, the price, and a shilling was given. My bonus, I suppose, was the slight detour to the shops.

After ten years or so, we decided to call it a day. In fact, I felt so depressed, I thought that if I stayed, one of us would sooner rather than later be dead and it would most likely be me.

There was the time when the boys might have been three, five, seven, and a glass was dropped, shattering on the floor with sharp pieces. I shouted at them to stand still, not to move, while I swept it up. I wasn't angry with the children but it broke something in me and I knelt on the floor with dustpan and brush and screamed to a god I never believed in to just let me die.

I can see them now, three small boys, half-afraid of this mad, demented woman, still as statues while I sobbed and scoured the floor for every fragment of glass. I believed the children would be happier and better off with one happy parent rather than in a house of submerged hostilities. I had assumed that I would go, with the three boys. My husband assumed that I would go. Period.

When our respective assumptions became clear to the other, things began to get a bit nasty. Until then, we had maintained civility and even close friends had no idea of our plans but, with the possible loss of his sons, my husband said he would leave the country, go home, and I would get no maintenance from him and, with having to work, how did I think I was going to look after three young boys. He had a point.

There were no government pensions for single mothers then and my family wouldn't help. I agonised over some decision. I never did doubt, or have doubted, the goodness of my ex-husband and the love he had for the boys. He had arranged that he would marry a young woman whom he had known since childhood and who stayed with us when she transited between her home and her teaching position in Hobart at the beginning and end of the long summer holidays. The boys would have an instant stepmother. I don't know how it happened, what contacts my husband had, but the decree nisi took place in record time.

I have it in my mind that the woman was the eldest of five girls and until she married, the second down the line could not. I might not be right but I think she was not really interested in marrying but the arrangement with my soon-to-be-ex-husband suited everyone. She must have made the proviso that she be allowed to keep working.

A *Sophie's Choice*; what was I to do? In the end, I felt for all concerned that I should go but that I would keep with me the son who was not my husband's biological child. Grieving for someone who has died, in this case two people, is easier than grieving the living, and my grief has been long.

I will never know the correct answer to the rightness or otherwise of making an only child of one, depriving two of a third brother. What

I lost is immeasurable. There were no court barriers to my seeing the children but my former husband and his new wife made that difficult. I was also supposed to be paid maintenance but that was seldom forthcoming. It amuses me when I think of the solicitor's letter to my former spouse, saying I was in 'a state of penury'. It is not a state to which I would willingly send anyone.

One time I was in Sydney trying to make arrangements to spend time with my sons; their paternal grandmother was visiting from Fiji and she insisted I be invited to dinner, to see her and also my sons. I think she really felt my loss. More than my own mother. Since they have been adults, I receive the rare phone call, a real spate of them from my youngest son when he broke his ankle. He was in the habit of getting a taxi home from work and the back of a taxi, stuck in Sydney peak-hour traffic, was just the time and place for a chat with one's mum.

It's always very difficult; I want to know about their life – their emotional state, are they truly happy, what are their dreams – but they don't want to go there with me. I have to stay bright and chatty, talk about the latest political fracas or books we've read. The conversation ends and I want to, and frequently do, howl. My African son, whom I made so independent, can also drive me to distraction with his infrequent calls and his lack of sharing.

I tried my best to provide a home, stability, for my son. I had made a promise to myself that I would not have any romantic entanglements until my son reached some mature age. I felt I had robbed him of so much, the least I could do was let him have all of me. I didn't become a nun but my first responsibility was my son. And I failed in that responsibility.

When I had my own family, my husband and I had an agreed set of values and what we wanted for the children. We agreed on discipline and neither ever smacked a child. Boundaries were laid down, extended as children grew and could handle wider horizons. I tried to maintain these standards when I became a single parent of one, not always easy when sharing a house with my sister and her two little boys and also when I was working and not at home when my son returned from school. I still feel the anguish I felt then at what was unavoidable neglect.

My son is grown now with a son of his own. I think he is over-protective of him, but if that is his reaction to my neglect of him, so be it.

I returned to Brisbane when the marriage did come to an end. For some symbolic reason, I decided my middle son and I would leave between the Christmas of 1968 and the new year of 1969, start a new life with a new year. That last Christmas will stay seared in my mind until the day I die.

My son had turned six the November before, the other boys would be nine and five in the coming April and August respectively. I was almost twenty-eight. I remember the preparations for Christmas, the trimmed tree and making paper chains to hang around the house along with the paper lanterns, also home-made by the boys. On Christmas Eve, we wrote a message on the blackboard to Father Christmas and arranged the supper for the man and his reindeer.

On Christmas morning, the three boys woke early with their usual exuberance and rushed to my husband and me to say 'He's been, he's been' and covered our bed with torn paper and the smaller presents that had been in their end-of-bed pillowcases. Later, three boys, still in their identical green-patterned pyjamas, collarless and almost sleeveless with extended shoulders, made to suit the hot summers, sitting on the floor opening the presents that had been placed under the tree. I can't remember what they received that year.

Halfway through the following week, my son and I prepared to leave. We travelled by train and we both wore suits, mine a beige skirt and jacket, my son's short pants and jacket, and I cried for hours. My son's sad, confused face and neither of us knowing, really, what we were doing. I think that sadness has stayed with us.

Getting through Christmas has been, still is, a struggle. My son has always been independent and now he has his own family, so mostly I am on my own. Friends have invited me to join their families for the day but that is more painful than being alone. Of course it is not just on the anniversary of my leaving that I feel loss, but missing out on special days, birthdays, weddings, graduations, school parents' days or being a volunteer, and later, grandparents' days; having no knowledge of their lives – the broad outline, yes, but not the daily minutiae. I didn't get to kiss bruises better but I remember the chocolate Sundays. We didn't indulge in soft drinks or junk food but on Sunday afternoons we would often eat chocolate. Lots of it, sometimes, but when it was finished, we all had to thoroughly clean our teeth and wait at least until the next Sunday for the next chocolate party.

If I expected a welcome, tea and sympathy from my mother at the end of my marriage and losing two children, I certainly didn't get it. My son and I stayed two days in the family house, leaving in tears with the recriminations from my mother ringing in my ears; I had made my bed et cetera and I could expect no help from her.

My sister, with her two sons, had also left her husband and was sharing a rented house with the woman who was to become my older brother's second wife. I moved in with them. My sister had been receiving a disability pension since the age of sixteen and this allowed her to stay at home with her children. She was now there to look after my son while I worked. Her sons, a little younger than mine, were very different in temperament and personality and this again must have been very confusing for my son.

Auntie M was the only adult, more adult than I, who spoke kindly to me, telling me my action was the most unselfish thing. My father quietly accepted me and my son.

My son's father

We talk about the chemistry between people, some magnetic force, the electric charge; something happens, unbidden, against any will, between two people. This is what happened between me and this very tall, very dark, very handsome man.

My young son and I had been sent to Brisbane and my sister and I were at a uni dance. Normally, I'd dance with a chap, sometimes exchanging first names and something innocuous about studies, but that was all. This time it seemed necessary to say I was married, as he said the same simultaneously. He was doing postgraduate veterinarian studies. His wife and two children had remained in Tanzania; he was living in one of the colleges. He later did much valuable work in Tanzania and also worked for WHO.

We spent a lot of time in each other's company; he was often at my parents' home for dinner and there he met my grandmother. She pronounced him a perfect gentleman. His college dean saw my photo on his dresser and advised him against seeing me. My friend told the dean to mind his own business. My first son then was about eighteen months old.

Eventually I was called back to Sydney and no contact was maintained. My mother never mentioned him in her letters and I got on with my life as best I could. Inevitably, there was another argument and another trip back to my parents, but this time I was to go by train. It might have been that my husband was going home to Fiji for holidays, so things were more planned. My family was informed of my ETA. The train pulled into South Brisbane station and the first person I saw was the Tanzanian. He had maintained contact with my family, who had told him of my arrival. One man rejects, another welcomes –

given the feeling that we had in the beginning, it is not surprising that on that trip my second son was conceived.

Unknown to me, he had become the local unofficial vet with the kids asking advice about their horses (kept on the vacant ground behind the family house) or cats and dogs. Of course he couldn't prescribe, he didn't have a licence to practise here, but he could give advice.

There was never any doubt in his mind that I and my then two children would return with him when he completed his studies. He was from a prominent family, two of his uncles were Oxford-educated lawyers who helped draft the constitution when Tanganyika became independent Tanzania. The family is written about in a book, *Politics South of the Sahara*. I can't remember the author and unfortunately it was left behind when I left Sydney; my youngest son later told me it had been burned.

My son's father said he would die for me; he said I would have my own house and servants and, in his heart, I would always be the number one wife. Our son was born in 1962. The Mau Mau had been through Kenya and north Tanzania as late as 1961 and it didn't ever feel to me the right thing to do. Whatever status his family had, a white woman wouldn't stand a chance and our son, a half-caste in whatever way you want to say it, would have been a target also. I couldn't, wouldn't, go.

My son was born in Sydney. I had been back living with my husband, who generously accepted my son as his own, never differentiated between what became three sons. I don't know whether it was through his accepting his part, his neglect, of me, or it was just easier to carry on. I had my third son with my husband. My second son has his surname. His natural father, however, continued to try to persuade me and all or one son, or just our son to go to Tanzania with him and then with anyone who was returning to East Africa after he had left. My answer didn't vary.

It is a pity my son does not have any of his father's names, has no tangible connection to his birthright. His grandfather was a king, head of the Chagga tribe. They and a tribe in Spain were the earliest peoples to practice agro-forestry. I have said his father is a veterinarian and for a time he had a position with WHO and my son, with his IQ, could have been anything. When he decided what he did want, it was in environmental studies.

The house or flat we were living in when my second son was born was cold and damp all the time and I would not put the growing baby down on the floor. I tried to take him to places that were dry, airy, so he could exercise, but it wasn't easy. Consequently, he was late in crawling and walking. He compensated with his language skills.

For several years, my son's father and I maintained contact through letters, his never wavering in his desire for us to join him and stating our son would forever be his son. When my son and I returned to Brisbane and my life became more difficult, complicated, my letter-writing reduced, gradually coming to a stop. He must have written to my mother at some point, asking what had happened to me; her reply, I was no longer interested in maintaining contact. I found this out many years later when I wrote to him telling him of my mother's death.

When my son was sixteen, I felt he should be in touch with his father. I had always felt that but at sixteen I considered him mature enough to cope with such a situation. I had no replies to letters, some returned marked 'wrong address'. I contacted the Red Cross who, in a relatively short time, found the correct address. Of course that was not given to me.

An official of the organisation wrote to him, explaining my mission and it was then up to him as to whether or not he chose to reply. He wrote to my son, his son, making it clear he would correspond with him, not with me. He was still under the impression I wanted no contact. Unfortunately, my son did not reply; he said to me that he wouldn't know what to do if it turned out they didn't like each other. Over the years, I have tried to persuade him to contact his father and his partner also has tried, particularly when they had their son, but my son is stubborn.

My story

Of course, this is all my story, but I hope this gives more insight into what makes me tick.

With no help or encouragement from my mother, although I have an idea my father might have applauded my ambitions, I'd decided from when I was very young that I wanted to teach. At sixteen I was finishing my intermediate years of high school. There were two more years to take students to matriculation level but this was the last year successful students could enter teachers' training college from year ten. I was a good student and felt confident of my future.

My nose wasn't in a book all the time now, though. I had noticed boys and boys certainly noticed me. I was experiencing admiring interest totally foreign to me: I had friends but really didn't know, had not felt, the depth of any real relationship, filial or fraternal. I lost – why do we say 'lost'? – I gave away my virginity when I was fifteen because I equated sex with love and I needed to be loved. It's possible I was still smarting about being forsaken, as I thought, by my school friend; the only physical contact we had was when we danced. We didn't even hold hands but we were definitely sweet on each other. The fairy story says we would have continued dancing until our feelings and hormones tried to get the better of us but he would have stayed the perfect gentleman until we decided to marry.

As I said, when I left Sydney – emotionally drained, bereft, shocked at what action I and my ex-husband had agreed upon – my mother's lack of understanding, devoid of sympathy, no empathy, caused her hospitality to last just two days. My sister, her two children and my older brother's mistress rented a big house just up the street and round the corner. They agreed I could move in. We seemed to be there for some time but the fog that envelops me changes in intensity and at that time was thick. The only other accommodation was the flat in Albion.

I was a public servant by then but the catalyst needed to buy my own house was the action and greed of the owner of the flat. His practice was to call in on Friday evenings to collect his rent, an amount agreed on when taking the flat. One particular evening he asked me if I would accept the receipt he was holding out to me. I looked at it and told him if I did accept it, he would be paid the amount written on it. He wanted me to pay the originally agreed amount but accept a receipt for a lesser amount. This would have shown his income as being less, which would in turn affect his tax bill. I was very angry that he could attempt to take advantage of people such as me.

The house I bought was the farmhouse moved to the suburban site, 646 Nudgee Road, Nundah. An ordinary suburb, with a high side and a low side. The house is on the low, working-class side of the railway line but the house was sound and I could afford it. If I could find a bank to lend me the money. The elderly couple selling really liked me and virtually took it off the market while I attempted to get a loan. It was 1971, I was thirty, single, divorced and a parent – according to the thinking of the times, not a good risk, regardless of the fact of having a good public service job. Women couldn't do anything without a male's signature somewhere, husband, father, brother. I kept presenting my case and finally the manager at the local ANZ decided I was worth the risk.

My son wanted to know why women had such difficulty in doing these things. I told him it was because there was always the possibility of a woman becoming pregnant, having to give up work and thus be unable to repay the loan. He looked up at me and said, 'But you're not, are you, Mummy?' He was assured, no, definitely not.

The old lady died soon after the move but her energy came back several times.

Friends helped me thoroughly clean the house, strip the old lino from the floors. For a while, they stayed bare and furniture consisted of wooden fruit boxes as side tables, covered with nice fabric, op shop stuff. My son had a proper bed; my mattress stayed on the floor for a time. Saris did duty as curtains. I was proud of being able to buy my house and I was not ashamed to invite friends to it. My friend Stephen, of the rug and prom concert, and his brother-in-law painted the outside of the house from a very dark blue to white, and also, by degrees, the inside. I remember only the kitchen colour, a lovely yellow. I had found the sunshine and I wanted to keep it.

Stephen worked for the taxation department and hated it. He spoke Russian and wanted to do other things at university. I persuaded him to give up work, move into my house and go back to study. We were sort of together for about six years. I was his first sexual partner but it wasn't a committed relationship. Once at university, he wanted and enjoyed time with his fellow students. I understood that but if he wanted to go away, camping or some such, for a weekend, he would contrive to pick a fight so he could go off in a huff. I told him he didn't have to do that; I didn't own him, he was his own person.

He is nine years younger than I and, had I been prepared to have a child with him, we might have stayed together. He was very kind and perceptive. I remember arriving home from work one day, feeling very crabby, snappy. He just took me in his arms and said, 'Bad day?' I can remember that feeling now of just letting go and letting him hold me. His grandmother used to continually say he had to marry a pleasant young woman. Obviously, in her eyes, I lacked both qualifications. Stephen and I used to laugh about it. He married a Japanese woman, five years his senior. I never did find out what his grandmother thought about that. But I was ever grateful for the books he chose to buy for my son. The two got along well.

My son spent a short time at Northgate State School before moving to Virginia State School. He did well there. He won a scholarship to Brisbane Boys Grammar so, in all, we spent about a decade and a half in Brisbane. Towards the end of that time, after my son had finished high school and decided against university, I remarried and in 1981 my husband and I went to the Solomon Islands. This is covered more fully elsewhere.

I have referred to myself as being a shy child but I think introverted might be more correct in describing me. It wasn't that I wasn't interested in things around me but that I internalised, thought about everything.

We were not a close family and, as I've said, I was told I was not as clever as my brother or as intelligent as my sister – the same sister my mother refused to educate and help in her socialisation. I was also discouraged from having friends, Australian friends, as they were descendants of convicts and therefore did not share our standards. I don't know what our standard was: we didn't have any money; getting by was a struggle.

We knew how to use our cutlery and which glass went with which wine but my working-class dad knew all that only through working in hotels. By marrying my father, my mother had cut herself off from whatever upper-class life she might have enjoyed in England. She worked hard all of her life, even mixing cement to make a path from the front steps of the Australian house to the gate. She didn't want any of that for her children. However, when I married, my domestic skills were nil. Often I used the French '*maman*' as I didn't want to use the familiar English 'mum'.

The literature tells us we choose our partners according to what we know of our parents. I had inherited the independence, strength, from my mother but such people are seen as competent, able to manage, don't need help. Consequently I have never felt I had the long-lasting support of another. Emotionally, I have lived a single life. Things might have been different had I felt safe enough to travel to Tanzania and live under the care of my son's father but, for both our sakes, I could not. There never was anyone upon whom I could totally lean, not all the time of course, but knowing that person was there with more strength than I at any particular moment, and I could take respite in it.

Many moves, dislocations. What I'm running from or trying to run to, I have no idea, unless it's the search for that perfect life. Which nobody has. And I have to say, at this end of my journey, it's all become very tiring. The very early moves were of course not of my making; my decisions started with my first marriage. As a young family, we had a few moves to different rental accommodation until the purchase of our house in Broughton Street, Drummoyne. Before I left Sydney, my husband had bought a piece of land in Ryde, on which he eventually built the house he and his second wife occupied and brought up the two boys. I was given nothing from the sale of the Broughton Street house.

Various friends think I have had a wonderful, exciting, adventurous life. I don't regret the places I've been or the people I've met but, like the rolling stone, I move and have to find another doctor, a dentist, a hairdresser, find the organisations which I might join and make yet more friends. All of this was relatively easy when I was younger; as one ages, it becomes more difficult. Other people are settled, have their own firmly established little groups and don't have the energy or inclination to shuffle things up a bit to allow for another member. Before I moved into my current apartment at the northern beach city of Redcliffe, I lived in an over-50s resort for four years.

That really was a mistake. The previous six years had been spent in Launceston being busy; I made, and have kept, friends, had a place amongst the writing fraternity and published my first book, which was launched most effectively by the mayor of the time. My second book also was launched there and my third was published just as I was about to leave. I had very good relationships with all the bookshop owners, all of whom supported local authors. I was friends with the person instrumental in bringing *Ten Days on the Island* into being and persuaded her to do a writers' ten days in the off year. But the mainland was calling me back. Money was not over-abundant and buying into an over-50s resort was affordable. Some, I'm sure, are better than others but I thought it would provide immediate friendship.

I was the wrong person in the wrong socio-economic environment and all I got out of it was deep depression. Conversation was restricted to food – price and menus at the nearby services clubs, which I didn't patronise, and health. I was homesick for Tasmania, a feeling that has not entirely left me after eight years. Those six years were the happiest, most fulfilling, I've had. Ah, yes, you might ask, why did I leave it? And why did I go there in the first place?

Travel between the mainland and Tasmania used to take most of a day. It was costly. Living in Tasmania is almost akin to living in another country. It is not a place one visits for a day, a weekend, although I did have friends come down to stay for a fortnight and more.

There is a saying, 'the past is a foreign country', and one cannot, at least so I have found to my cost, go back. My brothers, the friends I had when I worked here, I, have all moved on and they too have their close groups of friends who have kept up with the nuances of each others' daily life. Yes, we have all kept in touch but letters and emails are very superficial; one needs the conversations, the face-to-face, that cover the deep and profound as well as the inconsequential. So I find myself in a strange place without a passport, a displaced person.

A miscellany

For the first few months of my first pregnancy, I had morning, noon and night-time sickness but still managed to put on weight and look the rosy picture of health. Tea lost its attraction, as did my desire for Indian food. I hoped my taste buds would go back to normal after the birth as I didn't fancy a lifetime of drinking just water, and what on earth was I going to eat? Fortunately, my taste buds reasserted themselves but I didn't get back to the slender 32.5, 18, 34 inches that I had been.

Labour lasted three days and I wondered why anyone would want to do this more than once. My son was finally born at about nine in the evening on 1 April 1960.

I'd been a pacifist and member of the Humanist Society for some time. I'd never been overly fond of meat and did become a vegetarian some years later for several years. It was an Ayurvedic doctor, himself vegetarian, who advised me to go back to eating meat as my body needed it. I try not to think of the killing and eating of an animal. And with my pacifism, I can't understand why, with the level of evolution we have reached, we humans can't live peaceably together.

When I first held my son in my arms, I knew I could kill, or attempt to kill, any person or animal that threatened my child. Or be willing to die in the attempt. My son slept in his bassinet by my bed. If and when he cried, he was attended to immediately. My belief was, still is, that the cry was the only way my new human being had of alerting me to some need he had. He was an alert, happy, wakeful boy who very early on slept through from the last feed at eleven or so to five or six in the morning. His waking hours were full of conversation, with me and everyone who lived in the house, and visitors. This was his first three months of life.

Conditions changed when we moved to Sydney to join his father. I no longer had the help and our surroundings were not so comfortable. But he was still the focus of my attention. He no longer received the variety of conversation but whatever he did get served him well. He became a great conversationalist. He knew the times children and parents would be going to and coming back from school and stand at our front fence having conversations with anyone who would give him the time. Many did. He also knew his father's time for returning home and would eagerly await him. They were definitely two peas from the same pod. He became a successful electronics engineer. His living monument is the passive-solar home he designed and built; it is a lovely building.

Son number two caused some discomfort in his time of being a dot to a fully formed person but when he decided to join the world, he slid into it as easily as a fish swimming in water. We had decided on his name, which in English translates to something like sunrise, all the things the rays touch and give life to. His sunrise was approximately 10 a.m. I'd gone into the private little hospital in Sydney about midnight and thought sunrise would suit us well. As the clock neared ten, I remember thinking, come on, we'll have to change the name if you don't arrive soon. My son took to heart his sunrise of 10 a.m. or thereabouts, with his circadian clock set to that. Unfortunately, the world doesn't work that way. Though perhaps now with the world working 24/7, his time has come.

I called him Pudding when he was a baby but he has grown and stretched to a too-thin string bean. His language skills are as extensive as his brother's, if not more so, but he is more reserved and speaks only when he needs to.

When he was just a few months old, my husband's mother came for a visit. I have often wondered about that and whether she was there to say yay or nay about my husband's acceptance of this son. It was yay. She was visiting again, years later after the family had fractured. I was in Sydney trying to see my sons. She insisted I be invited to a dinner and meet her again. We have language problems but she was happy to see me and made me welcome in her son's home. I always felt she knew how I might be feeling, understood what I had lost.

My son has the tight curls of the negroid and his hair was always kept short. Until he went to high school. The rule was, no hair over the collar. My son let his hair grow and grow but it was so thick he could train it to stick out on each side of his head. It didn't reach his collar but it did look as if he had elephant's ears. I did not nag him to get it cut; I might have made the odd suggestion but it was up to him to deal with any consequences at school.

I had to wait a few years for the hair-raising moments occasioned by my second son. And even then I sometimes did not find out until he chose to tell me. There was one Warana Day when I'd spent the day in town with my American friend of the green eyes; I travelled home about five and on opening the front door immediately saw the trail of discarded outer clothing. Leather boots, jacket, socks, his helmet, of course. To say I was alarmed would be a gross understatement.

I found him semi-comatose on the lounge; he'd had a nasty fall. I asked him to wriggle his toes and fingers but I didn't want him to make any big moves. I asked if he thought he could move his head from side to side. We decided I would drive him to the hospital. Nothing broken but he did have deep tissue bruising which is very painful. He was difficult in accepting my help and would sit on the floor and wriggle his way to the toilet. And I thought I'd taken the motorbike accident to cover the family of two. (The other two didn't seriously ride.)

The small private hospital in which he was born looked after young single pregnant girls who did light housekeeping duties during their time there.

The third pregnancy was trouble-free. Again, I needed to go to the hospital at some time in the middle of the night. I woke my husband to take us to King George V (I think) which was in the same direction, roughly, as Sydney University, where my husband worked. So that was where he took us first. A quick redirection delivered us to the hospital. Unfortunately, my son was not in the correct position and he made a shoulder presentation after several hours of labour. We were both in a bad way and I didn't see him for something like twelve hours. I was very weak.

The conversations continued and he became a lawyer. He was a feisty number three; he was not going to be subdued by two older brothers. He could climb a six-foot fence almost as soon as he was walking – which he was doing at nine months. He was talking in proper sentences at the same time. He'd climbed a very tall tree when he was four and shouted for me to come and see. He was over the roof of the house. And of course, when he looked down he had doubts about his being able to climb down. I thought of ringing the fire brigade to rescue him but decided we'd try it on our own first. And of course I considered he might fall. – he could do that just waiting up there for help to arrive. So very calmly, I talked him down. He had a sense of achievement and I went to jelly, as I had with my first son, when he was safely in my arms. He slid the last few feet and had a graze on his inside leg. His badge of courage.

He might have been twelve months old when we gave refuge to my sister and her two boys; he took exception to the demands of one cousin who didn't want to share a toy so he hit him over the head. I had to hide my amusement at his method of applying our law, which was one of sharing, and talk to both small boys about fairness and not hitting.

All were always in the midst of the activity, never shut away. All three are extremely good-looking, clever, personable people.

When we have children of our own, we begin to distance ourselves somewhat from our families of origin. It is still our family but concentration is now on nurturing this new unit. For the time we were a complete family, I watched my sons grow, gave them the lessons for living, my husband and I hopefully passing on the values, the kindness, the generosity – the behaviour we believed helped make the world a better place.

We discussed budgets and university educations and what

aspirations the boys might have. We wanted them to know the world was theirs if they applied themselves. In every parent's mind is the belief in the dynasty they are creating. With that belief comes the feeling of love, safety, care returned as we, the parents, age, become infirm.

Families, generation after generation, keep rebuilding the nests that provide those feelings of belonging. In leaving, taking one son with me, I fractured the one I had set out to nurture. I encouraged my son to be independent; determined I would not do anything that remotely felt as if I were tying him to my apron strings. I did such a good job of that I think my son must have felt I abandoned him. We have lived apart, except for brief periods, since he left school at eighteen and I went to the Solomon Islands. He has been living in a different state for many years and I see him rarely. He is almost as much a stranger as my other two sons. And none of that was meant to happen. His son, my grandson, barely knows me.

My other grandchildren really know me only as the biological mother of their respective father. My first son's daughter has turned twenty and I could count on the fingers of one hand and have fingers to spare, the number of times we have met. My third son has three sons – the same applies.

We cannot change the past and, as I have said, we have to work with what we have so *non, je ne regrette rien*.

Solomon moments

Up to and immediately before our marriage, I understood Kris to have accepted a job in Malaysia building a major rail line. It seemed suited to his work and training in India as a senior civil engineer. He had project-managed the building of rail lines and bridges, among other things. India Rail and the army, which he'd also been accepted for when he graduated, were India's two top employers. He did, actually, accept the army offer first and lasted four days. He refused to submit to the induction/indoctrination exercises, which he declared stupid and juvenile. He refused such punishments for this behaviour, such as hopping frog-like around a barracks building. He was entering the service as an officer, lieutenant, and considered the whole rigmarole highly unseemly. After lengthy discussions with the senior officers, it was decided he would be released. He did get a taste of the army at war, however, when India and China were having border wars and many workers with India Rail and Kris's skills were made into a regiment and under orders from the army. With these stories and his natural charm, I thought we would go far.

It was only when no move was being made towards an imminent departure that I queried what was happening. He had changed his mind and turned it down at the last minute. I did ask if he had thought to tell me but there was no satisfactory explanation. This, I suppose, was the first puzzlement of Kris's character. Soon after, the position in the Solomon Islands was advertised.

The job looked interesting and the pay good, but first we had to find where the place was. In 1980, no one we knew had heard of the Solomon Islands and we even had trouble finding it in our atlas. However, find it we did and an application went off, leading to interviews, both in Brisbane and Honiara, the Solomon Islands capital. For him, that is. It was duly noted that he had a wife but, apart from being told I wouldn't be allowed to work, I might as well have not existed. He was offered the position of chief engineer, and accepted.

When we told our friends we were going, invariably their response was, 'How lovely. Where is it?'

When I told my family about our going, my sister looked down her pretty nose with her bright blue eyes – people say we look alike, but we don't; my eyes are a greeny-grey, my nose large and fat and she would have been nearly three inches taller had her spine been straight – so looking down her patrician nose she said, 'You'll hate it. You're a city girl and there'll be nothing there.' She went on about the kind of life that so many of the women were, indeed, having, but Kris wanted the job and as his wife I was prepared, no, eager, to explore something new.

It wasn't as if I was going very far and, anyway, I didn't have an Australian passport in those days, which meant if I wanted to re-enter Australia without a visa, I had to do so within twelve months of my leaving the country. So they weren't exactly getting rid of me. And for some, seeing me annually was quite enough, I'm sure.

The information package had stated that expatriate wives were not allowed to work and even voluntary work was limited. It was a newly independent country and, as far as was possible, work and any kind of work experience, as in volunteerism, had to go to Solomon Islanders. But I loved my husband and, being ever hopeful, thought things would work out.

Then the flurry of packing; we would be supplied with a house and furniture but we thought we should take as much as possible to ensure comfortable living. This included many books, both technical and encyclopaedic as well as others of more general interest. I, at least, would be glad of them in the months to come. As would a handful of Solomon Islanders. Finally, we had to interview and select suitable tenants for our apartment situated in a leafy suburb of Brisbane, close to the University of Queensland. We loved our green suburb with its abundance of trees and birds but later I would come to think of it as a sedate maiden aunt when compared with the riotous growth and colour in the Solomons. My own house had been rented out since our marriage and when my son finished school he shared a house with friends.

Our major belongings had been packed and prepared for a sea voyage but we still managed to have seventeen pieces of luggage, which a large taxi deposited at Departures, along with its owners. I knew I should keep a cool head for our arrival. Kris's new employers had not met me yet, which might say something about the status of women there at that time, and I wanted to make a good impression. The combination of excitement and nervousness encouraged a little over-imbibing of alcoholic beverages on the four-and-a-half-hour flight. Much to my regret. Even before we got off the plane, I knew it was going to be hot but I'd put money on that day being the hottest, muggiest, on record. Processing us, and everyone else on the flight, took hours. Our seventeen pieces of luggage seemed to require minute scrutiny and I was beginning to think it was like India where a little baksheesh could work wonders. However, we were expecting to be living there for an indefinite time, so maybe not a good way to begin.

I later got into the habit of carrying water with me but then, in the mid-afternoon tropical heat, my thoughts ranged from the simple – Oh, God, what have we let ourselves in for? – to my imminent death right there, in line, with large, sweaty, mostly men in front, behind and all around, my head swimming, my knees threatening to buckle.

Finally we were out, in the fresh air, still hot and sticky, and now I had to contend with the glare of the sun and the undisguised gaze of a great throng of people. We were being met and foolish I, now wanting only a cool room, cool flat sheets on a bed and several cups of decent tea, was looking around for a saviour and, if not suited, at least someone in slacks and neat shirt. Our welcoming committee consisted of about twenty men, including the manager of Solomon Islands Ports Authority, the finance manager, the foreman of each department such as carpentry, machinery, ship loading/unloading, housing and several more. Kris recognised the manager, now dressed in a sarong and T-shirt, but I couldn't take my eyes off the man who seemed to be in charge of loading our many bags onto a truck. He was as round as he was short, wearing torn and patched baggy shorts and a slightly torn shirt that might once have been white and once had sleeves. But it was his ears that fascinated me. The lobes had stretched to below his jawbone, the original decoration possibly being large bones pierced through the lobes themselves; now they held dangly earrings, each side different and each set of decoration dancing about his shoulders. Each side was a collection of shells, stones and smallish-sized bones. I couldn't help wondering if the latter were the remains of past dinners and of whom (or what) they had consisted. Much later he and I had several conversations about his custom belief and what he thought the missionaries had done to the people.

We have all seen processions of noteworthy people, British royalty among them, either in person or on TV. Our trip from the airport to our hotel was like one of those – a long collection of vehicles but none so grand, and no horses and no uniforms. We were, apparently, a big event – indeed, the first Ports Authority chief engineer had arrived but also, my husband was the *only* engineer. And when crowds are waving madly at one, one has to wave back. I always say that was when I perfected my royal wave. One gains in sympathy for those subjected to public display, as I thought, they, too, must sometimes feel like death but have to smile and wave, looking as if they haven't a care in the world.

Beyond the dusty road and the waving, laughing locals, the lush, green hills stood against the blue sky. I thought our minders would never finish with getting us installed in the beautiful international hotel, the Mendana, named after the Spanish explorer Alvaro de Mendana de Neira who landed there in 1568. He mistook the iron pyrite used by the locals for gold, and named the islands after the legendary treasure mines of the biblical king, Solomon.

Once installed, I was left free until the following evening, when there would be a reception. Kris had discussions with various levels of management in the morning. I didn't know which I wanted more, the shower or the bed. Or to book a seat on the next flight back to Brisbane!

We had thought the tenure would be long and comfortable and really I was looking forward to a good life with Kris in the Solomons. But it was where our marriage really came undone. We had met in February 1978 and, until our marriage in April 1981, we had been good friends; conversation was good, I was doing a second degree and also enjoyed being part of his group, which was doing a joint Masters project as part of the members' psychology degree, and our sex life was great. We shared our houses, staying overnight wherever it suited. My son was still in high school and we all got along really well. Kris did and does, practise transcendental meditation which, when we met, consisted of two sessions of thirty minutes each, every day. I could live with that. After a while, he undertook courses for higher levels and his meditation time increased to two hours morning and afternoon, and our sex life came to an end six months into our marriage. And even with that, I thought, okay, it will revive after a while. It never did. But I considered there was more to life and relationships than just sex and the conversation continued.

When I met Kris, it was if all the words I'd never uttered, about the things I really cared about, the metaphysics, history of the world, people who interested me, came tumbling out to someone who understood what I was talking about. Before that, my conversation had been not much more than trivial. I did want the whole package but what I had was more than I'd had before. We went to the Solomons at the end of December 1981 and I was hopeful there'd be a revival there.

The view from our hotel room's balcony was a travel agent's poster; golden sand, coconut palms, umbrellaed tables and chairs took up the foreground. Then the sea, occasionally hiccupping over visible tips of reefs and, to the left of the picture, the volcanic island Savo. Straight ahead, the sea just went on and on until it met the sky.

From the first day, we enjoyed drinking our early morning tea on the balcony and every morning, bathed in the golden light, there was a young boy fishing from his small canoe. We shared his joy when he caught something and gauged how good a breakfast his family might have that day. I would have thought that he had no knowledge of our being there but we learned that the senses of the Solomon Islanders were more finely honed than ours and it was quite possible that he was aware of our presence several hundred metres away.

In later moments of quiet reflection, gazing at that pacific expanse, the vision of warships, planes, bombs and submarines exploding the calm would lodge in my mind. The sea around Honiara was named Iron Cove, for the ocean floor was not sand but the wrecks of ships. In the sunlight, the rainbow slicks of oil could be seen shining on the surface, the slow, unceasing release from the dead vessels.

Our visitors invariably wanted to see war relics so, depending on age and fitness, we would take them to see collections or through the jungle to come across rusting machinery, vines and pawpaw trees or coconut palms forcing their growth through the broken spaces. Once we came across a one-man mini-submarine, the moving ocean shifting it about until it beached, its guts spilling across the sand.

There was a permanent museum, a large rough table with thatched cover and divided down the length by a long plank, something like a wide fence paling. On one side, US memorabilia was displayed while the other showed Japanese pieces. I will never forget the helmets of the airmen and the ground forces, from both sides, with two holes opposite one another, a straight trajectory through the wearer's head. And all I could think was these were someone's son. The declared participants of that war have nearly correct figures of their respective dead; I wonder if the Solomon Islanders have. If they did take censuses, they would not have been accurate and I don't know if anyone ever tried to put a figure on their losses.

Later, we witnessed other, newer, wrecks, machinery originally worth thousands of dollars, rotting and rusting for the want of technical knowledge, all leftovers from various aid programmes. This led to many discussions on the advisability of aid, how it should be administered and the efforts made towards making sure those for whom it was intended knew how to maintain it. This often began discussions on the readiness of some peoples in taking on the responsibilities of self-determination. In the Solomon Islands then and many countries since, the world has witnessed the tribal conflicts still extant.

Our welcoming reception was held at the hotel; I wasn't overly concerned, apart from hoping it didn't go on for too long. I surmised that with the general poor grasp of English, speeches might be somewhat rambling. I'd wear something simple, maybe one up from smart casual, in keeping with the weather and my surroundings. I met the Australian and British high commissions' staff, expatriate men working in other fields and their wives, who, I thought, were rather over-dressed. A thought repeated as time went on. I began to wonder what had happened to the Solomon wives of the almost entire male staff of the Solomon Islands Ports Authority when the manager of Ports introduced me to his wife with instructions to her to introduce me to other wives. Not James's but those of the other workers.

They were all sitting under the potted palms ranged around the large room, all wearing dark synthetic jersey dresses, printed with large bright flowers and fruit. The central lighting did not reach them, they were hard to see, but I was reminded of large dark purple plump plums in a huge bowl of vegetation. Everything about them, their round, soft faces, the large plump bosoms, the round, soft flesh of their arms, all with the faint glow you get from a bowl of the fruit only just illuminated by dim light. It could have been a painting by one of the old European masters.

We were soon to learn that the electricity supply was not constant and quickly overloaded, resulting in total breakdowns or at least brown-outs. Again, the royal handshake and how does one vary 'How do you do' and 'I'm so happy to be here'? Many of them I was never to meet again; others, our paths crossed but seldom.

Kris was busy getting to know the Ports' personnel, their methods of working and what, exactly, was required of him. This proved to be as fluid as the seas around us and probably began my loss of faith in the man I thought I could lean on. He somehow seemed reluctant to take charge or perhaps was unable to see the larger picture of which he was in charge. Many years later when it been suggested that he might be an Asperger's sufferer and the scales dropped from my eyes, I could see how it would have been impossible for him to use his imagination; he needed the straight lines of order and what naturally followed the previous step. It was the fluidity he couldn't cope with. He blamed everyone else for what he could not grasp but this was slowly building up and in the beginning I put his frustrations down to the peculiarities of the job, lifestyle and language.

In the meantime, I was left to my own devices. Still at the Mendana, I was in the city, which took hardly any time to explore. It held the British and Australian High Commission buildings, the Australian, at five storeys, being the highest and actually containing a lift. There was a newsagency with gift shop, a good second-hand clothes shop, others around corners and, further out though still walkable, a very good bookshop. There was a Chinatown selling everything, fabric, food, fake label shoes, handbags, leather jackets, plastics, party stuff, Chinese papers, pins – if one couldn't get it in Chinatown, one couldn't get it. There was the government store, which was empty most of the time but stormed each time a ship came in with stocks of western food. Nothing sedate about the rush to get what expatriates wanted. On the outskirts of town was the daily market, selling the best fruit and vegetables I've tasted. Back in the centre of town there was also a boutique with expensive haute couture, and the Mendana had a section selling local jewellery and souvenirs. Dotted about, there were carvers selling their work and children always, trying to sell their trinkets.

No one from either mission sent word to invite me to anything – morning tea, a chat, or anything else. I spent many hours sitting in the outdoor setting of the hotel, examining the people who frequented it, 99% expat, and writing the first of countless cards and letters to people in Australia. It appeared to double as office space for many, as I witnessed several business deals being done – as good a place as any and better than many, I would say. This might have been where and when I began to get a good name. Of course all of the staff, and probably many patrons, knew I was the wife of the Ports engineer but I did nothing more to distinguish myself than treat the staff with the same courtesy as should be afforded every human being. I didn't mind expressing my ignorance on many things and asking for help. I didn't buy anything from the roaming children selling their trinkets – had I started, it would never have ended – but I wasn't rude to them and tried to engage them in conversation. And they knew I was going to be around for quite some time, so I could wait. Our various visitors made up for my non-buying habits.

Just into our second week, our luggage arrived. I went down to the port to overlook its unloading; this was my first brush with Solomon Islands officialdom. The country was still newly independent and I think it must have been like new parents, not quite sure how it all works and playing it safe by going by the book. In this case, the book was very thick.

Our various and many pieces were not in a container but had been placed in the hold of the ship as they were when they left our Brisbane home. The bulging net swinging overhead was lowered to the wharf in stops and starts and eventually bumped onto the wharf, contents spilled out, the crane going back for another fishing trip, dropping the net into the depths of the boat. Boxes were opened there, on the wharf, to check for damage, I was told, but as neither owner of this particular cargo was called upon to inspect, I'm not sure by whose criteria damage might be ascertained. I believed more damage would occur right there on the wharf, our now uncovered belongings sitting in the blazing sun for what looked likely to be several days. My presence wasn't appreciated – looking back, I think they would have considered me a meddling member of the former colonisers. I remembered one of the chaps from the reception who appeared to be in charge here, so in a quiet moment and away from most eyes, I asked if he could get our belongings off the wharf as quickly as possible. And this was the port my husband was chief of.

Through the complicated system of communication within departments, it was arranged for our goods to be transferred to the house in the hills. One of the Ports staff, helping to put all our belongings in the house, kept stopping and looking out at the glorious view. It covered the thick green growth to the dusty road leading into and out of town, the town itself, the port, the beautiful sea and the islands dotting the horizon. I could understand his appreciation of it but couldn't understand his words, '*Numbawaan, numbawaan.*' He simply meant it was a first-class view, number one. I learned later that he was a bush man, not a coastal man, so his appreciation of the scene was the more remarkable. I was beginning to warm to these people who were friendly, quick to smile and give a helping hand, and honest.

The house was up on one of the many ridges but I always called it the Hill House. There was a separate building for staff but initially many of our belongings went into this while the main house was cleaned to my satisfaction and I decided where things were to go. It would be several days before we actually moved in but I had to interview prospective domestic staff and generally find my way about. We had survived the first two weeks, with 208 more to look forward to.

One of the workers had recommended two sisters who would like to work for me. I thought I might as well try them out as I didn't know anyone and there wasn't an agency for that kind of thing, so Weilat and Hadini became my first house-girls. Language was a bit of a problem; their English was minimal and my Pijin non-existent but in the beginning it was simply a matter of getting sorted. Pointing and other sign language saw things unpacked and arranged. One of the Australian women had told me at the reception, 'The natives are not to be trusted' and I should have any valuables locked away, the pantry locked at all times and definitely they should not be in the house if I wasn't. She hadn't, however, given any clues about how to go about finding suitable staff. Her system was not one I could work to; I needed to be able to trust the people who worked in my house.

Weilat and Hadini were trustworthy enough but we didn't really get along. Weilat was more interested in the young men who found it necessary to visit often and Hadini would often be found with a duster, sitting in front of a bookshelf, book open although she couldn't read, and a hand down the front of her knickers. However, I thought I'd try to maintain the status quo at least until I found my feet on this new terrain. I didn't want to be seen as someone who couldn't handle staff and anyway, at this point, I didn't know of anyone else. I talked to the two sisters about their hours of duty and what I expected of them. They agreed with everything I said and went on their merry way. It was during their reign that the only breakage not due to tremors happened. Weilat dropped a small glass elephant whose trunk snapped off.

Kris was busy at work and dealing with his own culture shock. At home in India there had been more servants than family members and when he graduated with a first class degree in civil engineering he moved straight into a job that put him in charge of many men, trained to varying but definite levels and there to do his bidding. As Chief Engineer of Solomon Islands Ports Authority, he was the only engineer and I think the only employee with a tertiary education. In applying for the position, the appeal had been the challenge of helping a newly emerging country at least have a highly functioning port and the other infrastructure that Kris's engineering skills could provide.

The process of winning trust, explaining in sometimes minute detail the things he wanted to do, the changes, repairs – not only to the port but also to workers' homes that were provided by Ports – took time. He had been in charge of multimillion-dollar projects both in India and Australia and was used to working with people who knew what he was talking about and what was expected of them. In India, he had grown up with the situation of clap hands and his bidding done. Australia not so obsequious of course, but a hierarchy just the same. Solomon Islanders certainly had a hierarchy but Kris's orders and expectations were ones not understood. He found it all much harder than he thought he would.

He soon learned of the great rivalry between each separate department. Each had its own workers and multi-skilling was not practised; each believed their contribution to the whole more important than that of the others. Hence the size of the welcoming committee – they were all important, they all had to come. Each department comprised men from different parts of the country, with their own language, custom practices and beliefs. They all spoke Pidgin but, not too long ago, would have been living in their own parts of the islands and frequently waging war on each other. Two men, each head of his department, had not spoken to each other for fifteen years and this was another situation my husband would deal with. As well as being a first class civil engineer, he was also an organisational psychologist. By the time we left, these two had become friends and proved the greatest allies of my husband.

In accompanying Kris to the Solomons, I referred to myself as his 'appendage'. A kept woman. Had there been a position advertised in the international press that I could have applied for and then got, I would, naturally, have also had a job. The many expatriate wives had little to occupy their time. Mah-jong, coffee mornings, bridge, shopping, not just for food but raiding the second-hand clothes shops, seemed to be the major pursuits. None of these things appealed to me, although the last activity was interesting in that it showed the inappropriateness of aid. I admit I did buy two dresses, exclusive labels and good as new, from one of these shops and they were the kind of garments the expatriate women sought.

Kris had to take a trip to Vanuatu and was away for ten days, leaving me to continue sorting things out on the home front. My mother had come for a visit and, not wanting to interfere, expected to be waited on. I was still disorganised but if she could cope with that, we managed. However, soon after Kris left, I collapsed to my bed with what, I didn't know. I had a raging fever interspersed with being freezing cold, my joints, every muscle, screamed; I wanted to tear my skin off, it was so itchy. In a matter of days, I lost several kilos. I thought I had malaria but we were taking our antimalarial tablets, so it couldn't be that, could it?

The two girls hovered but didn't know what to do about Missus, and I, too weak to even organise my thoughts, was unable to give orders. They fled. Mother ate whatever was in the house and I tried to keep my fluids up but was getting weaker by the minute. Initially, I slowly made my way to the kitchen to make up an Indian preparation that I believed could cure anything – stomach upsets, fevers, any imbalance at all. One of the ingredients was ginger and one day my mother offered to prepare it for me. I was concentrating on dry-frying seeds when I noticed my mother was cutting the ginger complete with skin and adhering mud. That was it. I told her she had to leave, go home immediately, now, go to the travel agent's and change her ticket. She went.

I really went downhill very fast from there and arrived at a point where I couldn't get out of my bed at all. I do remember thinking that dying wouldn't be so bad; the days were not too hot and the sunshine gave a soft glow to everything. I thought I would just drift from this life into oblivion.

I was alone in the house for several days, sipping water when I had the strength. Just as I thought I was at death's door, Kris arrived back. He immediately took me to a doctor, who didn't seem to know what to do either. He did prescribe penicillin, to which I seemed to have developed an allergy. Kris then took me to the hospital, where I refused, point blank, to be admitted. I was, though, diagnosed as having dengue fever. No particular treatment, just see it out. And keep up the fluids.

I asked Kris to send up a couple of fellows I'd met on the evening of the reception and sounded them out about a girl for the house. One was recommended, a relation, so I thought, well, here we go again, but I needed someone. Betsy came and probably saved my life. She also worked for another English expatriate who, on Betsy's urging, came with a friend to see me. She asked if I needed anything, food and such like. All I could think of was ice cream, I wanted ice cream. Betsy came a couple of times to clean the house and make simple meals for me but I was out of her way and without transport, I was difficult to get to. I was never Missus to her but Jacqueline, as I was to every other person who worked for me.

I hadn't met Dorothy or her friend Jenni because, like me, they shunned the mah-jong and coffee circles. Dorothy's Caribbean husband was a lawyer, she a teacher, working her way up from primary levels to university. When we met, she had retired from teaching but saw the need for a quality bookshop, so she became a naturalised Solomon Islander and went into business. None of the true confessions magazines that took pride of place in the one and only newspaper and gift shop ever crossed her doors. She sourced the books required for schools, the novels she thought students would enjoy and the broader stuff the rest of us might get our teeth into.

Dorothy and I became very good friends. Although they were invited often, she, her husband and their three children, rarely accepted invitations to dinner. She would come for lunch or afternoon tea or, when we had joined the musical circuit, come when it was our turn to host the monthly concert. These concerts were compiled from the various LP vinyl records we all had then. We would see her and the children, all high school age, at community gatherings, but rarely her husband. When I knew her well enough, I would ask how she had got a particular bruise or scratch. Her reply was that she had slipped, on wet concrete garden steps or rough paths, and I accepted those replies. It took me some time to question the truth of her stories and one day, particularly bruised, I challenged her. She then admitted her husband beat her. And I started to encourage her to do something about it.

When I had gained a little strength, Kris and I returned to the hospital to discuss malarial and dengue prophylactics. We had, on advice from the Australian health department, started taking antimalarial medication before our departure. The doctors in the Solomons were furious with that advice. We were told that no medication could totally prevent an attack of either disease but by taking the tablets unnecessarily there was then nothing with which to fight the illness if we should be unlucky enough to get it. We stopped popping pills and tried to keep our skin covered especially at dawn and dusk, when mosquitoes seemed to be around more.

Slowly my health and strength returned. I decided I needed transport. It was inconvenient having to rely on Kris to get me in and out of town when I wanted, so I bought a Honda motorbike. In those days, there was a total of about twenty-six kilometres of sealed road in Honiara; any other sealed road was private, and precious little of that. I managed very well on the gravel roads and was never menaced by snarling dogs. Most of the local drivers and many expats would not have passed a driving test in Australia, but in Honiara one had to just front up at the counter of Main Roads and grease someone's palm. I hasten to assure you that I had been used to riding bikes in Australia and had an Australian licence. Of course I was a bit of an oddity, riding around on my little bike, but it got me around town and outlying areas, and I was able to visit the friends I was making.

My son back in Brisbane didn't care for it, however. He pointed out that the potholes were as big as my bike and me together, and the trucks towered over me – and went faster. I kept on with it until Kris borrowed it one day to go to work. Coming home for lunch, he misjudged the corner and loose gravel at the entrance of our driveway, and had a spill. My bike, his accident, but he and my son applied pressure for me to sell it.

The Hill House needed plumbing repairs so the Ports plumber came with a dozen men. Copper pipe needed to be used and the tiles around the bath replaced. The head plumber measured the length of pipe needed by placing his hands either end of the area to be piped. Then he would stand, his hands positioned in front of him and in the position he thought they should be. This measurement was passed on to his second-in-command who, hands positioned in front, took the measurement downstairs to pass on to the person in charge of cutting. Hand to hand, the head of cutting passed it on to the actual cutter, the one to snip the length of copper pipe from the coil. This length of pipe would be transferred upstairs by way of the ascending order of workers, handing at last to the head plumber.

Of course it didn't fit. It was too long; it was too short. When a little pile of discarded pipe had been made, I could stand it no longer. I got my tape measure from my sewing basket but then had to show them how to use it. My help was not appreciated. After that, I took more notice of body adornment and found many necklaces had pieces of copper pipe amongst the various other bits. I always say that was when I earned my plumbing degree.

They had never done tiling before and so an entire job that should have taken no more than a day and a half, lasted for weeks. I showed them how to do it and get even spacing by using matchsticks. This was the only bathroom in the house but fortunately both Kris and I were comfortable with the Asian bucket baths, using a bucketful of water and a ladle. It's fine if the weather is warm, hell in a cold winter.

I was not earning myself any brownie points by my meddling in plumbing. To restore my equanimity I'd sit at my desk placed in front of a window and when I wasn't writing I gazed at the *numbawaan* view. I enjoyed the many hours, sitting there, taking it in, and trying to write – to family, friends – my thoughts. Early mornings, I would see little dots of boys in canoes, catching fish, and sunrises turning the bay into molten gold. Bigger canoes, with outboard motors, would be coming in, laden with produce for the day's market. Those canoes were so heavily stocked it looked as if the occupants and their goods were supported directly by the water. What looked like Matchbox cars and trucks trundled to and fro far below me, dots of people making their way on foot. Savo hadn't erupted in a very long time but was still considered active; as one does, I wondered if we might be lucky enough to witness a blow during our stay. Megapode birds dug holes in those parts of the crater that gave the right temperatures for their eggs to hatch but many of the eggs found their way to the local market. However, there were always enough left to hatch to ensure the continuation of the species.

Some time after my original girls had fled and I was managing whatever needed to be done, they, reluctantly I thought, came creeping back wanting to be taken on again. I knew their family would be angry with them for losing good jobs but I thought it was a good time to show that I was not a weak pushover and that I was, in this case, the boss. I refused to have them back. It was unheard of that the Missus should or could do her own housework and cooking and I was conscious of the Solomon Islanders' need for employment and Western wages to pay for a lifestyle imposed on them by first British then German colonialists, and then their independence and, with that, their dependence on trade.

My husband decided he didn't like our neighbours at the Hill House. We stayed there for a very short time and before I'd been offered work. We were there when I bought my motorbike and also where I had my dengue fever. It was also where our first visitors came. Friends of my mother's, really, but a couple I related to very well. They had come with her for the first three weeks of my mother's longer, second, sojourn.

Arthur would have been right at home with the drama group. I remember a particular act he used to perform at fund-raising events in Brisbane. The stage would be black and then the lights would show just a pair of glittering gloves and a top hat. To the music of 'She', these gloves danced. One had no trouble imagining a loving couple; it was brilliant. The lights would go up and there was Arthur, in black, except for his gloves and hat, those hands, female, caressing an unseen male back, evidenced in the top hat. A superb performance. He was a dab hand in the kitchen, too. He offered to make scones one lunchtime and the loaded plate was carried triumphantly from the kitchen by Arthur wearing shorts, singlet and a tall chef's hat. We ate. Dinner time came around and the question of what to have arose. My husband said he couldn't eat anything, he'd had such a heavy lunch. I wasn't the only one to make the odd faux pas.

Our neighbours could be noisy at night, admittedly, but they didn't bother me. I was still settling in and I had my desk and the view. I'd sit at my desk and write – all the letters back to family and friends in Australia and several other countries. During our stay, I wrote many letters, all handwritten as one properly brought up does. It wasn't until my first visit back and meeting with friends that I discovered there was a problem.

One friend said how much she enjoyed about one-third of my letters, to which I exclaimed, 'Oh my goodness. What's wrong with the rest?' It transpired that after that, my handwriting deteriorated and became illegible. You must understand my letters were averaging five thousand words apiece. I switched to typing; a practice that remained a sin in the eyes of my mother – only business letters were typed. I remember my early years at school when we were required to carefully copy copperplate letters and my thinking that my own writing was going to have my own individual stamp upon it. Foolish one. Had I practised what the teachers were trying to teach me, people today would be able to read what I write.

With the bike and my writing, I could not feel isolated and I had an idyllic view, but Kris couldn't sleep. The Ports management was prevailed upon to find something more suitable. The company bought a house on the beach which I named PortSea Lodge. It was beautiful and bigger with a large compound and a cottage in the corner closer to the street and not visible from the house. This would have been for domestic staff originally. Kris offered it to his clerk and family. The back of the house looked over about one hundred metres of grass, trees, flowers before meeting the sandy beach. Many meals and conversations were taken on the very wide tiled veranda that stretched the length of the house. A few metres out, in the ocean, a reef stretched across the width, and more, of our property. Especially when the tide was out, I liked to walk along the beach and examine the tiny fish caught in the many rocks pools. Many people have fish tanks and bird cages but for me, watching creatures in their own habitat beats anything that's locked up.

The locals used our property as a conduit between road and beach. Apparently an earlier tenant had a Solomon Island girlfriend so the property was open ground to the locals. On the front, or back, whichever way one wished to consider it – the laundry was dried on the side away from the beach so perhaps the street side was the back, but whatever, it was far enough away and with intervening foliage, we were barely aware of the traffic. On the side not used as a public pathway, there was a trellis of orchids. They were beautiful and grew so prolifically, nothing could destroy them, not even the unseen neighbours' chooks. Funnily, the chickens never laid an egg in our garden. I could pick long stems of the blooms and, making sure no dirt adhered to them, airmail them in boxes to my mother in Brisbane.

Betsy had been happy and willing to help at the Hill House when asked and after I had okayed it with her full-time employer. However, it was not easy for her to get from her house to mine so I didn't ask very often. However, once we were settled in PortSea Lodge and after I ascertained that she wasn't really fully occupied with my now friend, Dorothy, between the three of us, we decided Betsy could manage us both. Fortunately, Dorothy and I agreed on proper wages for whatever staff we employed. Betsy had to speak with her husband before making a decision.

Andrew worked in the ANZ bank and was a very pleasant, hard-working man. He was very shy, which made it difficult to have a proper conversation and, although he did very well at work and was highly thought of, I always considered Betsy to be more intelligent. Her formal education had been very short, as was the case with females, but she did know how to read. She had a very quick mind, and wit, assimilating new information easily. She laughed often, was a diligent housekeeper and cooked like an angel even though she couldn't understand how we stayed alive without eating meat. She learned to cook our vegetarian meals and even cooked some of them for her own family but she truly mourned over our fried rice. In fact, she couldn't bring herself to honour it with that title, it just became 'your rice'. She and Andrew had two little boys, one their own natural child, the other, the elder, adopted. A classic case of not being able to get pregnant but doing so as soon as they adopted.

Kris and I were invited to visit them at their home. They were paying off a lovely place and Andrew was working hard to fence it and create flower and vegetable beds. They had a small dog and everything was beautifully kept. The two little boys were, like all Solomon children, well behaved. Well, except one little boy, but I'll discuss him later.

Before we could move into PortSea, the beautiful wooden floors needed to be resealed. My husband bought the sealants, parts A and B, which needed to be mixed immediately before painting over the prepared floor. Kris explained in detail and in various ways what must be done and then had to go off again to some other Pacific port. I was left in charge and you will remember the lovely time I had with the plumbers. However, I was better acquainted by this time with many of the staff of Ports and didn't foresee any problems. It was, after all, a straightforward job, wasn't it?

Well, no. My mother was with me again, so to get us both down from the Hill House to PortSea, I had to ask someone from Ports to transport us and with one thing and another, I perhaps didn't get to the house as often as I should, or at least not early enough to forestall the disaster. Yes, they got it wrong. A comes before B, right? So the contents of tins A were painted over the large floor. It didn't seem to be drying, so should the contents of tins B be applied over sticky A? Yes, there was a dim recollection that they be mixed, so obviously they would mix on the floor. It was about this time I made a visit and I have to admit, I laughed. Do you remember that game we played as children where the crowd would have to be active until the one 'in' called freeze and we would have to hold our pose at that instant? I think it was called Statues. It did cause a lot of falling over. I could imagine stepping onto the sticky mess and the positions we might get into in trying to get off.

My laughter certainly eased things before I told the men that Mr Kris was going to be very angry and had reiterated the correct procedure. I made them think what might be the remedy. They knew it had to be removed and hot water and soap and scrubbing had not worked. I suggested that the head man, a few others and I go and talk to a couple of expats with a knowledge of industrial chemistry. We hadn't really solved the problem before Kris returned, and I was happy to hand it over to him. Whatever method it was in the end was messy and stank. I was sure it wasn't exactly healthy for the workers to be breathing in the fumes it gave off and I wanted them to wear heavy rubber gloves. But they were men, had been warriors, and weren't going to act like sissies.

In due course, we moved in and the house and Betsy were running smoothly. Kris's clerk's sister-in-law lived with him and his wife, Judy, who worked for ANZ, so her sister, Edna, helped them out. She also began helping Betsy, doing more of the heavier work, like cleaning the windows. Because of the proximity to the sea, the glass was forever salt-grimed. It was about this time, as things seemed to be settling nicely, that my sister's predictions about there being nothing there started to make an impact.

No bakery, no cinema, the only building with a lift belonged to the Australian High Commission. There was the Guadalcanal Club, where one could drink, play cards, have trivia nights, and several other occupations, I suppose, but it was not the sort of place Kris cared to go. And without him, I could not go either. There was a substantial

Chinese population whose members seemed to have the monopoly on shops, which were full of Chinese goods. No takeaway food, though. But they did monopolise the many mah-jong games and gambling. I think it was a government-run shop in town that stocked the goods that came in by ship every several months. Timing wasn't regular, so one could run out of flour, sugar, tea. Our diet consisted of more than fifty per cent Indian cuisine and a lot of mornay-type dishes, so my pantry filled up with lidded buckets of white flour, wholemeal flour and another one that was ground differently and suitable for making the Indian flat bread, roti or chapatti. I eat very little bread now but then I wanted good, fresh bread, so I made my own. The aroma of proving bread spreading throughout the house was definitely one I wouldn't banish with commercial sprays. We could buy local milk but were not sure about levels of pasteurisation, but butter and cheese, tofu were not available. I would stock up on them and freeze them.

When the supply ship came in, queues would start forming at the shop's door. When it opened, there was nothing sedate about the mad scrambling rush to get to the areas each shopper was most interested in.

Things I never bothered with were the European vegetables; I never missed cabbage or cauliflower, carrots or broccoli, preferring to buy locally grown vegetables daily from the market. We were spoiled with the fresh fruit and to this day I have not enjoyed a pineapple after eating those of the Solomons. I bought long-life milk to stock in the pantry and the buckets of flour, as well as the stuff for the freezer.

We had brought various other grains, protein-rich dried beans et cetera, with us, and we knew they were items we would have to procure for ourselves in other ways. Once the authorities became used to us, they would telephone to say another packet of spice was stinking out their work space, or a parcel of something whose name they couldn't pronounce. When we started inviting people in for dinner, I think they were initially somewhat apprehensive about getting enough to eat. With no meat, what kind of meal could it possibly be?

But the Solomon Islands honesty went so far as to actually tell one what they really did think. After the first dinner party, we were told how good the food was and how full they were when they had thought they'd have to return home and have another, late, dinner. After that, it seemed many wanted to be invited to dinner, maybe to find out for themselves what these strange non-meat-eating people could produce that was so satisfying. Meat, and fish for the sea people, was an important part of their diet.

Even before we'd found our feet, the Ports Authority harbour master died. We were honoured guests at his funeral. At the graveside I was unfortunately overheard saying to my husband that it was a pity the body wasn't cremated and the energy used to run a bakery or something useful. Yes, tactless, I know.

We'd had to visit the house beforehand and pay our respects to the body lying in state for several days. We saw the various holes being dug, different depths and different fuel for the many and various kinds of flesh that would be cooked in them. After the body was finally buried, we had to go back to the house for the party. Meat, meat and meat. I managed to wander around with a piece of chicken on my paper plate, every now and then surreptitiously passing it to a dog and taking another small piece so anyone looking might believe I was honouring them by actually eating. Kris could not be so generous. As is the custom, we gave generously to the widow.

Kris and I were getting about a bit more and I decided, if the high commissioners and their staff weren't going to invite us, I'd invite them, so invitations went out. We had been to the frequent official Australian and less frequent British parties, so we were getting to know and be known. We really had not been in the islands for very long when, at a British cocktail party, the second secretary asked if, by any chance, I used a British passport. I told him that was the only one I had.

'Oh good,' he said. 'Would you like to be my secretary?' With regret, I had to explain that I really wasn't an office worker, could only just type but couldn't take shorthand.

'Not to worry,' came the reassuring reply, 'you'll get by.' So I became the secretary to the second secretary of the British High Commission. I was also the front counter receptionist, which might have been a more correct description of the job, and I was in charge of local staff.

The work wasn't hard and I managed whatever typing I had to do. I enjoyed everything about it. The office of the High Commissioner's secretary was adjacent to my reception area and I could hear her when she answered her phone. I got to be able to tell what kind of person she was talking to. Her voice changed according to the nationality and status of caller. Her friends would have been among the British stationed there while mine were predominantly Solomon Islanders.

In those early 1980s, life in Honiara seemed tranquil. I did know about the tribal undercurrents but life seemed to be flowing smoothly enough. Enough to cause laughter one time when I updated the official notice on the wall about what to do in case of an insurgence. It was unimaginable that such a thing could happen. Before we left, there were serious fights between the Malaitans and Guadalcanal people, on whose island we were.

The medicos at that time were trying to spread information about vasectomies. Prince Phillip, on one of the royal visits, had famously made disparaging remarks about the birth rate. He was rude but it was true that the birth rate was very high. The men didn't like their wives to have tubal ligations because then the women might have sex with others knowing they wouldn't become pregnant. So the doctors spread all the good news about vasectomies. It so happened that I had good relationships with the Ports workers, perhaps because I was interested in them and their lives, customs, et cetera. So, whenever I could, I added my few words on the benefits of the men taking responsibility for limiting their families. I had my husband to hold up as an example of one who had had it done.

I'm happy to say many did go ahead with having the cut. And they were not to know that my sex life had stopped six months after the marriage. Nothing to do with medical intervention, I'm sure. My fame spread and one day a chap from one of the outer islands came up to my counter on the first floor of the building we used. He certainly had his wood carvings with him and most certainly wanted to sell them but he also wanted to ask me about this way of limiting his family. Like many families, he already had more children than he could afford to educate and most did consider the size of the land each male child would inherit once he died. They could do their maths and the allotments were getting smaller and smaller with all the divisions.

So we were having a serious discussion about such intimate medical matters, he using Pidjin, I trying as best I could to make myself understood. My boss came out from his office, wanting me for something, and stood behind me while this was going on. He can't have looked intimidating or my visitor would have fled but I was being paid to do a particular job and so I wrapped up the conversation as quickly as I could. I turned round and said I was sorry about all that but my bemused senior just shook his head with a smile that asked what would I do next. I know I rather shocked the HC's secretary.

The expats had formed an excellent amateur dramatics society, which did have a couple of Solomon Islands members. They put on some excellent shows while we were there and I think I saw the best ever *Fiddler On the Roof* in Honiara. Christmas was approaching and the drama group devised and performed another of their excellent pantomimes.

There is a detergent in England with the brand name Fairy and one of the skits had been built around this. Three tall and well-built men, one with a grey beard, another with a red one, both natural to their faces, the third clean-shaven, dressed as fairies. Pulleys raised and lowered them as they needed to fly or not and they performed a hugely comedic act. The expertise among the expats was evidenced in the faith those weighty fairies had in the mechanism above and behind the scenes. Kris and I saw the show twice, it was so funny.

One day there appeared at my counter a tall, red-bearded man. After I'd made all the necessary checks, I issued passports as part of my duties, but before the chap in front of me could make his request, I said, 'Oh, hello. You're one of the fairies.' There was that split second where I thought, whoops.

He was taken aback but after several seconds said, in that very English way, 'I beg your pardon?'

Of course I tried to explain that just a few nights before I had seen the panto and I obviously had mistaken him for one of the actors. I was trying to apologise and he was saying he could sue me and I could visualise my ignominious ending as an employee of the Solomon Islands British mission. Imagine what a newspaper like *Truth* could make of it: 'Brit Govt Official accuses Family Man of being Fairy'.

The fellow did look unmollified and I had to redeem myself. 'Oh, come on,' I said, 'you looked familiar, or as familiar as someone dressed up on stage can look to a member of the audience. I have obviously mistaken you for one of the actors. Who, incidentally, was very funny.' Maybe I shouldn't have added the last bit but my petitioner was being stuffy.

It all ended, if not quite happily, at least with some equanimity. I added the latest addition to his family to his passport and resolved to think first, speak second. A resolve that might have slowly improved over the ensuing decades.

The Solomon Islands are situated on a fault line and there were tremors every day; I was particularly sensitive to the earth's movements and was often correct in my assessment of their strengths. Usually the most damage was a book or two fallen from the top shelf of a tall bookcase.

I remember once when my son was visiting; we were sitting at opposite ends of the dining table and we both looked up at one another as we both felt the wobble beneath us. He asked, 'Was that...?' to which I replied in the affirmative.

If there was going to be anything major, ants changed their behaviour, the birds were silent and the dogs cringed and hid.

I was sitting on my office chair one day, talking to my standing boss, the second secretary. Suddenly I said, 'Quake! Get everyone out.'

Then Derek felt it and started the evacuation procedure. First the cipher room had to be closed down. (Of course there was a cipher room. Even a tiny mission in the Pacific has to have a cipher room.) The rest of us were supposed to leave as quickly as possible and certainly without bothering to tidy our desks. Going down the stairs was like being at a funfair except it wasn't funny. The walls moved in and out, like a breathing monster, while the stairs slowly undulated up. They were very difficult to negotiate and I think J.K. Rowling might have experienced an earthquake at some time before writing her famous bestsellers with Hogwarts and the moving staircases.

Once outside, I remember a group of us stood under a tree. Maybe not the best place, but I made some crack about if the earth was going to swallow me, I'd rather go without sunstroke. Everything was engaged in a macabre dance; parked vehicles waltzed and heaved to an unheard melody, while the tallest building, the Australian High Commission, swayed and bopped. Kris was engrossed in his office and did not hear any warnings. It wasn't until he became aware of the eerie silence that he looked out of his window to see huge cranes dancing, the wharf itself copying the ocean's waves, his own floor moving beneath him. That was when he left the building.

When we went back to our house, more than books had fallen to the floor. China and glassware, foodstuffs in the pantry, a beautiful vase, full of flowers, had broken. Betsy and Edna had cleaned up but kept the spilled and broken pieces in bags and boxes to show us, before throwing them out. The epicentre was some distance away and out to sea; no lives were lost. I sent Betsy home to check on her house.

Later, I tried to impress on all domestic staff that in future they were to leave immediately they sensed a sizeable quake and attend to their own homes and families.

It made the news in Australia, so of course we had many phone calls from family and friends making sure we were okay. Savo didn't erupt, and hasn't, which is a good thing for the villages located on its sides but at least I had this to write home about.

I mentioned that conjugal relations had ceased between my husband and me. We'd met in 1978 not long after I'd started work with the Department of Children's Services and just after my father had died in England at the end of what was supposed to be a holiday. I missed him and was sorry that I didn't know him better than I did, but I did not grieve his death. He was very young, sixty-five, still working, but I felt he had never been happy in Australia and knew he had never been happy with my mother and he had really engineered his death by not taking care of his health and not taking his medication for diabetes. He developed pneumonia, lapsed into a coma and died. I felt he was happy to have died in England and would remain there forever.

So on my first date with my eventual husband, I did not feel wrong in dancing and having a good time. I'd worn one of my many saris and while I'd been quite adept wearing them and looking after children at the same time, rocking and rolling was a bit different.

We didn't go dancing again, which should have rung bells, as should the strong feeling I had that he was seeing other women, or at least one other. But I was captivated by his mind. For the first time in my life, I felt as if someone really knew what I was talking about and I had someone with whom I could converse about the deep and meaningful metaphysics of cosmology. He was doing a second degree, psychology, and I also was doing a second, so our free time was not great. I refused to see there was a lot he was not telling me. We met, stayed over in one or the other's house from time to time until we married three years later in 1981. I had thought, with the three years we'd had, we had a good basis for marriage.

He was, is, a transcendental meditator. Just before our marriage he was doing further study which would give him higher status with the organisation as well, one supposes, as greater enlightenment. So with work, uni studies and the two hours meditation morning and night, I could accept that sex might need to take a back seat and that soon everything would get back to normal. But, as I said, six months into the marriage, there was no physical contact at all. You might well ask why I stay stayed. I thought, well, sex wasn't everything and I'd been attracted to his mind first. We had our first mutual friends in the Solomons and this was where we started to really unravel.

He and I would have discussed a particular topic and come to our mutual or otherwise conclusions. Sometimes the same topics would come up when we were with friends and Kris would often abandon his previous point for that held by the group. I would tackle him on this but he would deny he'd switched and that was when he started to question my own state of mind. No one else seemed to think I was losing it and it was becoming more and more difficult to live with him.

It became easier after I started work again and I'd also been asked by the head of the English department of the University of the South Pacific, Honiara campus, if I would compose a programme suitable for teaching English to young adults who were moving into the capital. A couple of evenings per week were used up in my teaching it. I developed more of my own pursuits.

I used to tell Kris he was a Sanyasi with all the comforts of a five-star hotel. A Sanyasi is one who gives up his domestic life, family, sex, and takes on poverty, wandering from place to place and surviving on that which is given. Personally, I think that kind of behaviour, be it in India or Christians joining convents and monasteries, is a bit of a cop-out. Holier than thou, no worries and depending on the goodwill of others who need nothing more from the enlightened one than a blessing.

Not long after moving into PortSea Lodge, my emotional health was not good. On weekends, I would often sit on the veranda gazing at the beautiful view. I wasn't there through the week so was not aware of the local traffic that walked through our grounds to get to the beach and onto the reef, from which they would fish, dive, watch the babies swimming on the shallow side. Those little ones could swim before they could walk.

One particular day, I was in a very low state. Suddenly there appeared from the side of the house, a young teenaged boy, sauntering his way to the beach. I shouted. I yelled, didn't he know this was private property; I was sick of everybody using it as a public thoroughfare, wasn't there a public path somewhere, there must be, use that. It was probably before I'd even finished my tirade when the poor boy turned and fled. Then I had time to reflect and I thought, oh God, what have I done? He probably wanted to fish; now he, his family, won't eat (the islands are rich in fruit and vegetables but they tend to sell that and eat the starchy yam; fish and meat are important to their diet); I felt worse than I had before his arrival.

I kept a lookout for him. It took some time before I had my first glimpse of him but when I shouted I wanted to speak to him, he, not unnaturally, fled. But eventually there came a day when I sort of ambushed him. I apologised. I stressed that he and anyone else could resume the PortSea Lodge pathway. I wanted to know what he did with his time and he said he just hung around. It was quite remarkable that we had a lengthy conversation that first time. I was struck by his obvious intelligence and on asking why he wasn't still at school, he told me his father could no longer afford it. We already had one gardener, elderly, supplied by Ports, so I offered Mark part-time employment as second gardener. I would pay him. When he wasn't in the garden, he could be found extending his knowledge by way of the encyclopaedia.

Both he and Betsy were keen students and in my spare time I helped them with English grammar and talked about the subjects of interest to them. Mark was willing to return to school and I did manage to get a school to admit him. Spaces in schools were scarce and to return, after a lengthy absence, was a rare occurrence. I was more than happy to pay the fees.

My reward was having a village named after me, Jaqui Village, and a niece of Mark's was called Jacqueline. And as often happens, Mark had insights that first-world sophisticates have lost. Many years later, I learned he'd considered Kris weak, selfish and not good enough for me. Dear boy. I didn't ever discuss my private life with him or anyone but he used to ask me why I wasn't happy and why I didn't leave Kris.

The old gardener said the tree at the side of the house was rotten and needed to be cut down. It was as tall as an old ghost gum and as fragile. It was a beautiful tree but if there was a likelihood it could easily blow down and damage our house or the one next door, then down it must come.

A huge crane came trundling out from Ports. The Ports workers would have told their families and anyway, a noisy piece of machinery rocking down a largely unpaved road was hard to ignore. Like the Pied Piper, it collected its followers. It barged into our yard but the retinue hid behind the greenery opposite or each other.

I suggested Betsy and Edna invite the children in and put them in a position to see well but at a distance so that falling limbs could not harm them. They resisted for some time. I went inside, taking Edna with me. I told her to make up some cordial and collect some glasses and biscuits and take them out, and to serve only when the children were in a suitable position. The men with the crane also encouraged them in. I didn't venture very far from the house – I think most of the interaction the children had with expatriate wives was not exactly full of bonhomie – but all in all, I think my actions went a long way in improving my image after the public thoroughfare debacle.

Apart from my dysfunctional marriage and Kris's strange behaviour, life was good. I enjoyed my jobs and we still could enjoy invited company over dinners. I wrote my first children's book, bits of poetry, endless letters. Friends had a daughter who turned three and I wanted to give her something nice. In those years of the 80s, the Chinese imports were all cheap, plastic and not inspiring. Kris had a good, beautiful honey-brown towelling robe with a pocket on which was embroidered a gold anchor.

And yes, folks, I cut it up and made a teddy bear. He became Captain Benjamin Bear (RN Retired) and needed a book to go with him.

There was much laughter in the house between me and Betsy, Mark and Edna. Often at weekends, Edna would stroll over and just do the odd thing. I think she found more peace in my house. I was also using spare time to sew children's clothes, which my staff distributed amongst those they considered needy. I'd discuss styles with Edna and offered to teach her to sew, but she wouldn't use my machine. She did make me endless cups of tea, just the way I like it.

While in the Hill House, Kris had developed what he called fatherly concern over Weilat. I told him his fatherly concern might be misconstrued by the locals and he could find himself in serious and costly bother if he wasn't careful. I tried to prevent even conversation between them.

Kris developed the same concern for Edna. Edna was the honeypot to the bees around town, so there were constant visits by young men on one pretext or another. Kris said he had to protect her. I told him that was not his job. She had her sister and brother-in-law but they were not there in the daytime; nor was Kris nor I unless one or other or both returned for lunch as we sometimes did. But we were not their keepers; their private lives were just that and although I did chat with Edna about sex and emotion, her life was no real business of mine. Or Kris's. And while we were having a marriage totally devoid of touch, Kris's interest in young women and the fatherly hugs they received hurt me greatly.

There was a particular day Kris was to collect me from under the tree outside of my workplace and we would have lunch at home. It was the same huge tree under which several of us had stood when the earthquake happened. I will always remember the ground around it heaving up and down like a prowling cat under a blanket. A few people were standing about, including Solomon Islanders whose main occupation seemed to be hanging about. I watched out for our car and, as it approached, stepped out towards the road only to have it drive right past me. General laughter from the onlookers with comments such as 'He's got something else on his mind' shouldn't have bothered me but, with the way things were, I thought some might have known more than I did. I should have just taken myself off to the Mendana but I waited for him to realise he'd forgotten me and return.

Once I started work with the BHC, I went to all of the parties, many of them cocktail affairs on board visiting naval vessels. Several Solomon Islands women would be present and I never wanted to outshine them in my choice of dress. I loved wearing saris and one in particular became my favourite for these occasions. It was a black French silk crêpe, perfectly plain, and I usually wore a black blouse, a *choli*, under it.

For the parties aboard ship, though, we often had to travel out in a small boat and climb up the side. On these occasions, I would wear long, loose, silk trousers with an easy to wear blouse. And flat sandals. A sari is long but has plenty of movement and is easily managed; I had lots of practice as a young mum but climbing up the side of a ship in one was out of the question. For other expatriate wives, their need to show off in their Paris originals was greater than trying to be sensible. As Robbie Burns said, about seeing ourselves as others see us… I could not resist a smirk as I watched the ungainly clamber in high heels and tight skirts. Naval personnel tried to look as if they couldn't see them, so they wouldn't have to offer assistance, but saw everything from the corner of their eye. Unladylike. It might have been at this time that I learned to talk about nothing with extreme intelligence.

Life went on. I wanted to explore but Kris was afraid I might hurt myself; it was easier to acquiesce to Kris's dictates.

It was several years later when I'd returned for a holiday, staying with my friend Dorothy and also going to stay at Mark's village on the furthermost tip of North Malaita Island, that I actually saw more of the group of islands that make up the Solomons.

To get to Mark's village, I first took a boat, small, crowded and stinking of diesel. There were live chickens and a goat and heaps of dead things as well as packs of rice, potatoes and other fruits and vegetables. It took several hours to get to Gizo and while the conglomeration of people and goods had not been tidy to begin with, it soon became an absolute mess. The women tried to keep the children happy while the men stretched out where they could and snored and farted their way to our destination.

Upon disembarkation, I had to climb up into the back of a truck and sit on my luggage while we bumped and ground and screeched our way further north for many more hours. I tried standing, holding on to the side of the truck, sitting and holding on to whatever was available, for if I hadn't held on to something, I would have landed on the hard floor of the vehicle. The sun beat down and a hat really was not sufficient cover.

The Solomon Islanders carry umbrellas with them at all times. We shared our food and I had quick naps until my loosening hold startled me awake again. At last, I was helped down, feeling more dead than alive, but I was still not at my destination. I had to spend a night in the place from which a canoe would take me the rest of the way. Tides determined the comings and goings of this, my last mode of transport. A few of us waited in a wall-less shed.

Then, at last the canoe, or at least the one that had come for me. I and my bags were put in and off we went. Again, several hours to the very top of North Malaita. We stayed close enough to the coast but not too close to the reefs. The sea was clear and beautiful, the fishes seen as clearly as if they'd been in a fish tank, with the colourful corals below. The coast was magnificent with the greenery overhanging the water creating lovely reflections as well as the patterns of light and shade.

At last, I was at Mark's village and here there was a difficulty: I was supposed to tumble into the water and swim a short distance in to the beach. I couldn't swim and, quite frankly, I was afraid of the water and wouldn't be in any depth in which I couldn't touch the ground. Couldn't swim? It was unheard of but, by and by, they accepted that this strange woman could not and so very carefully, avoiding the coral crops, they managed to get me close enough to walk. A couple of the men looked after my bags.

At that time, I was going through the menopause, my periods being very irregular, and it had actually been several months since the last. I was hoping against hope that it wouldn't happen while I was there, as I thought I might have to go to the women's house for the duration. I had bought several sarongs for my trip as I knew that the three or four showers were positioned around the edge of the clusters of houses and one washed in the open covered with a sarong.

It so happened that the only colour was red and I had not had time to wash them before I left Honiara. As I stepped under the running water, I noticed several women looking with alarm. I looked down and the water around my feet was running red. 'No, no,' I said, 'it's the dye from the fabric,' as I tried to grab a handful of the stuff and wring it out, showing the red running from it. My onlookers seemed satisfied and I had a blood-free stay, thank goodness.

I slept with a family, on a mat on the ground, as did everyone, and shared their food as I helped with the chores. The senior men asked me to a meeting at which we discussed the best positions for digging latrines, men one side of the village, females the other. I did question the need to have the women's lavatories situated just past the pig pen. We also talked about schooling for both sexes and the need for girls to have an education in the changing world.

Eventually, I had to make the reverse trip back to Honiara, a fitter, healthier person than the one who arrived.

Kris had never wanted to be anything but friends before and after our divorce but I went through stages of deep anger and animosity towards him. Dorothy bore the brunt of all this in the letters I sent her. While I was at Mark's village, it so happened Kris turned up in Honiara on some work he was doing. He called in to see Dorothy at her bookshop. It became obvious he did not know I was in the islands and Dorothy felt she had to alert me to the fact of his being there before I returned to the capital. No direct telephones to outlying areas, everything went through the radio, but she didn't want to be so public about letting me know. She contacted the police. So one day the senior police officer ordered me to his house to tell me that my (former) husband was in Honiara and he was required to protect me. No amount of protests from me were going to prevent him doing his duty and I stayed with him and his wife for several days before I could get back to Honiara (where Kris was staying in our old hotel) and Dorothy. If I needed to be safe, I was better off with Mark and his family, who all thought it a huge joke. I thought, this is an Agatha Christie farce.

Once back, I contacted him at the hotel; we arranged to meet for dinner. He picked me up, we ate and talked. Well, mostly he talked, about himself, his ups and downs, what had happened to him, the troubles he'd been through.

Sometime between eleven and midnight, I thought I could draw the evening to a close. I looked at him and said, 'You know, Kris, not once in the last few hours have you actually looked at me and asked me how I was.'

He looked surprised, replying that he could see how I was and I looked fine. And that was and still is, Kris. Self-centred.

For my sixty-ninth birthday, I invited him and a few friends for lunch. One friend, a former social work colleague, had not met Kris for several years. After he had abruptly left the luncheon, she remarked did I think he had Asperger's syndrome and it hit me, yes. All the years I'd known him…but perhaps being too close and emotionally involved blinds one.

One day on this holiday trip, I was coming out of the Honiara newsagency (which apart from the overseas newspapers still did not sell anything more uplifting than the true confessions type magazine) when I came face to face with one of my former English students. He pumped my arm up and down and kept telling me how happy he was to see me. I have to say I was surprised. He was not my most promising student and certainly didn't graduate from my classes with top honours. However, he had been given a dream, he said, of what might be possible. He worked hard and applied to study commerce at the university, a subject he had more than successfully completed. I was so happy for him. He was probably my only student to go on and gain a degree.

My experiences in the Solomons were interesting both when I lived there and then when I visited. It was unusual for a female to have anything to do with men's business but I was invited to meetings of chiefs and quizzed on all manner of things from health, plumbing which included placement of toilets, which of course could not be of the water closet variety, education, and whether or not having multiple wives was a good or bad thing.

I read too much into this advanced thinking. When running my classes, the young men and few women segregated themselves; I tried to mix them up. This was very wrong of me and initially I lost all my female students; by the next enrolments, I allowed them to sit where they wished.

Change comes slowly and nearly thirty years later, Solomon Islands women have more say in the running of things.

Somehow, a little boy, he said he was about ten, called Pelix, attached himself to Kris. His home and family were on another island but he used to travel to Honiara with his father with market vegetables. Kris considered him bright, with potential. I was already paying for Mark's education and I think Kris wanted to at least match what I was doing by fostering Pelix's education. I thought he was just an opportunist. He wasn't the studying type but he did want Kris to adopt him and take him to Australia. He would turn up at the house and expect me to answer to his beck and call. In no uncertain terms, I told him repeatedly that was not the way things happened in my home nor in Australia, so he became truculent with me and wheedling with Kris.

Pelix had a sister-cousin, the term given to first cousins on one or the other side of the family. He insisted we also house her. She was of similar age but had not been so often to Honiara and so not used to Europeans at all. I think Pelix meant her to be one of my house-girls but I was not about to start employing children and I certainly was not going to pay her. I did try to educate her in matters of personal hygiene and that it was not sufficient to wash her dress while she was wearing it in the shower, but to no avail. Pelix's English was passably good but his sister-cousin's was hardly there. She was miserable being with us and I was at a loss as to what to do with her.

I demanded to speak to Pelix's father when next he was in town. I told him he must take the girl home and that he must take back the control of his son. He pretended he couldn't understand me but I just kept on insisting. The little girl was relieved but Pelix continued to pester Kris at work and, although he stopped coming to the house, he gave me very dirty looks if we passed in town. Kris, of course, couldn't have a child hanging about at his workplace, so he had to become firm with him as well. Kris blamed me for creating bad vibes.

Our departure from the Solomons was as abrupt as Kris leaving my birthday luncheon. The couple in the house next door had gone away for a holiday, leaving their sixteen-year-old son in charge. A ship with a large component of Fijian crew was in port and the couple's estranged daughter decided to use the house in their absence and have a party, inviting the crew. It was in its fourth non-stop day and Kris complained to the local constabulary, to no effect.

After six days and nights of no sleep, constant noise of music, shouting, swearing, breaking bottles, Kris thought they might respond to reasonableness. He decided he would speak to them. They did not hear his knocking, so he thought he'd attract their attention by throwing rocks on the roof. I said they might construe that as aggression. He said he'd throw small pebbles and I said I didn't think they'd measure the size of the missiles. They didn't. They jumped over the fence and started bashing Kris. I screamed, alerting Judy and Barnabas, who then rang the police, who did, in the middle of the night, come out in force.

Kris's facial bones had been broken, including his upper palate, and he had severe bruising down the right side of his body. An ambulance took him to the hospital, where he was immediately X-rayed and given painkillers. I was told he needed to be taken back to Australia for treatment. He returned to the house while the Australian High Commission arranged our transport.

During the ensuing four days, there was a constant stream of visitors, all Solomon Islanders, expressing their sadness that this had happened in their country. I was very touched by their concern for his welfare. Some would have spent more than they could afford on getting lifts into town but they had to come. I maintained a stock of cakes, biscuits, sandwiches, and Edna made endless pots of strong tea, as they like it, not the very weak Earl Grey of my choice.

To feed Kris, I had to purée cooked vegetables and make them liquid enough for him to painfully swallow. He couldn't speak and was in great pain. Barnabas asked if he could bring in a custom medical man. Both Kris and I had great faith in the ancient art/science of the Indian Ayurvedic practitioners of medicine, so we were not going to deny the ancient medical science of the Solomons. We said yes. The old man came and made up a concoction with various plants he had brought with him. He waved his hands over Kris's head while muttering incantations and then squeezed drops of the liquid onto his crown. It all took about half an hour and he was gone. He wouldn't take any money but later I gave Barnabas a sum to give to the village headman. Later Kris related how he'd seemed to go into a haze and the pain abated. He slept a really deep sleep.

We were flown back to Brisbane and an ambulance took us straight to the Brisbane General Hospital. Kris was taken off and X-rayed again while I attended to his admittance details. The first set of X-rays clearly showed the breaks; the second only where bones had not quite properly aligned; and in others the thin line indicating a healed fracture. The medical staff could not believe the damage shown in the first could heal in the few intervening days and of course were most sceptical of the medical man's intervention. Some of the bones had to be rebroken and reset but Kris did recover in time, the deep bruising probably taking longer and leaving more inner scars. He decided that was the end of his time in the Solomons and went back only to tidy things up. And of course, it was an abrupt ending to my life there. I don't think I ever took official leave from my jobs. A correspondence between me and my immediate boss, the second secretary, went on for some time and particularly when he retired and returned to the UK with his wife.

I kept in touch with Barnabas and Judy and Mark for quite a long time. I am particularly sorry I allowed my contact with Mark to come to an end. Judy came to stay with me for a holiday and I wondered at her persistence to know about the Gold Coast. I learned later she had been having an affair with an Australian bank colleague who had promised to marry her and bring her to his home on the Gold Coast. Barnabas wouldn't allow her to take the boys and he had the law on his side. The Solomon Islands government was still operating with ancient British laws, changed to keep up with changing thinking in most other former colonies, but not the Solomons. I felt very sorry for them all, but particularly Barnabas as he was truly in love with Judy.

Mark had long since finished school and trade training and was successfully working in Honiara but there was a girl in his village he was keen on and spent more and more time there. He did try to get her to live in town but she wasn't keen.

Once back in Australia, Kris and I decided to put our respective properties on the market. We were living in his unit but it really was too small. We thought whoever sold first could buy the next house for us, in that person's name, of course, the other rented out. I sold mine. We selected another in the western suburbs, complete with swimming pool. I thought water exercises would be good for Kris after his body was so badly damaged. It was also brick on slab and we had been in it only a few weeks when we found it needed new underpinning. So much for the skills of my civil engineering husband in checking construction. He had procured a job in Fiji, as part of an Australian government aid programme, so it was decided he would go while I stayed behind and organised the work on the house. Once that was done, it was definitely more comfortable to be out of the house while the work was going on, so I joined Kris for a few months.

It was while I was on a trip back, checking on things, that I received his letter telling me he wanted a divorce. He said he was in love with a young girl, one I'd met actually, serving my lunch at a Hare Krishna restaurant. She really was just a child. He assured me his passion for her was never consummated and he never declared his feelings but he did end up going to bed with her mother. And of course, all of his young passionatas cost a lot, as he insisted on sending money and gifts to help them out.

I was friends then with Kay McGrath, the TV newsreader, and her husband. They were a tremendous support to me at that time.

My marriage wasn't perfect but I hadn't wanted a divorce either. I went through periods of hating Kris, not speaking and being friends, the latter situation he wanted from the start and the level we should have stayed at.

He fell in love with another girl in Fiji, one more cunning and conniving and who really played on his weaknesses. Kris's son had to go over at one stage and try to sort things out. That was when Kris shaved off half his beard – better than an ear – and he really was out of his mind. She continued to be troublesome for some time. I think he was doing voluntary work in Tonga when he fell in love again and married a girl forty-two years his junior. He fought government red tape to get her to Australia and then expected me to act as mentor for her. They are divorced now and I still haven't met her; and won't.

I sold the house after one year and purchased a lovely place, again in the western suburbs, on a ridge with fantastic views. It was this house I closed up to look after my mother and then rented out when I went overseas.

Ten days of normal

Many decades ago, I was talking to my friend and doctor about a city from which I had just returned. I was looking for a word to describe it and he supplied 'civilised'. And it was and is. It is not Rome or New York or Paris or London but Melbourne, Australia.

My life and for many years since was normal – working, studying, working; buying, selling the domestic homes, travel; working, studying, working; buying and selling the domestic homes, travel, working, studying, bringing up a son; voluntary work, many friends, much laughter. Now, I am about to clock up three years of 'not normal', with no end in sight. I made a mistake. My actions seemed valid at the time, I was approaching, have since passed, that pivotal point of three-score years and ten, so it seemed reasonable to move closer to what I thought was family. We hear often enough that old adage 'blood is thicker than water' but I have found that in my case it counts for nothing. I could proffer another old adage, 'too much water has flowed under the bridge'. I have been away from the family seat for too many years.

So, I find myself in an over-50s so-called resort in south-east Queensland. The weather is too hot and sticky, the intellectual climate is barren both within the complex and in the suburbs immediately surrounding, which are home to large numbers of unemployed people and school truants, and the crime rates are high; very young teenage parents appear to be in large numbers.

Fortunately, several months ago, I found a book group which provides much needed succour. On the days we meet, once a month, I listen, talk, laugh, engage in friendly banter and intelligent argument. From the group, four of us have banded together to meet more often for a meal or just a coffee and we all get a shot of life's best medicine, laughter. These are my isolated moments of normal when I forget the outside heat, where I live, and what my life has become.

Someone said, somewhere, that we don't die from lack of sex(ual intercourse) but from the lack of love. I don't have and have never had that abiding love but being busy, engaged in the community and surrounded by friends has supported me. It must be difficult to impossible for anyone to understand the depths of despair to which one can sink when isolated from life as it was.

Yes, I can travel for almost an hour and a half to get to this state's cultural centre, appreciate the art in its many forms, have lunch and return. By myself. Such an activity would once have been a must on my calendar, in company or alone, but either way, able to discuss it with a friend or two at some point. As I am ageing, I do not relish the travelling and I find no pleasure in going over the event in my own mind. But I did look forward to my short return to Melbourne, staying with an old friend recently relocated there.

My friend is seventeen years my senior. Time and disease have taken their toll on her body; I was not expecting that we'd go tap dancing but her mind is as sharp as ever it was. She lives in a bayside suburb next to her son and daughter-in-law, and two grandchildren when they are not away at university. My friend's sense of humour is not impaired, nor is her acuity of mind.

The streets are tree-lined, shading fruit and vegetable shops, flower shops and plant nurseries that pop up like special beads on a necklace of houses, all lovely, different, all separated by a halo of green foliage. Opposite her house is a park, child-friendly, with a large sandpit in a human-dug hollow, and man-made mini-hills. The sandpit is equipped with the usual paraphernalia – shovels, graders, et cetera. These toys are part and parcel of the pit. They are used and left for the next visitor and, I have no doubt, should one break while being used by a particular child, the parent would replace it, such is the community attitude. All this would once have been my kind of normal.

My friend took me to one of what have become her favourite

cafés. The food was delicious, the service excellent, ambience sublime. Schoolchildren were still on holiday and several accompanied their parents to dine while we were there. There was no shouting, no running about, adults discussed the menu with their three, four-year-olds and, from my point of view, all had a good time. No mobile phones heard or in evidence, no background music – my normal. There was also a certain frisson between the maître d' and me, an old normal. The chemistry, not the maître d'.

It happened that my friend and I went again before I left and during a conversation in front of the sweets cabinet, in which I complimented the maître d' on the establishment, he said we should get married. I calmly replied, yes, we should. I didn't know his name and he was wearing a wedding ring but we were having fun. I did give him my business card before we left, saying he should at least know who he was marrying. He told me his wife was a writer and he was a songwriter in disguise. It was a lovely interlude of mild flirtation that reminded me I was a woman and even one who could still inspire some playfulness in a good-looking man. Another normal.

Another day, another café, very different from the first; funky might, I think, be the word to describe it. It consisted of two very old shops made into one establishment, half of the common wall removed to allow a flow from one side to the other. It had not been made to look new, modern. One felt its age, its history when one entered, but it did not weigh one down. It was owned by two women, had young female staff, one of whom greeted us and showed us to a table, asked if and what we would like to drink. As with the other, this also provided excellent service and delicious food. And much with which to feed the eyes and imagination.

The entrance, one shop, contained the refrigerated sweets counter on which rested the till as well as various bric-a-brac which was for sale. It also separated customers from the kitchen beyond, but people waiting for a takeaway, while sitting on a well-padded metal garden seat and peering around the end of the cabinet, could view the progress of their nourishment. The café part contained a variety of unmatched tables and chairs, bright cushions and every part of the wall and ceiling displayed every imaginable item, all for sale. On shelves next to me was a tassel with a human clown-like top and multicoloured silk-ribbon skirt; painted wooden boxes in various sizes and colours; carved Chinese balls; dye of all colours, sizes, fabrics; puzzles. Behind, around, above, were cards, paper napkins, paper flowers, baskets, multicoloured beaded chandeliers, vases, very large Nepali umbrellas, brass hangings and well, really, a cornucopia of exotica. Again, children were dining with parents or what, in this case, looked like mother, aunts, grandmothers. Again, well-behaved and again, no intrusive music.

Both establishments were popular as evidenced by would-be patrons being turned away because of lack of table space, both served a range of food, well-prepared, delicious and reasonably priced. Both had staff who knew how to serve, attend to customers' needs and look happy, interested and friendly. At both places, I could happily eat alone and know I would be nourished both physically and intellectually. My normal.

My friend had a podiatry appointment so I elected to walk home. I took the opportunity to browse in adjacent shops. I certainly had no intention of buying anything, my luggage already overflowing, and I didn't need anything. The dress shop. Well, really, it was calm, with some lovely garments, Italian labels, and surely one skirt, different from anything I would find in my current locale, wouldn't take up so very much room…my kind of normal.

A wander around the Turkish shop made me want to book a ticket to that country. I conversed with the Turkish owner about his country and examined the pottery, jewellery, the brasses and rugs but no, this time I did resist. Next time. I posted some letters from the tiny post office and delighted in the scenes and scents emanating from the continental shops. My normal.

There was the family dinner, catered by my friend's twenty-year-old granddaughter and her friend, who cook because they enjoy it.

Both are engaged in intellectual studies at their respective universities and they produced three beautiful courses, none from a recipe book. Sat around the table were my friend, her son, daughter-in-law, the granddaughter and grandson, the other cook, her parents, and myself. Conversation was lively, flowing back and forth. A little while after the last morsel had been consumed, not counting the wine, liqueurs, chocolates, a table game was produced. We were divided into three teams; the young team cheated outrageously, the older team demanded extra time and privileges, we shouted, laughed, accused, played on. And oh, my kind of normal, long gone.

There were the shopping days, to the supermarkets, the greengrocer, for the stuff that maintains us. My friend is not yet familiar with the shop's layouts but, busy as they were, a staff member was available to attend to her needs. Courteously. My normal.

I bumped into a former acquaintance, a TV and stage actor, so we filled in several years of having not met. Then there was the occasion my friend and I creaked our way out of her car while five little boys, I would guess between four and seven, tumbled out of theirs. There must have been a set of twin there somewhere but I didn't work that out. They were accompanied by their mum and Big Bear and Little Bear. Big Bear was bigger than the biggest boy but was in the charge of one younger. BB sported a denim jacket and quite hid his minder. LB wore a pair of infants' shoes and kept his feet on the ground, his minder bent double to make it so. I thought, Teddy Bears' picnic.

Children are sometimes shy in speaking to an adult so I addressed myself to BB and LB. The latter was just out for an excursion but BB's shopping list consisted of honey, honey and honey. Yes, there were giggles but the boys spoke well, articulated ideas and their mother benignly allowed this interruption into what must have been another busy day. Another part of my once normal.

Four of us – my friend, her daughter-in-law, her friend and I – went to see a film; a serious film which we all enjoyed and enjoyed discussing afterwards. Another normal.

I had to return to my own house, leave the salubrious suburb of the so civilised city, each kilometre, each step bringing me closer to this gated community in which I do not fit. For how long can I be sustained on ten days of normal?

www.ingramcontent.com/pod-product-compliance
Lightning Source LLC
Chambersburg PA
CBHW071813080526
44589CB00012B/779